UNDERSTANDING ADAPTABILITY: A PREREQUISITE FOR EFFECTIVE PERFORMANCE WITHIN COMPLEX ENVIRONMENTS

ADVANCES IN HUMAN PERFORMANCE AND COGNITIVE ENGINEERING RESEARCH

Series Editor: Eduardo Salas

Volume 1: Advances in Human Performance and Cognitive Engineering Research, Edited by Eduardo Salas

Volume 2: Advances in Human Performance and Cognitive Engineering Research: Automation, Edited by Eduardo Salas

Volume 3: Advances in Human Performance and Cognitive Engineering Research, Edited by Eduardo Salas and Dianna Stone

Volume 4: Advances in Human Performance and Cognitive Engineering Research, Edited by Michael Kaplan

Volume 5: The Science and Simulation of Human Performance, Edited by James W. Ness, Victoria Teppe and Darren Ritzer bio-psycho-socio dynamic

complex & multi-faceted

per
rel.
coll

multi- discipline
multi - level
multi - phasic

systemic

ecological

emergent & planned

KSAO's

macro-cognitive / regulative principles

evolve rather than design or 'blueprint'.

team adaptivity (p122)

"it's about change"

"understanding, measuring & studying & interacts 'eco-change' is a very difficult problem.

'proximal & distal antecedents'

ADVANCES IN HUMAN PERFORMANCE AND
COGNITIVE ENGINEERING RESEARCH VOLUME 6

UNDERSTANDING ADAPTABILITY: A PREREQUISITE FOR EFFECTIVE PERFORMANCE WITHIN COMPLEX ENVIRONMENTS

EDITED BY

C. SHAWN BURKE

University of Central Florida, USA

LINDA G. PIERCE

US Army Research Laboratory, USA

EDUARDO SALAS

University of Central Florida, USA

ELSEVIER
JAI

Amsterdam – Boston – Heidelberg – London – New York – Oxford
Paris – San Diego – San Francisco – Singapore – Sydney – Tokyo

ELSEVIER B.V.
Radarweg 29
P.O. Box 211
1000 AE Amsterdam,
The Netherlands

ELSEVIER Inc.
525 B Street, Suite 1900
San Diego
CA 92101-4495
USA

ELSEVIER Ltd
The Boulevard, Langford
Lane, Kidlington
Oxford OX5 1GB
UK

ELSEVIER Ltd
84 Theobalds Road
London
WC1X 8RR
UK

First edition 2006

British Library Cataloguing in Publication Data
A catalogue record is available from the British Library.

ISBN-10: 0-7623-1248-3
ISBN-13: 978-0-7623-1248-1
ISSN: 1479-3601 (Series)

∞ The paper used in this publication meets the requirements of ANSI/NISO Z39.48-1992 (Permanence of Paper).
Printed in The Netherlands.

CONTENTS

LIST OF CONTRIBUTORS

Mike Barnes	Army Research Laboratory, AZ, USA
Hall P. Beck	Appalachian State University, NC, USA
Paul D. Bliese	Walter Reed Army Institute of Research, MD, USA
C. Shawn Burke	Institute for Simulation & Training, University of Central Florida, FL, USA
David W. Dorsey	Personnel Decisions Research Institutes, Inc., VA, USA
Mary T. Dzindolet	Department of Psychology and Human Ecology, Cameron University, OK, USA
Kathleen P. Hess	Organizational Training and Development Team, Aptima, Inc., MA, USA
David Hillis	Army Research Laboratory, MD, USA
Georgiy Levchuk	Aptima, Inc., MA, USA
Patricia McDermott	Micro Analysis and Design, CO, USA
Krishna R. Pattipati	Department of Electrical and Computer Engineering, University of Connecticut, CT, USA
Linda G. Pierce	Army Research Laboratory, MD, USA
Robert E. Ployhart	Management Moore School of Business, University of South Carolina, SC, USA
Elaine D. Pulakos	Personnel Decisions Research Institutes, Inc., VA, USA

Jerzy Rozenblit	University of Arizona, AZ, USA
Eduardo Salas	Department of Psychology and Institute for Simulation & Training, University of Central Florida, FL, USA
Daniel Serfaty	Aptima, Inc., MA, USA
Kevin C. Stagl	Department of Psychology and Institute for Simulation and Training, University of Central Florida, FL, USA
Liana Suantak	University of Arizona, AZ, USA
Janet L. Sutton	Army Research Laboratory, OK, USA
John Warner	Army Research Laboratory, AZ, USA
Susan S. White	Personnel Decisions Research Institutes, Inc., VA, USA

PREFACE

Adaptability is becoming a hallmark of effective performance at all levels and types of organizations. Individuals within both public and private organizations are having to adapt to technological changes and the tempo of operations in dynamic, competitive environments. Corresponding teams within these organizations have to adapt to changes in structure, membership, and environmental conditions. At an organizational level public and private corporations are competing in an environment that is increasingly global, technological, and high-risk. The increased need for adaptability is not only seen within public and private organizations. The US military is facing an increasingly complex geopolitical environment that also demands adaptability in order to be effective. For example, within the military, individuals are having to adapt to asymmetric threats, increased joint operations, and network capabilities. Teams are having to adapt to a wide variety of environmental and team composition factors (e.g., warfighting-peacekeeping, teams comprised of coalition partners of multiple nationalities), and at an organizational level the military is having to adapt to changes in the geopolitical environment. The above conditions are but a few which highlight that as complexity rises it is no longer acceptable to only be able to perform well when things go as expected; instead individuals, teams, and organizations must be able to continuously adapt their knowledge and skills in order to remain competitive in environments which are fluid, ambiguous, and where multiple pathways to goal attainment exist.

While the concept of adaptability is not new, the focus on understanding adaptability in terms of human performance capabilities with regard to organizations has received increased attention within the last 10 years. This increased attention is coming from a wide variety of disciplines that are intimately involved with maximizing human and organizational performance. It is only now that researchers and practitioners are truly beginning to unravel the complexities surrounding adaptability and, in doing so, identifying the antecedents, KSAs, and processes that contribute to this elusive construct. This work is leading to more practically based tools for selection, training, decision aides, and maximizing organizational structure within complex uncertain environments. To assist in furthering understanding around the topic of adaptability this volume takes a multi-disciplinary approach by integrating cutting-edge work done by experts in the field and compiling it in one volume. The volume takes a systems approach in that chapters describe the manifestation and antecedents of adaptability at individual, team, and organizational levels. Correspondingly, the volume is organized around sections, which represent work on adaptability conducted at the individual, team, and organizational levels, respectively. Section I, representing work conducted primarily on adaptability at the individual level, begins with a chapter by Ployhart and Bliese, which introduces a mid-range theory of adaptability that conceptualizes adaptability as an individual difference. Ployhart and colleagues then use the presented theory to develop and test a self-report measure that assesses individual differences in adaptability. Similar in topic, but not approach, Chapter 2 by Pulakos, Dorsey, and White explores the concept of adaptability in the workplace, specifically how to define and measure adaptive performance and how to select individuals who will effectively adapt in the workplace. Rounding out this section Chapter 3, by Barnes and colleagues, presents a cognitive model of visualization developed to address complex military environments where adaptation is needed. The authors present research on cognitive biases and their impact on the ability to visualize uncertain environments. Results of this research are being used to develop better visualization techniques for humans in uncertain-high risk environments wherein the decision cycle is too rapid to even consider traditional decision theoretic analyses. The chapter concludes by describing one such tool.

Chapter 4 begins Section II of the book, which represents work on adaptation conducted at the team level. Moving from primarily examining adaptation as an individual level phenomenon Stagl, Burke, Salas, and Pierce (Chapter 4) provide a multidisciplinary, multilevel, multiphasic theory of adaptation at the team level. Within this chapter, team adaptation and the emergent nature of adaptive team performance are defined and centered in an Input-Throughput-Output framework. This framework illustrates the core processes and emergent states that unfold and compile over time to emerge as adaptive team performance and result in team adaptation. While the next two chapters (Chapters 5 and 6) keep the focus at the team level the authors consider adaptation within the context of multicultural teams. Specifically, Chapter 5 by Sutton, Pierce, Burke, and Salas discusses the need for and potential barriers relating to cultural adaptability. Based on a combination of conceptual and field-based research these authors present a framework that researchers can use as a guide to understand the impact of cultural diversity on teamwork. Chapter 6 keeps the focus on multi-cultural adaptability, but from the perspective of the team leader, Burke, Salas, and Hess describe the challenges facing leaders of multi-cultural teams. These authors then describe a training tool that is being created to assist team leaders in gaining both the cultural awareness and skills needed to lead such teams; thereby enabling the creation of a third culture. Finally, to complete the focus on adaptability within teams Chapter 7 by Dzindolet, Beck, and Pierce discusses adaptability within the context of human-automated 'teams'. Dzindolet et al. use the Framework of Automation Use to examine a number of factors that determine how individuals can effectively integrate their activities with machine partners within fluid environments which call for adaptability.

The final section of the volume, Section III, completes the multi-level treatment of adaptability by taking an organizational perspective. This section is comprised of the final chapter of this volume, Chapter 8. Within this chapter, Levchuk and Serfaty discuss a program of research which has culminated in the development of an adaptive design process. This design process incorporates the notions of congruence and robustness. In turn, it promotes the development of cost-efficient adaptation strategies to achieve high performance in the presence of uncertainty and/or a changing environment.

SECTION I:
INDIVIDUAL LEVEL

INDIVIDUAL ADAPTABILITY (I-ADAPT) THEORY: CONCEPTUALIZING THE ANTECEDENTS, CONSEQUENCES, AND MEASUREMENT OF INDIVIDUAL DIFFERENCES IN ADAPTABILITY

Robert E. Ployhart and Paul D. Bliese

In terms of biological survival, seemingly inconsequential random differences in genetic makeup may very well explain why some organisms successfully adapt to changes in the environment and why others fail (Gould, 1989). That is, adaptability may be nothing more than simple chance variability in DNA that happens to favor one organism over another. In the social sciences, we also consider adaptability to be a key determinant of whether an individual successfully adjusts to changes in the social or work environment. Presumably, however, we are much less comfortable with the notation that successful adaptation is merely a chance process. Rather, we are inclined to think there is some predictability in how individuals react to change in their environments. Unfortunately, despite the

Understanding Adaptability: A Prerequisite for Effective Performance within Complex Environments
Advances in Human Performance and Cognitive Engineering Research, Volume 6, 3–39

ISSN: 1479-3601/doi:10.1016/S1479-3601(05)06001-7

sense that individual social adaptability is somewhat predictable, relatively little work has been conducted examining the nature, structure, and function of adaptability in social and work settings.

In this chapter, we review work on adaptability as part of a program of research we have conducted over the last several years. This experience has led to the development of a new theory of individual adaptability, called Individual ADAPTability (I-ADAPT) theory. The purpose of this chapter is to review past research on adaptability, propose the I-ADAPT theory of individual differences in adaptability, and compare and contrast I-ADAPT theory with other approaches. In creating I-ADAPT theory, we have drawn from several individual difference domains to conceptualize and place adaptability within a nomological network of existing constructs and processes. Finally, we conclude the chapter with the presentation of a self-report measure developed in a manner consistent with the theory. As such, it is broadly useful for understanding the multiple dimensions of adaptability across a range of applied contexts. As will be clear in later sections, we believe that understanding individual differences in adaptability will contribute to a better understanding of a variety of performance criteria. Thus, understanding individual differences in adaptability should prove useful to applied researchers attempting to improve human performance in complex, changing environments.

ADAPTABILITY IN MODERN WORK

Work organizations and the employees within these organizations face considerable environmental pressures requiring adaptive change. Several forces have contributed to this need for great adaptation. These are described in many excellent sources (e.g., Cascio, 2003; Ilgen & Pulakos, 1999); here we briefly review their implications for individual adaptability.

Technological changes have perhaps been the most pervasive and dynamic of all recent changes. In the current era, nearly every work environment has become dependent upon computers. This, in itself, has required considerable adaptation from a generation of employees who grew up in a world without computers. In addition, however, the speed at which computers and software change require employees to constantly learn new systems, thereby ensuring technological adaptation is a continual part of modern work (Hollenbeck & McCall, 1999).

A second change has been prompted by the shift from manufacturing to knowledge-based work. The new emphasis on knowledge work requires employees to constantly update their skills and expertise. But a more fundamental change comes from the fact that specialization is typically required to be proficient in one's occupation, yet many work tasks require the combined expertise of several individuals. Thus, there is an increasing trend toward more project-based teamwork, where members of distributed expertise come together, work collaboratively to solve a problem, and then disband when the project is completed. This requires not only adaptability in terms of working with people with diverse expertise, but also adaptability in working with people from diverse backgrounds and interests (Hesketh & Neal, 1999; Pearlman & Barney, 2000).

Tighter economic resources over the last 25 years have led to intense organizational competition. This competition required organizational decision makers to incorporate a variety of organizational-level adaptations that in turn required individual employee adaptation. For example, organizations frequently acquire, merge, or form alliances with other organizations to take advantage of strategic firm-specific resources (e.g., physical, financial, geographic, market penetration). Many of these mergers require a considerable amount of "growing pains" as the organizations try to align their practices, policies, and procedures, and this often results in dramatic stress and strain for employees. Likewise, to remain competitive many organizations downsize or outsource their labor force to control costs. Such concerns in conjunction with constant technological changes have led employees to adopt a "continuous improvement" perspective and view skill acquisition as a life-long activity – a modern requirement to adapt.

Obviously, contributing to organizational competition are changes to the more general environment in which business takes place. Today's business world is very much a global business world, and competition may come as much from across oceans as it does from across the street. The dramatic rise of globalism and organizations' continued expansion into foreign markets has led to a need to adapt to people with different cultures and languages (Cascio, 2003).

Together, these changes contribute to a strong need for employees to exhibit adaptability in ideas, values, and behaviors. Notice that most of these changes have occurred only within the last 30 years. Therefore, it is no surprise that much of the research we review in the following section has been conducted even more recently.

PREVIOUS RESEARCH ON INDIVIDUAL ADAPTABILITY (BROADLY CONCEPTUALIZED)

In this section, we review previous research on individual differences in adaptability. However, we take a broad perspective by reviewing research on performance adaptability, training, cognitive adaptation, coping, and reactions to organizational change. We believe these research areas share a considerable degree of conceptual overlap that can be usefully integrated when exploring the nature, structure, and function of adaptability. The research areas we review share a common conceptual frame: individual differences (e.g., cognitive ability) influence mediating processes (e.g., goals) which in turn influence how people perceive and respond to some change event (performance). Although the specific independent, mediating, and dependent variables differ across studies, this basic model is consistent across research areas. Our purpose in this section is to summarize these research areas to illustrate the following perspectives: (a) adaptability as task performance, (b) adaptability as changes to cognitive processing, (c) adaptability as coping, and (d) adaptability as responding to organizational change.

Adaptability as task performance. Most recent applied research has studied individual adaptability as a response to changing environmental situations. In the typical study, participants will perform a task (e.g., decision making, computerized) until they are reasonably proficient, and then some feature of the task will change and participants' responses to the change will be observed. Thus, adaptability is defined as how well an individual performs on a changing task. Within this paradigm, the antecedents of adaptability are defined in terms of the knowledge, skill, ability, and other characteristics (KSAOs) that relate to adaptive performance. For example, LePine, Colquitt, and Erez (2000a) manipulated the decision rules necessary to successfully complete a decision task, such that adaptability was defined by how well participants reacted to new decision rules. They found the effects of individual differences such as cognitive ability, openness, and conscientiousness on performance became stronger after the change in decision rules. This research suggests that specific individual differences may be particularly important predictors of adaptive performance.

Recent research by Thoresen, Bradley, Thoresen, and Bliese (2004) confirmed the idea that specific individual differences may be particularly predictive of adaptive performance. Thoresen et al. (2004) contrasted individual difference predictors of performance between (a) a transition group of sales representatives forced to adapt to an entirely new sales product and (b) a maintenance group of sales representatives working with an established sales product. The results of the study showed that the personality characteristic of openness to new experience was predictive of sales performance in the transition sample, but not the maintenance sample.

A broad perspective on task-related adaptability is based on the training literature. This literature argues adaptation is reflected in how well individuals generalize and transfer knowledge in performance transition situations (Baldwin & Ford, 1988). A persuasive program of research by Kozlowski and colleagues has shown the value of this approach, arguing that transfer and generalization may represent two specific forms of adaptability (Kozlowski, 1998; Kozlowski et al., 2000; Smith, Ford, & Kozlowski, 1997). For example, Kozlowski et al. (2001) examined how training goals (performance and mastery) and individual differences (ability, performance, and learning orientation) predicted performance adaptability (through knowledge), where adaptability was conceptualized as generalization of knowledge and skills to a new task.

Likewise, if one conceptualizes transfer of training as representing one form of task-related adaptability, then studies such as those conducted by Brown (2001), Colquitt and Simmering (1998), Ford, Smith, Weissbein, Gully, and Salas (1998), Martocchio and Judge (1997), Mathieu, Martineau, and Tannenbaum (1993), and Phillips and Gully (1997), among others, have important implications for understanding adaptability. Indeed, in the majority of these studies, performance is defined in terms of affective, cognitive (learning), and/or behavioral (generalization of task performance) outcomes on a changing task (see Kraiger, Ford, & Salas, 1993). In each of these studies, various individual differences (KSAOs) are expected to interact or be mediated by context-specific state-like processes to influence the dependent variable. Unfortunately, the majority of these studies examine only a few individual difference variables (primarily goal orientation, cognitive ability, and/or personality), presumably most relevant to predicting the criterion construct. While this is certainly an appropriate way to conduct such research, it makes it difficult to summarize findings across studies. That is, because the criterion construct differs across studies, the KSAO predictors change as well. Consequently, it becomes difficult to integrate and summarize this literature into a unified perspective.

Thus, a consequence of conceptualizing adaptability in terms of changing task demands means that adaptability is defined in task-specific terms, and this makes it hard to determine whether the same KSAOs contribute to adaptability across tasks and contexts. For example, does successful adaptation on a decision task require the same KSAOs as successful adaptation on a physical task? It is extremely unlikely that the same KSAOs will be equally, or even similarly, important across different tasks. Consequently, findings in this research area are partially confounded with task and performance context.

A broader perspective has sought to identify the underlying dimensions of tasks and performance that require adaptability across all major tasks and occupations. Pulakos, Arad, Donovan, and Plamondon (2000) provided the first comprehensive study of adaptive performance. They examined critical behavioral incidents from 21 different jobs that spanned private industry to military occupations, and identified eight latent dimensions of adaptive performance. They subsequently supported this eight-factor structure using confirmatory factor analysis (CFA). Pulakos et al. (2002) then developed measures to assess individual differences in adaptability on these eight dimensions (biodata, interest inventory, and self-efficacy types of measures). The eight-factor structure was confirmed in the individual difference study as well, and the measures helped explain performance in adaptive contexts.

The impressive program of research conducted by Pulakos and colleagues suggests that adaptive performance can be captured using eight dimensions. These eight dimensions consist of (1) handling emergency or crisis situations; (2) handling work stress; (3) solving problems creatively; (4) dealing with uncertain and unpredictable situations; (5) learning new work tasks, technologies, and procedures; (6) demonstrating interpersonal adaptability; (7) demonstrating cultural adaptability; and (8) demonstrating physically oriented adaptability. See Pulakos, Dorsey, and White (this volume), for more additional details.

Adaptability as change in strategy selection. A second approach that falls outside of the typical industrial/organizational orientation, but has several interesting implications for understanding the process of adaptation, is research on individual differences in strategy selection. This approach is unique because rather than focusing on individual differences in KSAOs, it focuses on individual differences in adaptive strategy selection and use. Adaptive strategy selection is further defined in terms of how well people can identify relevant situational cues, draw from a repertoire of strategies, and choose the best strategy for the situation.

Probably, the most well-known research in this area has been conducted on the topic of adaptive expertise. This research shows that experts use different ways of interpreting tasks and therefore chose different strategies to accomplish tasks (Chi, Feltovish, & Glaser, 1981; Ericsson & Polson, 1988; Holyoak, 1991). Interestingly, however, this research does not fully account for why individuals – whether novice or expert – might use *different* strategies. Part of an answer to this question comes from Lovett and Schunn (1999). They proposed and tested a model of strategy selection known as RCCL: Represent the task, Construct strategies appropriate for the task, Choose a strategy with the best chance of success, and Learn new success rates as the strategy is applied. The model explains how people use base-rate information and characteristics of the situation to make choices, and adapt these choices toward most successfully solving the problem. Schunn and Reder (1998) further describe several studies that measure and show the effects of individual differences in strategy selection. As might be expected, the individual differences are moderately related to cognitive ability, but appear to be sufficiently different to suggest strategy selection is something different (although what that "something different" refers to is not exactly clear). As with the research noted in the previous section, adaptability is defined in terms of performance on a changing task, but it focuses more on the strategies individuals develop in responding to the changing task.

Thus, this perspective considers adaptability largely in terms of strategy selection, and describes the processes through which it occurs. While there have been a few studies in training that have recognized the importance of strategy selection (Ford, Smith, Weissbein, Gully, & Salas, 1998), these are not as theoretically developed as those conducted within the cognitive arena. This is obviously an important component of adaptation that deserves additional study within the organizational literature.

Adaptability as coping. There is an abundance of literature examining how individuals cope with stressful events. We do not try to summarize this literature (instead see Beehr, 1995; Jex, 1998; Sonnentag & Frese, 2003); rather, we explore the obvious overlaps between coping with stressful events and adaptability. Importantly, several forms of coping are conceptually similar to adaptability and fit within a similar nomological network. That is, coping presumably mediates the effects of stressors (or appraisal of the event) on various dependent measures (Lazarus & Folkman, 1984; Pearlin & Schooler, 1978; Pearlin, Menaghan, Lieberman, & Mullan, 1981). Coping describes how people handle stressful events, and is therefore fundamentally similar to individual adaptability.

Theoretically, coping is typically broken into distinct styles. At a very general level is the distinction between active and passive coping (Taylor & Aspinwall, 1996). As the title suggests, active coping involves proactive responses to resolving or addressing stressful events. For example, an individual may quit a stressful and threatening job in favor of a job the person feels is less likely to overwhelm his or her resources, as a form of active coping. Avoidant coping still involves an individual trying to reduce beyond coping.

the stress, but here the approaches try to ignore the stress rather than eliminate it. For example, the employee may start drinking as a way to reduce the stress caused by a demanding job. Research suggests active coping is more effective than avoidant coping (e.g., Jex, Bliese, Buzzell, & Primeau, 2001). It is important to emphasize that much of the coping-styles literature suggests they are dispositional in nature. These can be distinguished from coping strategies, which tend to be more problem-specific in nature. Carver, Scheier, and Weintraub (1989) identify a variety of coping strategies, such as acceptance, humor, and behavioral disengagement. Others suggest two general strategies, problem- and emotion-focused (Pearlin & Schooler, 1978). These context-specific coping strategies may be affected by a dispositional coping style, such that those with an active coping style might use different strategies than those with an avoidant coping style.

While coping has not typically fallen within the realm of adaptability research, there are many conceptual similarities. Pulakos et al. (2000) identified an ability to deal with stressful situations as a form of adaptability (see also Pulakos et al., this volume). Individual differences may influence what is perceived as stressful (primary appraisal), and how individuals will cope with the stress (secondary appraisal; e.g., Lazarus & Folkman, 1984). It can be argued that one's psychological resources, which are largely individual differences, help determine the nature and type of coping (Pearlin, 1999). Coping strategies may be chosen just like strategy selection in the RCCL model (Lovett & Schunn, 1999). Thus, in our opinion, coping represents another form of individual adaptation.

Adaptability as reacting to organizational change. Our final example of adaptability research considers the literature on individuals reacting to organizational change. As we noted earlier, such a change has been common over the last 20 years, but surprisingly little of the research on organizational change has studied the person within the organization (Armenakis & Bedian, 1999). There are some recent exceptions. Judge, Thoresen, Pucik, and Welbourne (1999) examined the dispositional antecedents (locus of control, generalized self-efficacy, self-esteem, positive affectivity, openness to experience, tolerance for ambiguity, and risk aversion) of a measure of coping with organizational change, and how coping with organizational change predicted job satisfaction, organizational commitment, career outcomes, and performance. Similar to the research on stress and coping, coping with organizational change was a mediator in these relationships. Similarly, a study by Wanberg and Banas (2000) examined the dispositional (self-esteem, optimism, perceived control) and contextual (information, participation, change self-efficacy, social support, personal impact) predictors of openness to organizational change, and openness was expected to predict job satisfaction, work-related irritation, and intention to turnover (and turnover behavior). Openness to organizational change operated as a mediator between the dispositional and contextual variables and the outcomes.

Notice that once again, we see a mediated model such that individual difference variables are (partially or fully) mediated by coping with change or openness to change. As such, these models are very similar to the studies described earlier defining adaptability in terms of task performance. However, notice that different individual difference variables are included in each study. Therefore, we must again question whether these findings will generalize to other contexts outside of organizational change.

Integration and critique. The research reviewed in this section enhances our understanding of individual adaptability from a variety of perspectives. In this section, however, we build upon this work by approaching the literature from an individual adaptability perspective.

First, notice that none of the studies that define adaptive task performance consider such performance dimensions as contextual performance, organizational citizenship behavior (OCB), or counterproductive work behaviors (CWB). Rather, adaptability is nearly always defined in terms of task performance. Certainly, however, these other dimensions are important types of performance that require adaptability on the part of employees. For example, volunteering to help coworkers (an aspect of OCB) might require one to adapt to changing coworker behavior (in fact, the "backing up" dimensions of teamwork would certainly require adaptability; LePine, Hanson, Borman, & Motowidlo, 2000b). Thus, it is unclear whether the research conducted to date is specific to task performance or whether it would generalize to other dimensions of performance in the full criterion space.

Second, while research that defines adaptability in terms of changes to task performance has identified several KSAO determinants, these findings may not generalize to tasks different from the one being manipulated. It is unreasonable to believe the KSAOs required for successful cultural-adaptive performance are the same as those required for adaptive physical performance. The aforementioned studies recognize this concern, but it does not eliminate this as a potential limitation toward building a generalizable theory of adaptability.

Third, across the studies reviewed we have seen a wide variety of individual difference variables, even though most research takes an "individual differences→explanatory construct(s)→outcome" model. Some studies examine cognitive ability and personality based on the Five Factor Model (FFM) (LePine et al., 2000a, b), other studies use goal orientation (Colquitt & Simmering, 1998; Phillips & Gully, 1997), and others use a multitude of personality constructs (Judge et al., 1999). This makes it extremely difficult to understand what KSAOs actually contribute to adaptability with different performance constructs. Because not all studies examine the same individual differences, who can say which are most important? This requires the use of strong theories, which is valuable to the field. Unfortunately, however, the theories that have been proposed tend to be quite context specific, which may not be a good thing. For example, is adapting to organizational change really different than adapting to training? There is clearly a need to integrate and synthesize this expanding literature.

A fourth and related concern is that research often focuses on different "explanatory" variables that are adaptive in nature. Wanberg and Banas (2000) use openness to change, Judge et al. (1999) use coping, Brown (2001) uses learner choices, Lovett and Schunn (1999) use strategy selection, and so on. Each study rightfully focuses on the explanatory construct or processes most theoretically relevant to the given context and criterion, but this again produces results that may be context and criterion specific. We suspect that a number of these constructs are conceptually similar and perhaps empirically indistinguishable. Therefore, a question is whether the proliferation of such explanatory constructs for individual change-related questions can be summarized by an overall adaptability construct.

A final issue is that nearly every one of the studies mentioned has largely considered the causal sequence to flow from individual differences to explanatory-mediating mechanisms to performance. However, we consider it likely that some form of feedback loop exists such that performance influences the explanatory mechanism. The kinds of longitudinal research that are necessary for determining whether the explanatory variables "cause" some adaptive performance are lacking (NB: repeated measures designs are often used where there are multiple observations within a given session, but not the kinds of long-term studies conducted over months or years). Indeed, few of the models mentioned above allow much provision for feedback and reciprocal causation.

Thus, what is missing from current research is a broad-based understanding of the determinants and consequences of individual differences in adaptability. We believe a mid-level theory of individual adaptability would greatly contribute to research and practice by integrating these multiple diverse streams of research. Pulakos et al. (2000, 2002) provided a great service by identifying the latent dimensions of adaptability, and it seems appropriate to now understand the KSAO determinants and consequences of adaptability across multiple contexts and settings. There is also a need for a broadly applicable measure of adaptability that can be used for research and development in a variety of contexts and settings. Such have been the goals of our program of research on these issues. In the sections that follow, we introduce a theory to accomplish such goals.

THE I-ADAPT THEORY

In this section, we describe the structure, function, and process of individual adaptability within the conceptualization of I-ADAPT theory. This helps place the individual adaptability construct within a nomological network of KSAOs, performance, and situations. The I-ADAPT theory guides research, determines the appropriate way to measure the construct, and directs the nature of design and analysis.

In I-ADAPT, individual adaptability is defined as follows:

> *Individual adaptability* represents an individual's ability, skill, disposition, willingness, and/or motivation, to change or fit different task, social, and environmental features.

Our definition obviously builds on the research mentioned previously, but there are some important distinctions and clarifications in our definition.

First, adaptability resides within the individual, and hence reflects individual differences. Individual adaptability is not a characteristic of the situation (although situations may require or demand adaptability), nor does it occur only in response to a change in the environment or task (as it has been frequently conceptualized). Rather, individual adaptability is a reasonably stable, individual difference construct that influences how a person interprets and responds to different situations. For example, suppose an individual's behavior in a given situation is not producing the desired effect. Although the environment may not have changed, a more adaptive person will recognize this and change his/her behavior to change the situation in the intended manner. This subtle but important fact needs to be recognized – adaptability need not only occur from a changing situation. We can therefore think of adaptability as either proactive or reactive. Adaptability is proactive when an individual perceives a need to change even though the environment has not. Adaptability is reactive when an individual perceives a change in the environment (see Schunn & Reder, 1998 for similar distinctions).

Second, adaptability as an individual difference is not the same as adaptive performance. This is an important point of departure distinguishing

I-ADAPT theory from most of the previously discussed research within the industrial/organizational literature (e.g., Kozlowski et al., 2001; LePine et al., 2000a, b). We describe and refine this distinction when we discuss the theory, but our conceptualization of individual adaptability is as a composite KSAO, not task performance.

Third, individual adaptability is determined by a multidimensional set of KSAOs, and therefore captures the shared variance of these KSAOs in the prediction of adaptive performance. In the real world, behavior is determined by multiple dimensions, and so too is adaptation. This means adaptability is not a pure, basic trait or skill, but rather a characteristic composed of those set of KSAOs that most contribute to adaptability. We shall see the nature of these KSAO determinants of individual differences in adaptability, but in general they reflect cognitive ability, certain personality traits, preferences, and stress and coping skills. But realize no single KSAO entirely captures the breadth and depth of our conceptualization of adaptability. In the language of Hough and Schneider (1996), individual adaptability would be called a compound trait (whereas cognitive ability, the FFM traits, and so on, would be called elements). In the language of Ones and Viswesvaran (2001), it would be a criterion-focused occupational scale (COPS). One implication of this is that adaptability should be more strongly related to performance in situations that require it because it is based on those KSAOs most determinant of adaptive performance.

Fourth, the definition emphasizes "change" and/or "fit." Whether imposed by the person (proactive) or the situation (reactive), change and/or fit capture the essence of individual adaptability, but both terms are necessary to conceptualize the concept. Consider common synonyms of adaptability: "change, alter, modify, adjust, vary, revise, amend, bend, fit, rework"; but also "to acclimate, become accustomed, familiarize, or get used to." Therefore, our definition is broad enough to capture the subtle differences between affecting the environment (change, modify, alter, etc.), reconfiguring oneself (to acclimate, become accustomed, familiarize, or get used to), and degrees in between (fit).

Fifth, the definition allows change to occur in multiple ways and dimensions – task, social, and environment. To be specific, we build from the work of Pulakos et al. (2000, 2002), and recognize adaptability that contains eight lower-order latent dimensions, which are subsumed within a single higher order overall adaptability factor. Fig. 1 shows this expected structure, and notice the similarities of this hierarchical structure to models of the Five-Factor Model of personality (e.g., Costa & McCrae, 1992) and Carroll's (1993) hierarchical model of intelligence. One consequence of this

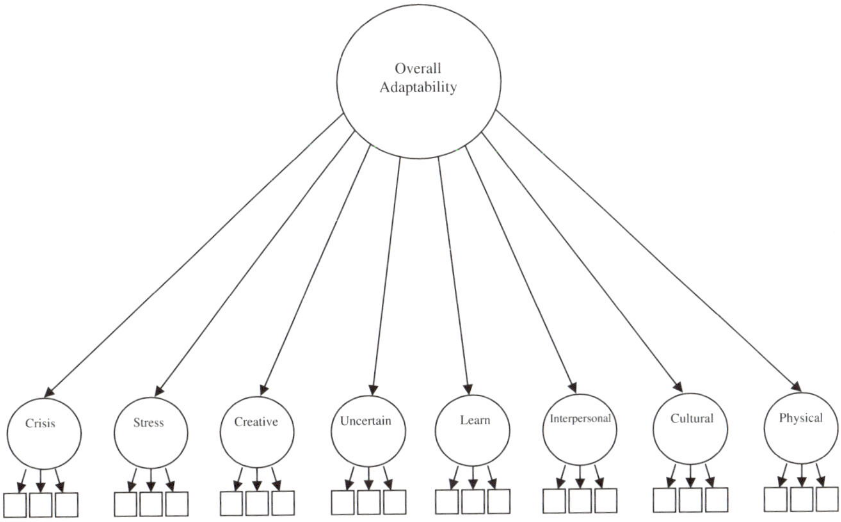

Fig. 1. Hypothesized Second-Order Factor Structure for Adaptability. Circles Represent Latent Constructs, Boxes Represent Measured (Manifest) Items *Note:* Not All Items are Shown; only Three Items per First-Order Factor are Used for Illustrative Purposes.

hierarchical structure is that not all types of adaptability are based on the same reasons. It also explains why we conceptualize adaptability as a broad-based summary of KSAOs most relevant for effective change and/or fit. For example, adapting to different social situations presumably requires different KSAOs than adapting to different types of technology. But an important benefit of using a broad-based adaptability conceptualization, rather than measuring the individual KSAOs, is that we often do not know which specific KSAOs are most important for a given type of change. Because the adaptability measure captures all such relevant variance (reflected among the eight lower-order factors), it should prove to be useful across a greater range of situations.

Please note that our purpose is not to claim adaptability to be all encompassing; such a definition has no theoretical value. If the definition says individual adaptability is predicted by everything, and explains everything, it obviously has no scientific purpose. But the definition is not so broad; as will be seen in the following sections we can make very specific – and falsifiable – predictions about the nomological network of individual adaptability. Thus, our goals lead us to define and study individual adaptability within the world of work and everyday life. Such a world contains multiple influences and consequences, and our conceptualization of adaptability must be broad enough to operate in this environment. We need to recognize that adaptability takes many forms – but always by an individual requiring proactive or reactive change to an environment.

I-ADAPT THEORY

Fig. 2 shows graphically the I-ADAPT theory, and how we conceptualize individual differences in adaptability fitting within a nomological network of KSAO-performance relationships. This nomological network builds from and articulates the definition noted above, as well as integrates previous research. We use the features of the theory to generate research propositions, but recognize that these propositions are general summaries of the nature of the relationships and effects. Space prohibits going into the detail necessary to fully articulate specific hypotheses, and such detail is the basis for future empirical research.

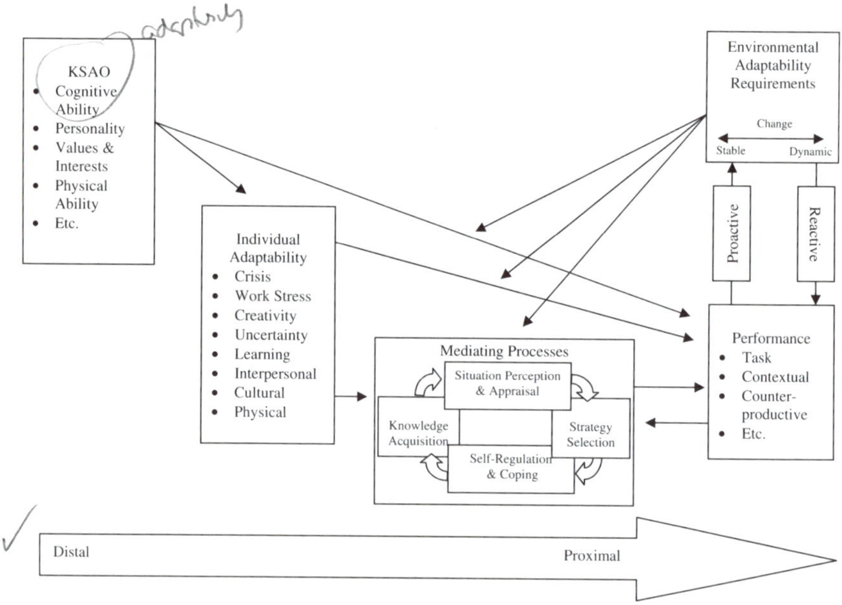

Fig. 2. Individual Adaptability (I-ADAPT) Theory.

Distal–proximal continuum. The first point to consider is that we conceptualize KSAOs, adaptability, proximal mediating processes, and performance as lying on a distal–proximal continuum. Distal predictor constructs tend to be more stable and trait-like; proximal predictor constructs tend to be more variable and state-like (George, 1992; Kanfer, 1990). Therefore, the most distal KSAOs contain such individual differences as cognitive ability, personality, interests/values, and physical ability. These KSAOs are relatively stable and enduring, unlikely to be strongly affected by situational factors and not quickly changed through experience. At the other extreme are proximal mediating processes such as self-regulation and strategy selection. These proximal mediating processes are more affected by situational factors, are more variable across time and situations, and relatively dynamic. As a general rule, proximal constructs are more strongly related to performance than distal constructs, but distal constructs work through proximal constructs and processes to influence performance. Thus, the theory is very much a process theory, and consistent with recent research in personality (McCrae & Costa, 1996; Mischel & Shoda, 1995), self-efficacy (Chen, Gully, Whiteman, & Kilcullen, 2000), performance (Campbell, McCloy, Oppler, & Sager, 1993; Motowidlo, Borman, & Schmit, 1997), and selection (Ployhart, 2004; Schmitt, Cortina, Ingerick, & Wiechmann, 2003).

KSAO-adaptability. Working now through the theory from the most distal to the most proximal processes, we see the distal constructs represent traditional, stable individual difference domains: cognitive ability (e.g., Carroll's hierarchical theory of intelligence, Cattell's fluid/crystallized intelligence, etc.), personality (Five Factor Model, Eysenck's two-factor model, etc.), values and interests (Holland's interest hexagon, Schwartz's values, etc.), physical ability (Hogan, 1991), and so on. These KSAOs are relatively unchanging and enduring; they may be altered only slowly over long periods of time.

Notice these distal KSAOs are hypothesized to be the only primary and direct determinants of individual differences in adaptability. This is consistent with the I-ADAPT definition that individual adaptability is not a measure of performance but a representation of KSAOs necessary for performance in such contexts. Being less distal and determined directly by distal KSAOs, adaptability is still reasonably stable and trait-like. However, it is more malleable than the KSAOs because it can be learned and changed to a degree (please note – while malleable, it is not easily changeable and thus more distal than proximal).

Although we have shown only a single, general summary relationship between individual adaptability and the KSAOs, we obviously expect more specific relationships between each KSAO and each sub-dimension of adaptability. For example, we would expect cognitive ability to be more strongly related to creativity and learning adaptability sub-dimensions than to work stress and physical adaptability sub-dimensions. We would expect the FFM trait neuroticism to be most strongly related to crisis, work stress, and uncertainty adaptability sub-dimensions. Extraversion should be related most strongly to interpersonal and cultural adaptability sub-dimensions. Notice that we do not propose or expect these relationships to be affected by situational cues, adaptability "is what it is." Therefore, one could conceptualize overall adaptability as the combination of adaptability sub-dimensions, with each adaptability sub-dimension in turn composed of various weightings of KSAOs (NB: the following notation is obviously not matrix notation in a statistical sense, only conceptually):

$$\begin{matrix}\text{Overall}\\ \text{Adaptability}\end{matrix} = f\left(\begin{pmatrix}\text{Crisis } w_1\\ \text{WorkStress } w_2\\ \text{Creativity } w_3\\ \text{Uncertainity } w_4\\ \text{Learning } w_5\\ \text{Interpersonal } w_6\\ \text{Cultural } w_7\\ \text{Physical } w_8\end{pmatrix}, \begin{pmatrix}\\ \textit{Weighting}\\ \textit{Matrix}\\ \\ \end{pmatrix}, \begin{pmatrix}\text{CognitiveAbility}\\ \text{Neuroticism}\\ \text{Extraversion}\\ \text{Openness}\\ \text{Agreeableness}\\ \text{Conscientiousness}\\ \text{Interests}\\ \text{PhysicalAbility}\end{pmatrix}\right) x$$

In this model, we see that the overall adaptability composite is a function of weighted adaptability sub-dimensions. These weights (denoted by w_1, w_2, etc.)

will most typically represent the dimension variances or factor loadings, unless there is a good reason to develop a different weighting scheme. Likewise, the KSAOs that contribute to each adaptability sub-dimension are based on weights defined in the weighting matrix (similar to factor loadings). This allows, for example, cognitive ability to more strongly be related (weighted) to creativity than to physical adaptability sub-dimensions. Altogether, this leads to:

Proposition 1. There will be differential weighting of various KSAOs to each adaptability sub-dimension.

Proposition 2. Overall adaptability is a weighted composite of the eight adaptability sub-dimensions.

Proposition 3. These weights are invariant across situations, contexts, and environments.

Adaptability-mediating processes. Adaptability, in turn, is the primary and direct determinant of psychological mediating processes. These mediating processes are state-like and dynamic, being affected by situational features and demonstrating varying rhythms and patterns over time. A variety of proximal mediating processes take place that are highly interrelated and dependent on each other in a system of processing. This conceptualization draws heavily from McCrae and Costa (1996) and Mischel and Shoda's (1995) cognitive-affective personality systems (CAPS). However, here we also see the various mediating processes described in previous research, including appraisal and coping, strategy selection, and so on, which have not been integrated into such a system. Although neglecting much specific detail, for present purposes we summarize all such processing in four major processing steps.

First, situation perception and appraisal represent how the individual perceives and interprets the situation, whether it is perceived as stressful versus challenging (appraisal), changing versus stable, the nature of the change, and related environmental features. Individual differences in adaptability directly influence how individuals perceive and appraise situations, events, roles, and tasks. We would expect highly adaptive individuals to more quickly recognize changes in key situational features and cues, recognize when the cues have not changed but should have, identify and interpret the situation as challenging rather than stressful, and identify how the situation needs to change. More adaptive people should therefore perceive tasks and situations differently than those who are less adaptive. Such expectations are consistent with a variety of studies (e.g., Lazarus & Folkman, 1984; LePine et al., 2000a, b; Lovett & Schunn, 1999).

Proposition 4. Individuals with more adaptability will be more likely to correctly identify the relevant situational cues highlighting a need for change.

Interpreting a situation that requires adaptability starts a chain of events for which the adaptive individual will be better suited. The more adaptive person will more correctly frame the situation and choose the appropriate strategy from a set of strategies (Lovett & Schunn, 1999). This strategy selection will contribute to regulating one's behavior in a manner consistent with the strategy and goal, coping with the nature of the challenging or stressful event, learning from the experience, and cycling back through these processes. We would expect more adaptive individuals to adopt more active coping styles and problem-focused strategies. By behaving in such ways, one learns the success base rates of the behavior and strategy (Lovett & Schunn, 1999), acquires knowledge about performance and situational contingencies (Kozlowski et al., 2001), and determines how behavior and environment are related (LePine et al., 2000a, b). Individuals with more adaptability will accomplish all such tasks more quickly and accurately.

Proposition 5. Individuals with more adaptability will be more likely to correctly select a set of relevant strategies, and the appropriate strategy, for the situation.

Proposition 6. Individuals with more adaptability will be more likely to appropriately regulate their behavior to change or create the change in the situation.

Proposition 7. Individuals with more adaptability will be more likely to adopt active coping styles, and implement problem-focused coping strategies.

Proposition 8. Individuals with more adaptability will be more likely to acquire the appropriate knowledge about the situation and how they are performing in it, to determine how well they are adapting to the change.

Thus, individual adaptability influences the processing and interrelationships of the mediating mechanisms. But notice the theory proposes no feedback loop from proximal processes to adaptability; the theoretical causal direction is one way from individual differences in adaptability to mediating processes. Further, it is not expected that every and all adaptability sub-dimensions will influence all mediating processes. We expect to find particular sub-dimensions most affecting specific mediating processes. This means, for example, individual differences in the cultural adaptability sub-dimension may most influence situation perception and appraisal when dealing with individuals from diverse cultures, while the crisis adaptability sub-dimension may be less important. But if summarized in an overall adaptability composite, the theory predicts:

> **Proposition 9.** Individual differences in adaptability affect mediating processes, but mediating processes do not affect individual differences in adaptability.

> **Proposition 10.** Different sub-dimensions of individual adaptability can demonstrate unique effects on each of the various mediating processes.

The nature of performance. I-ADAPT theory makes no specific claims about the nature of performance. Performance may represent task performance, contextual performance, CWB, or related dimensions, and each dimension may require adaptability to perform successfully. For example, adaptive task performance may involve the switch to a new technology, adaptive contextual performance may involve learning to help new co-workers from different cultures, and adaptive counterproductive performance may involve innovative ways of stealing from the company (obviously a bad thing, but adaptive nonetheless). This is in contrast to the work by Pulakos et al. (2000), who identified dimensions of adaptive performance. We agree that these latent dimensions capture the breadth of adaptability within most organizational settings, but in contrast, I-ADAPT theory proposes any type of performance – task, contextual, counterproductive, teamwork, etc. – may be adaptive depending on the adaptability requirements in the situation. Thus, the extent to which performance is determined by individual differences in adaptability is not inherent in the criterion construct, but rather driven by the environment. When the environment requires adaptability in performance, this criterion-construct variance will be related to individual adaptability. Notice this distinction is similar to research on typical and maximum performance (Sackett, Zedeck, & Fogli, 1988), which defines the difference between typical and maximum in terms of environmental features (time pressure, evaluative context, instructions). Therefore, just as the distinction between typical and maximum performance is driven by contextual factors (see Lim & Ployhart, 2004; Ployhart, Lim, & Chan, 2001), so too are the adaptability requirements of performance.

Proposition 11. The adaptability requirements of performance are not inherent in the criterion construct, but determined by the adaptability requirements in the environment.

Proposition 12. Any dimension of performance (e.g., task, contextual, counterproductive) may be determined by individual differences in adaptability, so long as the environment requires adaptation.

Determinants and consequences of mediating processes. As shown in Fig. 2, mediating processes operate in a continual dynamic loop such that situation perception → strategy selection → self-regulation and coping → knowledge acquisition → situation perception → etc. However, these mediating processes produce an overall effect directly onto performance. We call this effect a feedforward mechanism because the causal arrow goes from the mediating processes to performance. The feedforward mechanism allows the relationship between mediating processes and performance to change as driven by variability in mediating processes.

Proposition 13. Mediating processes in combination produce a direct effect on performance (feedforward), but the magnitude and direction of this effect may be variable across time and situations.

Why does the effect size of the feedforward mechanism change? Answering this question requires examining the three direct effects on mediating processes. First, we have already mentioned the direct effects of individual adaptability on mediating processes. Second, performance may itself influence the mediating processes, such that performance allows feedback into the processing system. How well the individual is performing provides feedback to influence situation perception, strategy selection, self-regulation, and the remainder of the cycle. This allows feedback from performance to alter and influence mediating processes, and hence is called a feedback mechanism. Third, there is a direct effect of the environment on the mediating processes. If performance behavior changes the situation, the situation will lead to different perceptions of the situation, strategies chosen, self-regulatory behavior, learning, and the reiteration of these processes. Thus, the mediating processes are affected by an open-loop system of adaptability, performance, and the environment.

Proposition 14. Individual differences in performance may influence mediating processes (feedback mechanism).

Proposition 15. The environment has a direct effect on mediating processes.

Proposition 16. The environment does not moderate the individual adaptability-mediating processes relationship, but rather directly effects the mediating processes.

The role of the environment and relations to performance. I-ADAPT theory makes a distinction between the environment in which performance and behavior occur, and the performance/behavior itself. We use a generic term "environment" to capture the breadth and variety of cues, features, and demands in the environment that will require adaptability (more detail on possible adaptability-invoking task characteristics may be found in Kozlowski et al., 2001; Wood, 1986). For our purposes, we summarize these in terms of a continuum of "change," such that at one extreme there is no change in the environment (stable) and at the other extreme there is continuous change in the environment (dynamic). We have represented this change continuum within the environment box in Fig. 2. This allows a variety of interesting relationships with performance and individual adaptability.

In particular, if the environment is stable it still allows individual adaptability to be present. Adaptability will be proactive because when there is no change in the environment, but the person perceives the need for such a change, she or he performs differently to produce a change in the stable situation. On the other hand, when the environment is dynamic and requires adaptability, we see it has a direct effect on performance and the adaptability requirements for performance stem from changes in the environment – a reactive form of adaptability to a changing environment. This is the conceptualization of adaptability proposed in most previous research (Kozlowski et al., 2001; LePine et al., 2000a, b; Pulakos et al., 2000, 2002).

Proposition 17. Proactive relationships between the environment and performance occur when the environment is stable, but the individual's performance influences the environment.

Proposition 18. Reactive relationships between the environment and performance occur when the environment is dynamic and hence demands performance adaptation.

Environmental moderators and direct effects. Although the I-ADAPT theory is about individual adaptability, an important part of the theory is its predictions for when individual adaptability will and will not be strongly related to performance. Thus, the theory is quite falsifiable in that it predicts when effects should be present and absent. The theory allows for such conditions via the nature of the environment, and thus the environment determines the "need" for adaptability. Fig. 2 shows how the environment produces these effects through one direct effect and two moderating effects.

The direct effect occurs on the proximal mediating processes. As noted above, they are more variable and state-like and hence affected by the environment (George, 1992). By influencing mediating processes, the environment constrains or enhances the effects of individual adaptability. Additionally, two moderating effects are present: one on the KSAO-performance relationship, and one on the adaptability-performance relationship. Thus, the environment may moderate the direct effects of the KSAOs and individual adaptability on performance – a three-way interaction. In environments or situations that are stable and have no need for adaptability, the direct effects of the KSAOs should be reasonably strong (where strong is defined as based on past research) and the direct effects of adaptability should be fairly weak. However, as the change continuum shifts to a more dynamic environment, the direct effects of adaptability will become strong and fully mediate the effects of the KSAOs (whose direct effects will become nonexistent). This occurs because the nature of performance variance changes from relatively stable variance to relatively dynamic variance.

These predictions are shown graphically in Fig. 3. Notice that the relationship between adaptability and performance is strong and positive (and the KSAO-performance relationship is weak) when there are strong adaptability requirements in situations (i.e., dynamic environments). On the other hand, when the situation requires little adaptability (static environment), the

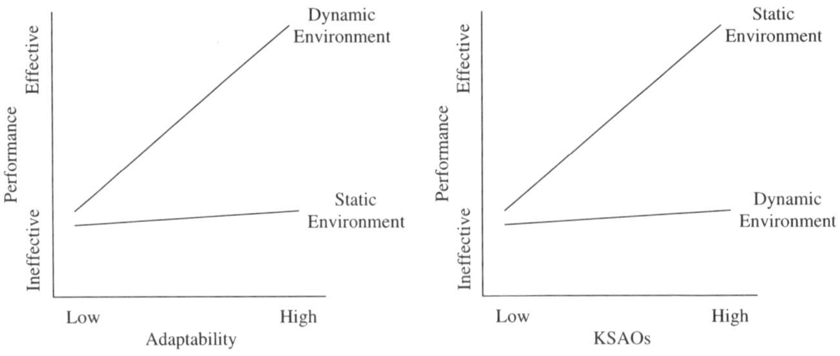

Fig. 3. Moderating Effects of Environment on KSAO and Adaptability Relationships with Performance.

KSAOs have a strong and positive relationship with performance, whereas adaptability has relatively little relationship.

> **Proposition 19.** When the environment is stable, the KSAOs will demonstrate a direct effect on performance and individual adaptability will demonstrate practically no effect.
>
> Thus, individual adaptability will play no role as a mediator.
>
> **Proposition 20.** When the environment is dynamic, the KSAOs will demonstrate practically no direct effect on performance and individual adaptability will demonstrate a strong direct effect. Thus, individual adaptability will partially (under mild dynamism) or fully (under total dynamism) mediate the effects of the KSAOs on performance.

The big picture. Although we have examined the intricacies of the I-ADAPT theory through the lens of a microscope, it is instructive to step back and see the gestalt of the theory that provides its real scientific value. To ensure that this "big picture" is not lost in the details, we reiterate the critical features:

- Individual adaptability is a reasonably stable, higher-order individual difference construct composed of eight latent sub-dimensions. In terms of its "distance" from performance, individual adaptability lies midway on a distal–proximal continuum. It is determined only by more distal KSAOs, and it effects more proximal mediating processes.
- Individual adaptability has both direct and mediated (through proximal mediating processes) effects on performance. Individual adaptability charges and directs these proximal mediating processes.
- Proximal mediating processes are where individual adaptability, performance, and the situation "meet." These mediating processes have both feedforward and feedback loops from performance, and hence occur in a dynamic system of processing.
- The effects of individual adaptability may take two forms. Proactive effects occur when there is no change in the environment but the individual anticipates the need for such change. Reactive effects occur when there is a change in the environment that must be accommodated.
- Adaptive performance is not inherent in the criterion construct but driven by the demands of the environment. Thus, adaptive performance requirements are really consequences of a changing environment. This means adaptive performance may occur for task, contextual, or counterproductive performance dimensions.

- The environment lies on a change continuum, from entirely stable to entirely dynamic. This results in a moderating effect of the environment on KSAO-performance and individual adaptability-performance relationships. The more dynamic the environment, the stronger the effect of individual adaptability on performance and the weaker the effect for KSAOs.
- The right half of Fig. 2 allows cause to move forward and backward in an open system. Forward causal influence goes from KSAOs → individual adaptability → mediating processes → performance → environment. Backward causal influence goes from the environment → performance → mediating processes.

COMPARISON OF I-ADAPT THEORY TO EXISTING CONCEPTUALIZATIONS

Let us now consider how I-ADAPT theory compares to previous conceptualizations of adaptability: performance-defined adaptability, strategy-defined adaptability, coping-defined adaptability, and reactions to change-defined adaptability. In particular, we shall see each of the previous conceptualizations fit well within I-ADAPT theory.

First, I-ADAPT theory incorporates the dominant performance-defined adaptability perspective, which treats adaptability as individual differences on performance to a changing task (e.g., decision making). In our model, the studies by Kozlowski et al. (2001) and LePine et al. (2000a, b) would equate adaptability with task performance and try to predict this adaptive performance with direct effects from KSAOs (LePine et al., 2000a, b) and mediating processes (Kozlowski et al., 2001). I-ADAPT theory draws a distinction between individual differences in performance with individual differences in adaptability. By adopting this perspective, we need not be concerned whether the specific KSAOs of adaptive performance generalize to other performance contexts because individual differences in adaptability should contribute to adaptive performance in all contexts in which it is required. Thus, in I-ADAPT theory individual adaptability is neither context nor task dependent.

Second, I-ADAPT theory can generalize and account for training transfer (i.e., generalization and maintenance). Much of the transfer literature would define adaptability in terms of learning new knowledge or generalizing behavior to new contexts (Kozlowski et al., 2001; Kraiger et al., 1993). In

I-ADAPT theory, the learning and meta-cognitive components are present in proximal mediating processes, and as such transfer is largely driven by individual differences in adaptability. However, unique to the theory is the pivotal and fully mediating role played by adaptability between transfer (performance), learning (mediating processes), and more distal KSAOs.

Third, it is both similar to and different from the conceptualizations of Pulakos et al. (2000, 2002). It is similar because our approach is based on the logic that adaptability requirements of performance are driven by the performance context or situation. That is, individual differences in adaptability are only likely to be important when they are demanded by the performance situation, and they are likely to be represented by eight latent lower-order factors subsumed within a higher-order factor. But it is different because the theory proposes so long as adaptability is demanded by the environment, it applies to any performance dimension and type of performance – task, contextual, and counterproductive. Thus, I-ADAPT theory proposes any type of performance can potentially have adaptive requirements, but these requirements are not inherent in the criterion construct but rather in the environment. This obviously expands the realms to which adaptability may be relevant, and in our opinion increases the relevance of adaptability to more "routine" forms of work. For example, the typical task performance of a postal delivery worker will become adaptive when she or he must learn how to use a new way of processing mail.

Fourth, it incorporates the perspective of Lovett and Schunn (1999) and Schunn and Reder (1998) on strategy selection as a form of adaptability. They used strategy selection as a dependent variable to study adapting to a changing situation. Our model incorporates strategy selection (and indeed, can incorporate the RCCL model) within proximal mediating processes. But notice that by doing so, individual differences in strategy selection are determined by individual differences in adaptability, performance, and the environment.

Fifth, I-ADAPT builds on and synthesizes research on stress and coping by incorporating them into proximal mediating processes. We see individual adaptability influences both the primary appraisal of the situation and the secondary appraisal of coping. We expect those with more adaptability to be less inclined to see events as stressful, and when they are, to respond with active coping styles and problem-focused coping strategies. However, an important extension to the stress and coping research is the pivotal role of individual adaptation. That is, the psychological resources that help energize coping are hypothesized to stem from individual differences in adaptability, such that those with more adaptability have a greater "reserve" of psychological resources.

Sixth, I-ADAPT theory incorporates the perspectives of individual differences to organizational change. For example, openness to change in Wanberg and Banas (2000) is likely to be similar (if not empirically identical) to individual adaptability. Likewise, I-ADAPT theory has no need for specific measures such as coping with organizational change (Judge et al., 1999) because they are subsumed within a general coping-mediating process. But again, we see that rather than KSAOs having a direct influence on these explanatory variables, the direct effect is individual adaptability with KSAOs operating through this direct effect.

Therefore, because I-ADAPT theory conceptualizes individual differences in adaptability falling between KSAOs and proximal mediating processes, and performance (broadly defined), it helps increase the generalizability of the individual adaptability construct to many different types of tasks and settings – so long as the environment requires adaptation. Individual adaptability is not task specific, context specific, or dependent on a particular set of KSAOs. Rather, individual adaptability is a broadly useful construct for explaining and predicting individual differences in performance in environments that require adaptation. I-ADAPT theory makes a variety of novel predictions describing when adaptability should and should not matter, how it should matter, and how KSAOs, individual adaptability, performance, and the environment are interrelated. Now that we have defined and conceptualized the individual differences in adaptability construct, we discuss a measurement system capable of assessing the breadth of individual differences in adaptability.

THE I-ADAPT MEASURE

Let us begin by making clear the goals of the I-ADAPT measure (I-ADAPT-M) measurement system. Obviously, the first goal is to assess the breadth and structure of adaptability as proposed from the theory. This means we must assess all eight dimensions denoted by Pulakos et al. (2000), and test the structure of these dimensions using second-order CFA. Second, because our goals are to study individual differences in adaptability across a wide variety of real-world contexts, we needed a reasonably short measure that could be completed quickly and easily. It is rare in "real world" data collection to have the luxury of administering long surveys. Our experience suggests few organizations are willing or able to add more than a page to existing surveys, and employees are less likely to complete surveys with more than about 60 questions. Third, we wanted a self-report measure to simplify administration and scoring, and to enhance applicability to multiple contexts. We chose a self-report inventory because such inventories can easily be administered using a variety of formats (e.g., paper-and-pencil, internet), are familiar to most people, and are easy to score. It was important to ensure that the items were not specific to any particular context, however, as this would decrease the generalizability of the measure.

Therefore, our goals were to develop a comprehensive self-report measure that assesses eight dimensions of adaptability, but is short enough that it can be completed in approximately 10 min. We call this measure the I-ADAPT-M. In what follows, we summarize the development of such a measure. We would especially like to thank Jessica Saltz and David Mayer for their work in developing the original version of the adaptability measure.

Development of the original I-ADAPT-M was based on a thorough review of the literature relevant to individual adaptability, with a particular focus on understanding the eight dimensions identified in Pulakos et al. (2000). Their work was so careful and comprehensive that we felt it appropriate to write items to reflect these eight dimensions. Remember, the I-ADAPT theory conceptualizes individual adaptability as a composite of those KSAOs most relevant for adaptation across situations. As such, the eight dimensions seemed perfectly suited as a useful taxonomy upon which to summarize these KSAOs.

As an aside, it is worth noting that this approach is not unique to I-ADAPT-M. For example, the FFM is a taxonomy based on the natural structure of normal adult personality, with five broad factors subsuming multiple lower-order factors. Yet, Hough (1998) has argued the taxonomy is too broad for prediction in organizational contexts, and should be refined to seven dimensions. The purpose of the taxonomy thus determines the nature of the taxonomy (Fleishman & Quaintance, 1984). Because our purpose is to assess individual differences in adaptability across a variety of real-world contexts, the eight dimensions identified by Pulakos et al. (2000) provide an ideal starting point.

After writing preliminary items to tap each dimension, they were subjected to a variety of subject matter expert reviews (e.g., translation and retranslation) and empirical assessments of item and scale quality. A construct validity study using a 40-item measure (five items for each sub-dimension) found strong support for convergent and discriminant validity, and a CFA found support for the second-order factor structure (i.e., Fig. 1). When using the I-ADAPT-M in practice, we identified some items in need of refinement and have since added new items to several of the sub-dimensions. Inclusion of these new items improved the fit of the CFA. We present a short,

55-item version of the I-ADAPT-M drawn from our research in the appendix. We have found this short 55-item format to be extremely useful. This instrument is freely available for research purposes.

FUTURE DIRECTIONS AND UNANSWERED QUESTIONS

We conclude our discussion of I-ADAPT theory with a consideration of the next evolution of this research, and what will be necessary to test and refine the theory.

The most pressing issue is to more specifically articulate and test the various propositions in the theory. There are a multitude of proposed relationships that occur in a particular sequence, and future research must be cognizant of these issues. These propositions are necessarily general, and future research will need to carefully explicate the various relationships for specific and testable hypotheses. For example, can one show differences in reactive versus proactive adaptability? Are the KSAO-adaptability sub-dimension relationships invariant across situations? Is the environmental moderator effect (Fig. 3) supported? What are the key features of an environment that requires adaptability? In answering such questions, the linkages of the theory will be strengthened as will our understanding of individual adaptability.

Another fruitful area of research is to identify how individual adaptability fits with other constructs that are mid-range on the distal–proximal continuum. Our review of past research identified goal orientation as being a key mid-range variable, and how goal orientation fits within the I-ADAPT theory is an open question. On the one hand, we can see it being a more distal concept that helps drive adaptability. Alternatively, we can see it being a consequence of individual adaptability such that those more adaptable will be more likely to adopt different kinds of goals (such as learning goals). Individual adaptability's relation to other such constructs, such as openness to change (Wanberg & Banas, 2000), could be an exciting area of research.

An additional area for theoretical extension will be to examine how I-ADAPT theory fits within group and team contexts. Clearly the entire theory has been conceptualized at the individual level, with the exception of contextual factors being represented from the environment. While that has been our goal, future theoretical and empirical work may attempt to integrate the I-ADAPT theory into team adaptation models and in team contexts. For example, one might examine how individual adaptability emerges to form aggregate unit-level adaptability (e.g., average group adaptability), and how this aggregate unit-level adaptability predicts unit-level processes and outcomes. Relatedly, one might conceptualize individual adaptability within a more dynamic system of individual and team processing (e.g., Kozlowski, Gully, McHugh, Salas, & Cannon-Bowers, 1996). How individual adaptability relates to role perceptions would clearly be important and could lead to a consideration of adaptive leadership. For example, what proximal mediating processes do adaptive leaders enact that contribute to better individual and unit performance (see Zaccaro, Gilbert, Thor, & Mumford, 1991)? Pulakos et al. (this volume) provide a nice description of the issues and a model of team adaptability that should prove useful for framing such questions.

When conducting research on adaptability, a variety of experimental and correlational methods will be required. An obvious need not just for the theory, but for this entire domain of research, is truly longitudinal models that can tease apart causes from effects. I-ADAPT theory is somewhat unique in its specification of feedforward/feedback processes and dynamic mediating processes, but a consequence of these propositions is the need to use designs that can capture both processes. Also important will be the use of laboratory manipulations. There is nothing in the theory that makes it context specific or dependent on "real world" participants, so laboratory studies will be a critical mechanism for testing many aspects of the theory. Indeed, laboratory studies will be particularly important in determining whether the hypothesized causal direction of the theory is correct. Assuming the study was appropriately designed, the theoretical implications of the theory testing should generalize to other contexts. However, field studies will be necessary to estimate effects sizes and determine whether these laboratory findings are supported in real-world applications of the theory. Clearly both methodologies are important for supporting or refuting the theory.

Researchers may need to investigate the feasibility of other measurement systems. We chose a self-report system because of its broad applicability, but issues of self-deception and other potential confounds to self-report measurement could be issues. Therefore, more objective forms of measurement may need to be considered. One possibility is to use a variation of a policy-capturing methodology. Different situations reflecting the eight adaptability sub-dimensions could be presented, with each situation varying in its degree of change and hence adaptability requirements. These data could be modeled in a growth model (discussed next), and the amount of change across the situations would represent adaptability. Likewise, reaction-time measures may be reasonable ways of inferring individual adaptability.

Finally, the appropriate analytical methods will be needed to capture adaptability. Here, we propose the longitudinal random coefficient (RCM) growth model as an especially effective analytical strategy. For example, one could model individual changes in task performance (e.g., slope, rate of change) to occur as a function individual differences in adaptability. That is, individual differences in performance are modeled as a change across situations via a slope parameter, and individual differences in adaptability will predict and explain such slope differences. There are a variety of analytical models that are perfect for this context; we refer the reader to several sources that describe such models and how to use them (Bliese, 2002; Bliese & Ployhart, 2002; Ployhart, Holtz, & Bliese, 2002). Such models could easily be used in existing paradigms (e.g., Kozlowski et al., 2001; LePine et al., 2000a, b) and have already been used in stress and coping research (e.g., Bliese & Jex, 2002; Garst, Frese, & Molenaar, 2000). Such models could provide more information about change and adaptability than existing approaches.

CONCLUSION

Most of us are painfully aware of the demands requiring our individual adaptation, and we can see the successes and failures of adaptability all around us. We propose I-ADAPT theory as a means to conceptualize and frame such questions, and research on the theory may contribute to a greater understanding of the antecedents and consequences of individual adaptability. Armed with the theory and measure, researchers may have a useful set of theoretical and methodological tools to carry out this research. We believe the future holds exciting times for research on individual adaptability.

ACKNOWLEDGMENT

We thank Jessica Saltz, Dave Mayer, Ben Porr, and Michael Camburn for their help in preparing this chapter.

REFERENCES

Armenakis, A. A., & Bedian, A. G. (1999). Organizational change: A review of theory and research in the 1990s. *Journal of Management*, *25*, 293–315.

Baldwin, T. T., & Ford, J. K. (1988). Transfer of training: A review and directions for future research. *Personnel Psychology*, *41*, 63–105.

Beehr, T. A. (1995). *Psychological stress in the workplace*. London: Routledge.

Bliese, P. D. (2002). Multilevel random coefficient modeling in organizational research: Examples using SAS and S-PLUS. In: F. Drasgow & N. Schmitt (Eds), *Measuring and analyzing behavior in organizations: Advances in measurement and data analysis* (pp. 401–445). San Francisco, CA: Jossey-Bass.

Bliese, P. D., & Jex, S. M. (2002). Incorporating a multi-level perspective into occupational stress research: Theoretical, methodological, and practical implications. *Journal of Occupational Health Psychology*, *7*, 265–276.

Bliese, P. D., & Ployhart, R. E. (2002). Growth modeling using random coefficient models: Model building, testing, and illustration. *Organizational Research Methods*, *5*, 362–387.

Brown, K. G. (2001). Using computers to deliver training: Which employees learn and why. *Personnel Psychology*, *54*, 271–296.

Campbell, J. P., McCloy, R. A., Oppler, S. H., & Sager, C. E. (1993). A theory of performance. In: N. Schmitt & W. C. Borman (Eds), *Personnel selection in organizations* (pp. 35–70). San Francisco: Jossey-Bass.

Carroll, J. B. (1993). *Human cognitive abilities: A survey of factor-analytic studies*. New York: Cambridge University Press.

Carver, C. S., Scheier, M. F., & Weintraub, J. K. (1989). Assessing coping strategies: A theoretically based approach. *Journal of Personality and Social Psychology*, *56*, 267–283.

Cascio, W. F. (2003). Changes in workers, work, and organizations. In: R. J. Klimoski, W. C. Borman & D. R. Ilgen (Eds), *Handbook of psychology* (Vol. 12, pp. 401–422). Wiley: Hoboken, NJ.

Chen, G., Gully, S. M., Whiteman, J., & Kilcullen, R. N. (2000). Examination of relationships among trait-like individual differences, state-like individual differences, and learning performance. *Journal of Applied Psychology*, *85*, 835–847.

Chi, M. T. H., Feltovish, P. J., & Glaser, R. (1981). Categorization and representation of physics problems by experts and novices. *Cognitive Science*, *5*, 121–152.

Colquitt, J. A., & Simmering, M. J. (1998). Conscientiousness, goal orientation, and motivation to learn during the learning process: A longitudinal field study. *Journal of Applied Psychology*, *83*, 654–665.

Costa, P. T., Jr., & McCrae, R. R. (1992). *NEO-PI-R professional manual*. Odessa, FL: Psychological Assessment Resources, Inc.

Ericsson, K. A., & Polson, P. G. (1988). An experimental analysis of the mechanisms of a memory skill. *Journal of Experimental Psychology: Learning, Memory and Cognition*, *14*, 305–316.

Fleishman, E. A., & Quaintance, M. K. (1984). *Taxonomies of human performance*. Orlando, FL: Academic Press.

Ford, J. K., Smith, E. M., Weissbein, D. A., Gully, S. M., & Salas, E. (1998). Relationships of goal orientation, metacognitive activity, and practice strategies with learning outcomes and transfer. *Journal of Applied Psychology*, *83*, 218–233.

Garst, H., Frese, M., & Molenaar, P. C. M. (2000). The temporal factor of change in stressor–strain relationships: A growth curve model on a longitudinal study in East Germany. *Journal of Applied Psychology*, *85*, 417–438.

George, J. M. (1992). The role of personality in organizational life: Issues and evidence. *Journal of Management*, *18*, 185–213.

Gould, S. J. (1989). *Wonderful life: The Burgess Shale and the nature of history*. New York, NY: W.W. Norton & Company.

Hesketh, B., & Neal, A. (1999). Technology and performance. In: D. R. Ilgen & E. D. Pulakos (Eds), *The changing nature of performance: Implications for staffing, motivation, and development* (pp. 21–55). San Francisco, CA: Jossey-Bass.

Hogan, J. (1991). Structure of physical performance in occupational tasks. *Journal of Applied Psychology*, *76*, 495–507.

Hollenbeck, G. P., & McCall, M. W. (1999). Leadership development: Contemporary practices. In: A. I. Kraut & A. K. Korman (Eds), *Evolving practices in human resource management* (pp. 172–200). San Francisco, CA: Jossey-Bass.

Holyoak, K. J. (1991). Symbolic connectionism: Toward third-generation theories of expertise. In: K. A. Ericsson & J. Smith (Eds), *Toward a general theory of expertise* (pp. 301–336). Cambridge, England: Cambridge University Press.

Hough, L. M. (1998). Personality at work: Issues and evidence. In: M. D. Hakel (Ed.), *Beyond multiple choice: Evaluating alternatives to traditional testing for selection* (pp. 131–166). Mahwah, NJ: Lawrence Erlbaum Associates.

Hough, L. M., & Schneider, R. J. (1996). Personality traits, taxonomies, and applications in organizations. In: K. R. Murphy (Ed.), *Individual differences and behavior in organizations* (pp. 3–30). San Francisco, CA: Jossey-Bass.

Ilgen, D. R., & Pulakos, E. D. (1999). Employee performance in today's organizations. In: D. R. Ilgen & E. D. Pulakos (Eds), *The changing nature of performance* (pp. 1–18). San Francisco, CA: Jossey-Bass.

Jex, S. M. (1998). *Stress and job performance: Theory, research, and implications for managerial practice*. Thousand Oaks, CA: Sage.

Jex, S. M., Bliese, P. D., Buzzell, S., & Primeau, J. (2001). The impact of self-efficacy on stressor-strain relations: Coping style as an explanatory mechanism. *Journal of Applied Psychology*, *86*, 401–409.

Judge, T. A., Thoresen, C. J., Pucik, V., & Welbourne, T. M. (1999). Managerial coping with organizational change: A dispositional perspective. *Journal of Applied Psychology*, *84*, 107–122.

Kanfer, R. (1990). Motivation theory and industrial and organizational psychology. In: M. D. Dunnette & L. M. Hough (Eds), *Handbook of industrial and organizational psychology* (2nd ed., Vol. 1, pp. 75–170). Palo Alto, CA: Consulting Psychologists Press.

Kozlowski, S. W. J. (1998). Training and developing adaptive teams: Theory, principles, and research. In: J. A. Cannon-Bowers & E. Salas (Eds), *Decision making under stress: Implications for training and simulation* (pp. 115–153). Washington, DC: APA Books.

Kozlowski, S. W. J., Gully, S. M., Brown, K. G., Salas, E., Smith, E. M., & Nason, E. R. (2001). Effects of training goals and goal orientation traits on multidimensional training outcomes and performance adaptability. *Organizational Behavior and Human Decision Processes*, *85*, 1–31.

Kozlowski, S. W. J., Gully, S. M., McHugh, P. P., Salas, E., & Cannon-Bowers, J. A. (1996). A dynamic theory of leadership and team effectiveness: Developmental and task contingent leader roles. *Research in Personnel and Human Resource Management*, *14*, 253–305.

Kozlowski, S. W. J., Toney, R. J., Mullins, M. E., Weissbein, D. A., Brown, K. G., & Bell, B. S. (2000). Developing adaptability: A theory for the design of integrated-embedded training systems. In: E. Salas (Ed.), *Human/technology interaction in complex systems* (Vol. 10). Greenwich, CT: JAI Press.

Kraiger, K., Ford, J. K., & Salas, E. (1993). Application of cognitive, skill-based, and affective theories of learning outcomes to new methods of training evaluation. *Journal of Applied Psychology*, *78*, 311–328.

Lazarus, R. S., & Folkman, S. (1984). *Stress, appraisal, and coping*. New York: Springer.

LePine, J. A., Colquitt, J. A., & Erez, A. (2000a). Adaptability to changing task contexts: Effects of general cognitive ability, conscientiousness, and openness to experience. *Personnel Psychology*, *53*, 563–593.

LePine, J. A., Hanson, M. A., Borman, W. C., & Motowidlo, S. J. (2000b). Contextual performance and teamwork: Implications for staffing. In: G. Ferris (Ed), *Research in personnel and human resources management* (Vol. 19, pp. 53–90). Stamford, CT: Jai Press.

Lim, B. C., & Ployhart, R. E. (2004). Transformational leadership: Relations to the five factor model and team performance in typical and maximum contexts. *Journal of Applied Psychology*, *89*, 610–621.

Lovett, M. C., & Schunn, C. D. (1999). Task representations, strategy variability, and base-rate neglect. *Journal of Experimental Psychology: General*, *128*, 107–130.

Martocchio, J. J., & Judge, T. A. (1997). Relationship between conscientiousness and learning in employee training: Mediating influences of self-deception and self-efficacy. *Journal of Applied Psychology*, *82*, 764–773.

Mathieu, J. E., Martineau, J. W., & Tannenbaum, S. I. (1993). Individual and situational influences on the development of self-efficacy: Implications for training effectiveness. *Personnel Psychology*, *46*, 125–147.

McCrae, R. R., Jr., & Costa, P. T. (1996). Toward a new generation of personality theories: Theoretical contexts for the five-factor model. In: J. S. Wiggins (Ed.), *The five-factor model of personality: Theoretical perspectives* (pp. 51–87). New York: The Guilford Press.

Mischel, W., & Shoda, Y. (1995). A cognitive-affective system theory of personality: Reconceptualizing situations, dispositions, dynamics, and invariance in personality structure. *Psychological Review*, *102*, 246–268.

Motowidlo, S. J., Borman, W. C., & Schmit, M. J. (1997). A theory of individual differences in task and contextual performance. *Human Performance*, *10*, 71–83.

Ones, D. S., & Viswesvaran, C. (2001). Integrity tests and other criterion-focused occupational personality scales (COPS) used in personnel selection. *International Journal of Selection & Assessment*, *9*, 31–39.

Pearlin, L. I. (1999). Stress and mental health: A conceptual overview. In: A. V. Horwitz & T. L. Scheid (Eds), *A handbook for the study of mental health: Social contexts, theories, and systems* (pp. 161–175). New York: Cambridge University Press.

Pearlin, L. I., Menaghan, E. G., Lieberman, M. A., & Mullen, J. T. (1981). The stress process. *Journal of Health and Social Behavior*, *22*, 337–356.

Pearlin, L. I., & Schooler, C. (1978). The structure of coping. *Journal of Health and Social Behavior*, *19*, 2–21.

Pearlman, K., & Barney, M. F. (2000). Selection for a changing workplace. In: J. F. Kehoe (Ed.), *Managing selection in changing organizations* (pp. 3–72). San Francisco, CA: Jossey-Bass.

Phillips, J. M., & Gully, S. M. (1997). The role of goal orientation, ability, need for achievement, and locus of control in the self-efficacy and goal setting process. *Journal of Applied Psychology*, *82*, 792–802.

Ployhart, R. E. (2004). Organizational staffing: A multilevel review, synthesis, and model. In: G. R. Ferris & J. Martocchio (Eds), *Research in personnel and human resource management* (Vol. 23, pp. 121–176). Oxford, UK: Elsevier.

Ployhart, R. E., Holtz, B. C., & Bliese, P. D. (2002). Longitudinal data analysis: Applications of random coefficient modeling to leadership research. *Leadership Quarterly*, *13*, 455–486.

Ployhart, R. E., Lim, B. C., & Chan, K. Y. (2001). Exploring relations between typical and maximum performance ratings and the five factor model of personality. *Personnel Psychology*, *54*, 809–843.

Pulakos, E. D., Arad, S., Donovan, M. A., & Plamondon, K. E. (2000). Adaptability in the workplace: Development of a taxonomy of adaptive performance. *Journal of Applied Psychology*, *85*, 612–624.

Pulakos, E. D., Schmitt, N., Dorsey, D. W., Arad, S., Hedge, J. W., & Borman, W. C. (2002). Predicting adaptive performance: Further tests of a model of adaptability. *Human Performance*, *15*, 299–323.

Sackett, P. R., Zedeck, S., & Fogli, L. (1988). Relations between measures of typical and maximum job performance. *Journal of Applied Psychology*, *73*, 482–486.

Schmitt, N., Cortina, J. M., Ingerick, M. J., & Wiechmann, D. (2003). Personnel selection and employee performance. In: W. C. Borman, D. R. Ilgen & R. J. Klimoski (Eds), *Handbook of psychology: Industrial and organizational psychology* (Vol. 12, pp. 77–105). Hoboken, NJ: Wiley.

Schunn, C. D., & Reder, L. M. (1998). Strategy adaptivity and individual differences. *The Psychology of Learning and Motivation*, *38*, 115–154.

Smith, E. M., Ford, J. K., & Kozlowski, S. W. J. (1997). Building adaptive expertise: Implications for training design. In: M. A. Quinones & A. Dudda (Eds), *Training for a rapidly changing workplace: Applications of psychological research* (pp. 89–118). Washington, DC: American Psychological Association.

Sonnentag, S., & Frese, M. (2003). Stress in organizations. In: W. C. Borman, D. R. Ilgen & R. J. Klimoski (Eds), *Handbook of psychology: Industrial and organizational psychology* (Vol. 12, pp. 453–491). Hoboken, NJ: Wiley.

Taylor, S. E., & Aspinwall, L. G. (1996). Mediating and moderating processes in psychosocial stress: Appraisal, coping, resistance, and vulnerability. In: H. B. Kaplan (Ed.), *Psychosocial stress: Perspectives on structure, theory, life-course, and methods* (pp. 71–110). San Diego, CA: Academic Press.

Thoresen, C. J., Bradley, J. C., Thoresen, J. D., & Bliese, P. D. (2004). The big five personality traits and job performance across time in maintenance and transitional job stages. *Journal of Applied Psychology*, *89*, 835–853.

Wanberg, C. R., & Banas, J. T. (2000). Predictors and outcomes of openness to changes in a reorganizing workplace. *Journal of Applied Psychology*, *2000*, 132–142.

Wood, R. E. (1986). Task complexity: Definition of the construct. *Organizational Behavior and Human Decision Processes*, *37*, 60–82.

Zaccaro, S. J., Gilbert, J. A., Thor, K. K., & Mumford, M. D. (1991). Leadership and social intelligence: Linking social perceptiveness and behavioral flexibility to leader effectiveness. *Leadership Quarterly*, *2*, 317–342.

APPENDIX. SHORT 55-ITEM I-ADAPT-M

This survey asks a number of questions about your preferences, styles, and habits at work. Read each statement carefully. Then, for each statement circle the corresponding number that best represents your opinion. If you need to change an answer, completely erase the incorrect response and then circle the correct response. There are no right or wrong answers.

Please circle the number that best describes your opinion. Circle only one answer for each question.

Item		Sub-dimension
1.	I am able to maintain focus during emergencies	Crisis
2.	I enjoy learning about cultures other than my own	Cultural
3.	I usually over-react to stressful news	Work stress
4.	I believe it is important to be flexible in dealing with others	Interpersonal
5.	I take responsibility for acquiring new skills	Learning
6.	I work well with diverse others	Cultural
7.	I tend to be able to read others and understand how they are feeling at any particular moment	Interpersonal
8.	I am adept at using my body to complete relevant tasks	Physical
9.	In an emergency situation, I can put aside emotional feelings to handle important tasks	Crisis
10.	I see connections between seemingly unrelated information	Creativity
11.	I enjoy learning new approaches for conducting work	Learning
12.	I think clearly in times of urgency	Crisis
13.	I utilize my muscular strength well	Physical
14.	It is important to me that I respect others' culture	Culture
15.	I feel unequipped to deal with too much stress	Work stress
16.	I am good at developing unique analyses for complex problems	Creativity
17.	I am able to be objective during emergencies	Crisis-N
18.	My insight helps me to work effectively with others	Interpersonal

APPENDIX. (*Continued*)

19.	I enjoy the variety and learning experiences that come from working with people of different backgrounds	Cultural
20.	I can only work in an orderly environment	Physical
21.	I am easily rattled when my schedule is too full	Work
22.	I usually step up and take action during a crisis	Crisis
23.	I need for things to be "black and white"	Uncertainty
24.	I am an innovative person	Creativity
25.	I feel comfortable interacting with others who have different values and customs	Cultural
26.	If my environment is not comfortable (e.g., cleanliness), I cannot perform well	Physical
27.	I make excellent decisions in times of crisis	Crisis
28.	I become frustrated when things are unpredictable	Uncertainty
29.	I am able to make effective decisions without all relevant information	Uncertainty
30.	I am an open-minded person in dealing with others	Interpersonal
31.	I take action to improve work performance deficiencies	Learning
32.	I am usually stressed when I have a large workload	Work stress
33.	I am perceptive of others and use that knowledge in interactions	Interpersonal
34.	I often learn new information and skills to stay at the forefront of my profession	Learning
35.	I often cry or get angry when I am under a great deal of stress	Work stress
36.	When resources are insufficient, I thrive on developing innovative solutions	Creativity
37.	I am able to look at problems from a multitude of angles	Creativity
38.	I quickly learn new methods to solve problems	Learn
39.	I tend to perform best in stable situations and environments	Uncertainty

APPENDIX. (*Continued*)

40.	When something unexpected happens, I readily change gears in response	Uncertainty
41.	I would quit my job if it required me to be physically stronger	Physical
42.	I try to be flexible when dealing with others	Interpersonal-N
43.	I can adapt to changing situations	Uncertainty-N
44.	I train to keep my work skills and knowledge current	Learning-N
45.	I physically push myself to complete important tasks	Physical-N
46.	I am continually learning new skills for my job	Learning-N
47.	I perform well in uncertain situations	Uncertainty-N
48.	I can work effectively even when I am tired	Physical-N
49.	I take responsibility for staying current in my profession	Learning-N
50.	I adapt my behavior to get along with others	Interpersonal-N
51.	I cannot work well if it is too hot or cold	Physical-N
52.	I easily respond to changing conditions	Uncertainty-N
53.	I try to learn new skills for my job before they are needed	Learning-N
54.	I can adjust my plans to changing conditions	Uncertainty-N
55.	I keep working even when I am physically exhausted	Physical-N

Note: Each item is scored on a five-point strongly disagree–strongly agree scale. Items followed by an "N" refer to new items added since the original version.

ADAPTABILITY IN THE WORKPLACE: SELECTING AN ADAPTIVE WORKFORCE

Elaine D. Pulakos, David W. Dorsey and Susan S. White

Today's organizations are characterized by changing, dynamic environments in which the need for adaptive workers has become increasingly important (Edwards & Morrison, 1994; Hollenbeck, LePine, & Ilgen, 1996; Ilgen & Pulakos, 1999; Smith, Ford, & Kozlowski, 1997). For example, employees must frequently adjust to new ways of performing their jobs, as changing technologies and automation continue to alter the nature of work tasks (Patrickson, 1987; Thach & Woodman, 1994). Furthermore, the environment of mergers, "rightsizing," and corporate restructuring is requiring employees to adapt and expand their skill sets to be competitive for different jobs (Kinicki & Latack, 1990). And, of course, today's global economy calls for many individuals to regularly adjust the way they do business in order to facilitate operations in different countries and with diverse individuals who may be different than themselves (Black, 1990; Noe & Ford, 1992).

Workers need to be increasingly adaptable, versatile, and tolerant of uncertainty to operate effectively in these changing and varied environments – and this need will only increase as the pace of change continues to grow. Accordingly, both researchers and practitioners in organizations have begun

Understanding Adaptability: A Prerequisite for Effective Performance within Complex Environments
Advances in Human Performance and Cognitive Engineering Research, Volume 6, 41–71

ISSN: 1479-3601/doi:10.1016/S1479-3601(05)06002-9

to take steps toward understanding and enhancing adaptability in the workplace. Yet, adaptability, flexibility, and versatility are elusive concepts that have not been well defined in the psychological literature and have therefore been difficult to measure, predict, and train effectively. In this chapter, we will explore the concept of adaptability in the workplace, specifically how to define and measure adaptive performance and how to select individuals who will effectively adapt in the workplace. In discussing selection issues, we will focus not only on individual adaptive performance but will also consider a multi-level perspective, specifically understanding and predicting team adaptive performance. We feel this is important because in today's world of work, individuals are often selected into jobs that require them to perform as part of a team, and adaptive performance requirements can occur at both the individual and team levels. In fact, Ployhart and Schneider (2002a) have argued that the traditional selection model is limited and fails to consider how selection practices and constructs may change through incorporation of a multi-level perspective. These authors presented a model that allows explicit consideration of multiple levels in personnel selection research, drawing on both the traditional selection model (Binning & Barrett, 1989) and general system-oriented human resources approaches (e.g., Dobbins, Cardy, & Carson, 1991; Jackson & Schuler, 1995; Ostroff & Bowen, 2000). Consistent with Ployhart and Schneider's call for consideration of multi-level perspectives and their implications, we will suggest how both individual and team levels can be incorporated into strategies to select an adaptive workforce.

The present chapter is organized into four major sections. First, we present a model of individual adaptive performance. We begin with a discussion of the criterion domain because to make effective selection decisions, one first needs to understand the performance one is trying to predict. That is, there needs to be a solid foundation for understanding "adaptive performance" before trying to predict it. We then present hypotheses about individual difference predictors of individual adaptive performance. We follow this with a presentation of a model of team adaptive performance, describing both the criterion of team adaptability and predictor constructs. Finally, we discuss specific selection procedures to enhance selection of an adaptive workforce.

A MODEL OF INDIVIDUAL ADAPTIVE PERFORMANCE

Although models have been published in the literature covering various aspects of the job performance domain (e.g., technical performance, contextual performance), researchers have recently recognized a void in these models and have called for their expansion to include adaptive performance components (Campbell, 1999; Hesketh & Neal, 1999; London & Mone, 1999; Murphy & Jackson, 1999). Toward this end, Pulakos, Arad, Donovan, and Plamondon (2000) developed a taxonomy of *adaptive job performance* similar to the model of job performance developed by Campbell, McCloy, Oppler, and Sager (1993). This model contained eight dimensions of adaptive job performance. Pulakos et al. began their research with a review of various literatures on adaptability and identified six different aspects of adaptive performance. These are shown in Table 1, along with the research references from which they were derived. The diversity of substantive areas that are represented in the research articles cited in Table 1 is a testament to the perceived importance of adaptability across a number

Table 1. Individual Adaptability Dimensions, Definitions, and Source.

Dimension Title	Dimension Definition	Sources
Solving problems creatively	Solve atypical, ill-defined, and complex problems	Hatano and Inagaki (1986); Holyoak (1991)
Dealing with uncertain or unpredictable work situations	Adjust and deal with unpredictable situations, shift focus, and take reasonable action	Ashford (1986); Dix and Savickas (1995); Edwards and Morrison (1994); Goodman (1994); Hall and Mirvis (1995); Murphy (1989); Weiss (1984)
Learning new tasks, technologies, and procedures	Anticipate, prepare for, and learn skills needed for future job requirements	Hesketh and Neal (1999); Kinicki and Latack (1990); London and Mone (1999); Noe and Ford (1992); Patrickson (1987); Thach and Woodman (1994)
Demonstrating interpersonal adaptability	Adjusts interpersonal style to achieve goals working with new teams, co-workers or customers	Kozlowski, Gully, Salas, and Cannon-Bowers (1996); Paulhus and Martin (1988)
Demonstrating cultural adaptability	Performs effectively in different cultures learning new languages, values, traditions, and politics	Black (1990); Chao, O'Leary-Kelly, Wolf, Klein, and Gardner (1994); Ilgen and Pulakos (1999)
Demonstrating physically oriented adaptability	Adjusts to various physical factors such as heat, noise, uncomfortable climates, and difficult environments	Edwards and Morrison (1994); Fiedler and Fiedler (1975); Weinstein (1978)
Handling work stress	Remains calm under pressure, handles frustration, and acts as calming influence	Critical incidents analysis; Pulakos et al. (2000)
Handling emergencies or crisis situations	Reacts appropriately and decisively to life-threatening or dangerous situations	Critical incidents analysis; Pulakos et al. (2000)

of behavioral disciplines. Although the idea that adaptive performance is multi-dimensional was reasonable based on the wide range of behaviors "adaptability" has encompassed in the literature (for example, adapting to organizational change, different cultures, different people, new technology), no published research prior to Pulakos et al. had systematically defined or empirically examined specific dimensions of adaptive job performance. Pulakos et al. conducted two studies to refine the six-dimension model of individual adaptive job performance derived from the literature. In Study 1, over 1,000 critical incidents from 21 different jobs were content analyzed, yielding an eight-dimension taxonomy of adaptive performance. That is, the critical incident analysis produced two additional adaptive performance dimensions that are shown at the bottom of Table 1.

Using these dimensions as a starting point, Pulakos et al. (2000) set out to more systematically define and empirically examine the dimensions underlying adaptive performance. The eight-dimension model was empirically investigated in a second study, with the development and administration of the job adaptability inventory (JAI), an instrument designed to describe the adaptability requirements of jobs. Exploratory factor analyses of JAI data from 1,619 respondents across 24 jobs yielded an eight-factor solution that mirrored the hypothesized eight-dimension taxonomy from Study 1. Subsequent confirmatory factor analyses on the remainder of the sample ($N = 1{,}715$) indicated a good fit for the eight-factor model.

The major results and conclusions of this research to define adaptive performance were first, that adaptive performance appears to be a multi-dimensional construct, as evidenced by exploratory and confirmatory factor analyses of the JAI data which supported an eight-dimension taxonomy. Another major conclusion of this research was that the adaptive performance components identified were more or less relevant to a given job. That is, the profile of a job's adaptability requirements vary along the eight dimensions identified in the model. Support for this notion was derived from both the critical incident analysis involving over 1,000 incidents collected from individuals representing 21 different jobs as well as JAI data collected from individuals in 23 largely different jobs. The jobs included were representative of 15 of 23 major occupational groups and all six of the highest level occupational categories contained in the standard occupational classification system (SOC), a job classification system designed by the federal government to cover all jobs in the national economy. Therefore, the dimensions appeared to represent adaptive performance requirements that exist across many different types of jobs.

Ployhart and Bliese (2005) in this volume have proposed an I-ADAPT theory of adaptability, which they have described as similar to and different from the above-described eight-dimension conceptualization of adaptive performance. These authors view our approaches as similar because both conceive of adaptability requirements as being driven by the performance requirements of the context or situation. Ployhart and Bliese further state that they concur that the adaptability requirements of situations are likely to be represented by the eight latent lower order factors subsumed within our model. However, these authors assert that their theory is different because it proposes that so long as adaptability is demanded by the environment, it applies to *any* performance dimension and type of performance – task, contextual, and counterproductive. Thus, they state that their I-ADAPT theory takes issue with the notion that the eight dimensions of adaptability defined above constitute new performance dimensions. Ployhart and Bliese thus argue that their conceptualization expands the realms to which adaptability may be relevant and increases the relevance of adaptability to more "routine" forms of work. They cite the example that "typical task performance of a postal delivery worker will become adaptive when she or he must learn how to use a new way of processing mail."

As a point of clarification, while the eight adaptive performance dimensions in our model are conceptualized as different types of performance requirements (with potentially different underlying knowledges, skills, abilities, and other characteristics (KSAOs)) than technical and contextual performance, we do not view adaptive performance requirements as occurring completely independent of technical and contextual performance. Rather, adaptability may or may not be required during the performance of technical and contextual work activities. Thus, a given technical task can be performed without any adaptive requirements or that same technical task can be performed in a context that requires adaptability, for example, if there is a change to the environmental circumstances that require the task to be performed in a new and novel way. Ployhart and Bliese's example of typical task performance of a postal delivery worker becoming adaptive when she or he must learn how to use a new way of processing mail is exactly the type of performance that would be covered under our dimension, titled Learning New Tasks, Technologies, and Procedures. Thus, we do not feel that the distinction that Ployhart and Bliese have posited between their theory and our adaptive performance model accurately depicts the relationship we intended to convey between our adaptability dimensions and technical and contextual performance components.

INDIVIDUAL DIFFERENCES PREDICTORS OF ADAPTIVE PERFORMANCE

Our next step in developing the model of adaptive performance was to conduct a review of the literature to identify individual differences constructs that would likely be effective predictors of adaptability. In addition to reviewing past research in which adaptability was predicted or assessed, we also gave consideration to the content of the eight adaptability dimensions to identify likely predictors. We not only reviewed research on individual differences, but we also reviewed social, psychological, cognitive, and other literatures to identify the constructs that may be important determinants of the ability to adapt. These different lines of research suggest numerous individual characteristics that are likely to be relevant for predicting adaptive behavior. Moreover, they all agree on the importance of individual differences in understanding and predicting adaptability. Individual attributes are expected to affect adaptability in two primary ways: (1) by predisposing individuals to perceive more or less stress when faced with a novel, changing, or stress-provoking situation (Koch, Tung, Gmelch, & Swent, 1982; Motowidlo, Packard, & Manning, 1986) and (2) by predisposing individuals to use more or less effective coping strategies to deal with these situations (Fleishman, 1984; Holahan & Moos, 1987; Kobasa, Maddi, & Kahn, 1981; Parkes, 1984).

It is interesting to note that Ployhart and Bliese (2005) similarly argue for a more systematic exploration of the individual differences constructs that underlie adaptive performance. These authors noted that while previous research has examined a few individual differences that were hypothesized to underlie adaptive performance, the fact that the criterion construct has varied across studies makes it difficult to summarize and integrate these research findings into a unified perspective across studies. These authors further noted that adaptability has typically been defined in relation to specific types of tasks and situations, which also has made it difficult to determine whether the same KSAOs contribute to adaptability across contexts. They hypothesize that it is unlikely that the same KSAOs will be equally, or even similarly, important across different tasks, for example, between circumstances that require creative problem-solving adaptability versus physical adaptability. We concur with this position and, in fact, explicitly set out to address the issue of criterion differences across studies by using the eight-dimension model of adaptive performance presented above as a comprehensive conceptual framework that would be used as the basis for examining similarities and differences in individual differences that underlie different types of adaptive performance.

Based on an extensive review of the literature, we identified several cognitive and noncognitive constructs that we hypothesized to underlie an individual's ability to adapt. Several of the hypothesized predictors are relatively common cognitive ability and personality constructs found in the literature. Others are more fine-grained personality measures that have been proposed as being potentially important for predicting adaptive performance, in particular. Although some of these more fine-grained constructs are components of larger (e.g., big-five) personality constructs, we felt there was a potential value in considering some of these constructs separately. This is consistent with Hough's (1992) research, which showed higher validities by considering component constructs of the big-five rather than measures only at the highest construct level. Table 2 presents the operational definitions of each construct that we propose as most relevant for predicting adaptive performance. Key findings from the literature regarding the relevance of each construct for predicting individual adaptive performance are discussed below.

Table 2. Descriptions and Definitions of Predictor Constructs.

Predictor Label	Definition
Cognitive ability	The ability to understand and use language
Practical intelligence	The ability to solve ill-defined problems, for which there may be multiple solutions and multiple ways of obtaining them; to learn and apply knowledge to everyday, ill-defined problems.
Originality	The ability to come up with unusual or clever ideas about a given topic or situation; the ability to develop creative ways to solve a problem.
Domain-specific knowledge	Knowledge of a specific content domain that may facilitate dealing with a particular adaptability dimension
Openness	Is receptive to new environments and events; is curious and broad-minded; displays broad interests
Cognitive flexibility	Perceives change as a challenge or opportunity for further development
Emotional stability	Remains levelheaded, even-tempered, and calm when confronted with adversity, frustration, or other stressful/difficult situations
Cooperativeness	Works effectively with others toward a common purpose; shows willingness to give and take in an effort to achieve group goals; develops constructive relationships
Achievement motivation	Shows desire to achieve results and master tasks beyond others' expectations; sets difficult and challenging goals and works hard to accomplish them; shows a drive to succeed
Sociability	Feels at ease in social situations; is outgoing; enjoys meeting new people
Social intelligence	Understands situationally appropriate social behavior; understands the feelings, motivations, and behaviors of others and acts appropriately upon them; finds solutions to interpersonal problems

Cognitive Ability

The ability to modify one's behavior or focus and deal effectively with a variety of different and dynamic situations may simply be a function of having higher levels of intelligence. In fact, Snow and Lohman (1984) suggested that fluid intelligence is the ability to adapt one's crystallized intelligence to novel tasks. Fluid intelligence will become increasingly indispensable for workers who must constantly be in a learning mode, particularly those who must learn complex new tasks. The research shows compelling evidence that cognitive ability can predict different dimensions of work performance as well as contribute to one's ability to adapt to and learn novel tasks (Ackerman, 1988; Campione, Brown, & Bryant, 1985; Fleishman & Mumford, 1989; Hunter & Hunter, 1984; Milgram, Pinchas, & Ronen, 1988; Ree, Carretta, & Teachout, 1995; Ree, Earles, & Teachout, 1994). Cognitive ability would be expected to enhance effective adaptability in situations that require learning and problem solving.

Practical Intelligence

Distinct from general intelligence, practical intelligence refers to the ability to solve ill-defined problems, for which there may be multiple solutions and multiple ways of obtaining them, and to learn and apply knowledge to everyday, ill-defined problems (Wagner, 1986). Practical intelligence may thus play an important role in one's ability to adapt effectively to novel and changing situations, and to solve problems creatively.

Originality

Originality is defined as the ability to develop unusual or clever ideas about a given topic or situation or the ability to develop creative ways to solve a problem (Fleishman, 1992). Since originality has been shown to contribute to solving novel, ill-defined problems, this construct should facilitate adaptability in such situations.

Emotional Stability

Emotional stability, one of the "Big Five" personality factors (McCrae & Costa, 1989; McCrae & John, 1992), refers to the ability to remain calm and level-headed when confronted with difficult or stressful situations. The well-adjusted or emotionally stable person also displays an awareness of mood and tends to be adaptable to even rapidly changing situations. Emotional stability has been found to be a valid predictor of several different types of job performance criteria, including irresponsible behavior, teamwork, and executive capacity, among others (Hough, 1992). In addition, in a study by Peterson et al. (1993), subject-matter experts (psychologists) hypothesized that emotional stability would be highly predictive of adaptability. Although it is likely to be related to several of the adaptability dimensions, we would expect particularly strong relationships between this construct and dealing with crisis/emergency situations and reacting to job-relevant stress.

Openness

Openness represents another of the empirical dimensions to emerge from factor analytical research of the "Big Five" personality factors (McCrae & Costa, 1989; McCrae & John, 1992). Openness refers to one's curiosity, broad-mindedness, and receptiveness to new environments and events. Individuals high on openness tend to display traits such as tolerance and curiosity when confronted with novel situations. Consequently, they are less likely to perceive change as stressful and are thus likely to adapt more effectively. McCrea and Costa (1989) found that openness was positively related to utilization of effective coping strategies in dealing with major life stressors. Whitbourne (1986) extended these findings to the workplace, noting that openness was positively associated with identity flexibility in work as well as family roles. Barrick and Mount (1991) also found that openness was related to training performance criteria. This finding is consistent with definitions of the trait, as one would expect that persons who are inquisitive and intelligent by nature would be effective in learning environments that present novel stimuli. Judge, Thoresen, and Pucik (1996) also found a positive correlation between openness and coping with organizational change. Since individuals high on openness exhibit tolerance and inquisitiveness when confronted with novel situations, this construct is likely to enhance effective adaptability across several of the adaptability dimensions.

Cognitive Flexibility

Cognitive flexibility, a component of personal hardiness, refers to one's tendency to perceive change as a challenge or opportunity for further development (Kobasa, 1979). Kobasa (1979) studied the effects of stressful life events on the health of middle- and upper-level executives and found that executives who viewed change as a challenge (i.e., cognitive flexibility) coped better with change and stress and remained healthier than those who viewed it as a threat. It appears that people who feel positively about change are more likely to explore their environment and have better knowledge of available resources that can help them cope with change (Moss, 1973). Since dealing with change represents a key aspect of adaptive behavior, we expect cognitive flexibility to be important in increasing one's effectiveness in regularly changing and volatile situations.

Achievement Motivation

Achievement motivation refers to one's desire to overcome obstacles, achieve results, and master tasks beyond others' expectations. Research has indicated that high achievers tend to possess a set of characteristics including a willingness to assume a substantial degree of responsibility for solving the problems they face and a tendency to set moderate achievement goals involving calculated risks (Greenlaw, 1972). Achievement motivation can also create positive performance expectations based on interest in personal success and increase the willingness to overcome obstacles. Research has shown significant, positive relationships between achievement motivation and success in adapting to new tasks or situations (Dweck, 1986; Schmeck, 1988). Borman, McKee, and Schneider (1996) also noted that achievement motivation may be more instrumental to worker success in the future than in the past, due to the fact that workers who are not driven to achieve will be tolerated to a lesser extent in the increasingly competitive global economy. We would expect achievement motivation to be particularly relevant for adaptation, which requires learning new tasks, technologies, and procedures as well as in situations characterized by difficult problems, which require perseverance to overcome or solve.

Cooperativeness

Cooperativeness involves the ability to work effectively with others toward a common purpose. Cooperativeness has been shown to be related to psychological adjustment, managerial performance, teamwork, public relations performance, customer service, and other interpersonally oriented criteria (Gellatly, Paunonen, Myer, Jackson, & Goffin, 1991; Hogan & Hogan, 1992; Hough, 1992; Peterson et al., 1993). Peterson et al. (1993) also reported that cooperativeness was judged by subject-matter experts (psychologists) to be moderately predictive of adaptability. Given the nature of this construct, we would expect it to be highly relevant for predicting the interpersonally oriented dimensions of adaptation.

Sociability

Sociability refers to the tendency to be outgoing and feel at ease in social situations. Sociability resembles positive affectivity, a personality disposition which is characterized by well-being, confidence, and affiliation (Tellegen, 1985). These qualities were shown to be predictive of effective coping with life events (Holahan & Moos, 1987). In addition, the affiliation aspect of sociability should aid individuals in forming positive and productive interpersonal relationships, which can themselves be adaptive or which can serve as a buffering mechanism for dealing with other stress or change situations (Schneider, 1992). In a study of the effects of personality characteristics on coping with organizational transformation, Judge et al. (1996) found a strong positive correlation between managers' positive affectivity and coping with change. Hence, sociability is expected to facilitate effective adaptability by enhancing individuals' ability to cope with change and stress, in general, as well as by directly impacting their effectiveness in dealing with situations that require interpersonal and possibly cultural adaptability.

Social Intelligence

Social intelligence is defined as "the ability to understand the feelings, thoughts, and behaviors of persons including oneself, in interpersonal situations and to act appropriately based on that understanding" (Marlowe, 1986, p. 52). Social intelligence is widely viewed as an adaptive personal quality (Costa & McCrae, 1992; Showers & Cantor, 1985), and recent work on the social–cognitive aspects of social intelligence is very relevant to the notion of adaptability (Cantor & Kihlstrom, 1987). Social intelligence is expected to enhance adaptive behavior, especially in interpersonal arenas.

Physical Ability

One of the dimensions emerging from the critical incident analyses was demonstrating physically oriented adaptability. This dimension involves adjusting to challenging environmental circumstances (e.g., heat, noise, cold) as well as adjusting weight and muscular strength to become proficient in performing physical tasks. Although physical fitness and ability constructs have not been associated with adaptability in the research literature, it is reasonable to expect that physically oriented adaptability will require physical abilities above and beyond other kinds of individual attributes that might be associated with it. Therefore, we proposed that physical ability will be highly relevant to predicting physically oriented adaptability.

LINKAGES BETWEEN INDIVIDUAL ADAPTABILITY ATTRIBUTES AND ADAPTABILITY DIMENSIONS

Next, we conducted an expert judgment task (Wing, Peterson, & Hoffman, 1984) to link the individual attributes (defined above) that were hypothesized to underlie one's ability to adapt to changing and novel situations to the eight adaptability dimensions. The definitions of the predictor constructs and adaptability dimensions were given to 17 industrial and organizational psychologists with extensive experience in selection/classification research. The experts were asked to judge which predictor constructs would be most relevant for predicting performance in the different adaptability dimensions. Each expert rated the relevance of each predictor for each adaptability dimension using a 6-point scale, where 0 = no relevance and 5 = very high relevance.

The results of the expert judgments are summarized in Table 3. A key finding of the judgment task was that while some attributes were linked to several adaptability dimensions, other attributes were linked to only a few dimensions. Overall, the relationships anticipated, based on the literature review, between particular individual differences constructs and dimensions of adaptability were supported by the expert judgment results. As we hypothesized, the judges indicated that noncognitive predictors such as openness emotional stability and cognitive flexibility would be important for predicting many of the adaptability dimensions, with the exception of physically oriented adaptability. All other predictor constructs were found to be relevant to only a subset of the adaptability dimensions.

Also as expected, cognitive ability was judged by the experts to be mainly relevant to cognitive-oriented adaptability dimensions such as learning new tasks/technologies and solving problems creatively. Alternatively, the interpersonal predictors (i.e., cooperativeness, sociability, and social intelligence) were linked only to the interpersonally oriented adaptability dimensions

Table 3. Predictor – Adaptability Dimension Linkages.

Predictor	Adaptability Criterion Dimension							
	A	B	C	D	E	F	G	H
Cognitive ability	◇		◆		◇			
Practical intelligence	◆		◆	◇	◇			
Originality			◆	◇				
Emotional stability	◆	◆		◇		◇	◇	
Openness			◇	◆	◆	◆	◆	
Cognitive flexibility			◇	◆	◆	◇	◇	
Achievement motivation			◇		◆			
Cooperativeness						◆	◆	
Sociability						◆	◇	
Social intelligence						◆	◆	
Physical ability								◆

Note: ◇ denotes predictor/adaptability dimension combinations with a mean rating between 2.5 and 3.5, and ◆ denotes predictor/adaptability dimension combinations with a mean rating above 3.5. The eight adaptability dimensions are: (A) handling emergency or crisis situations, (B) handling work stress, (C) solving problems creatively, (D) dealing effectively with unpredictable or changing work situations, (E) learning work tasks, technologies, and procedures, (F) demonstrating interpersonal adaptability, (G) displaying cultural adaptability, and (H) demonstrating physically oriented adaptability.

(i.e., demonstrating interpersonal adaptability and displaying cultural adaptability). And last, the physical predictors were found to be highly relevant for predicting physically oriented adaptability. The results of the expert judgment task suggest two primary implications. First, the different predictor constructs seem more or less relevant for forecasting adaptability in each of the eight adaptability dimensions. Second, measures should be designed that facilitate identification of the type(s) of adaptability required for a given job, so that appropriate predictors can be selected based on the types of adaptability required on the job.

MODEL OF TEAM ADAPTIVE PERFORMANCE

The above discussion summarizes research on defining adaptive performance and identifying the constructs that might be considered in selecting adaptable workers. However, many workers today find themselves working not as individuals, but as members of teams. It therefore may not be enough that they be individually adaptable – the team as a whole may also need to function in an adaptive manner. In this section, we thus present a model of team adaptive performance, both defining adaptability at the team level and outlining constructs that are hypothesized to predict it (White, Dorsey, Pulakos, Smith, & Incalcaterra, 2002). The model suggests factors beyond those discussed above for selecting adaptable individuals, taking into consideration several team-level variables that are of importance to creating teams with the capacity to be adaptable as integrated wholes.

As with the individual performance literature, there has been increasing attention paid to adaptability at the team level in recent years, and many models of team performance include some capability of the team to adapt or adjust to novel circumstances (Kozlowski, Gully, Nason, & Smith, 1999; Marks, Zaccaro, & Mathieu, 2000; Waller, 1999). However, despite the consideration of team adaptability in general, there has been little work on providing an explicit definition of what it means for a team to be adaptable. As Klein and Pierce (2001) note, "It is commonplace for organizations to assert that they want to encourage their teams to be adaptive. Yet little has been written about what it means to be an adaptive team."

Just as it was critical to understand the individual adaptive performance we are trying to predict, it is equally critical to first define what we mean by team adaptive performance before trying to predict it. Accordingly, we propose a definition of team adaptive performance in Table 4. The primary

Table 4. Team Adaptability Dimensions and Definitions.

Dimension Title	Dimension Definition
Solving problems creatively	Develop and share solutions to atypical, ill-defined, and complex problems
Handling unpredictable work situations	Adjust and deal with unpredictable situations, shift focus, and take reasonable action; clarify roles and structures of team activities to provide focus in dynamic situations
Learning new tasks, technologies, and procedures	Develop shared understanding of team tasks and approaches for handling different situations (e.g., learning other members' roles through cross-training); anticipate, prepare for, and learn skills needed for future job requirements
Handling interactions across team boundaries	Learn about the climate, needs, values, etc. of other groups; adjust approaches to maintain positive relationships with other groups
Handling work stress	Remain calm under pressure, handles frustration, and acts as calming influence; demonstrate resilience in the face of setbacks or other stressful circumstances
Handling emergencies or crises	React appropriately and decisively to life-threatening or dangerous situations, orchestrate team members' responsibilities with little need for overt communication and planning, and perform backing-up behaviors as necessary

basis for our model of team adaptive performance was the Pulakos et al. (2000) model of individual adaptability (see Table 1). We began with the eight dimensions of individual adaptive performance and considered the relevance and appropriateness of each dimension for teams. We considered whether the dimensions could be meaningfully measured at a team level as well as whether they could be supported by the research literature (e.g., adaptability research, teams research, social networks research, social capital research, social ecology research). In addition, we considered whether the research that we examined suggested any dimensions or aspects of team adaptability that had not been captured in the model of individual adaptive performance.[1] This process resulted in the six dimensions in Table 4.

PREDICTING TEAM ADAPTABILITY

Like at the individual level, developing an explicit definition of team adaptive performance allows us to consider the types of factors that are likely to predict adaptability at the team level – and, accordingly, the types of factors that might be useful for selecting individuals into teams that are able to effectively respond to change in their environment. Teams are more than the sum of their parts, and creating an adaptable team involves more than bringing adaptable individuals together. As Ployhart and Schneider (2002a) point out, it is important to consider team-level factors – in addition to individual ones – when selecting individuals for teams. Of course, as we will discuss, individual adaptability plays a major role in adaptable teams, but there are a number of additional considerations as well. Fig. 1 describes our model of the factors that predicts team adaptability.

Individual Adaptability

First, note that individual adaptability is one of the predictors of team adaptability – it follows that a team composed of adaptable individuals is likely to be more adaptable. For example, to the extent that individual team members solve problems creatively when working on their own, they will likely contribute ideas about potential solutions to team problems. If team members learn new technologies and procedures to facilitate their independent work, the team is likely to display greater levels of learning new tasks, technologies, and procedures as well. Support for the relevance of individual differences and individual-level performance to team performance is prevalent in the research literature. For example, Barrick, Mount,

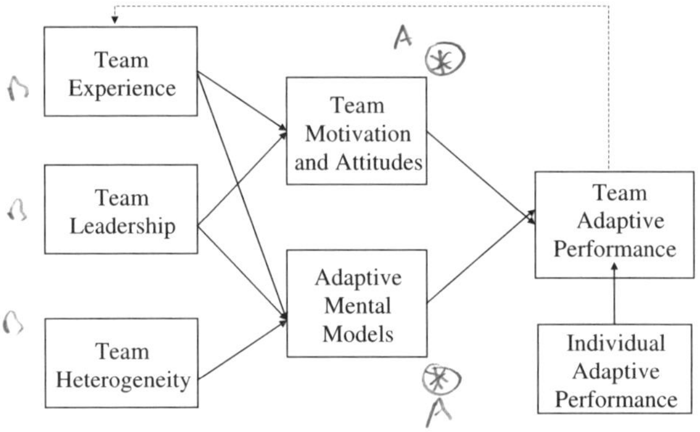

Fig. 1. Model of Team Adaptive Performance.

Neubert, and Stewart (1998) demonstrated that including even one team member with a low level of general mental ability, extroversion, agreeableness, or conscientiousness can significantly reduce team productivity.

The predictors of individual adaptability discussed above are therefore relevant in predicting team adaptability as well, and for selecting an adaptable team. However, the predictors may not have the same relationships to adaptability at the individual and the team levels. For example, we discussed cooperativeness above as an important factor when selecting an individual for a job involving high levels of interpersonal adaptability. However, cooperativeness likely plays a role in all of the different facets of team adaptability (see Table 4). To the extent that team members cooperate with one another, the team will likely be able to handle crises and solve problems more effectively – in addition to handling interactions outside team boundaries.

Individual adaptability, and its predictors, are likely to be useful in selecting individuals to be part of an adaptive team. In addition, we have proposed team-level predictors that would likely be useful to consider when composing an entire team. These team-level variables take into account the relationships among the individual characteristics of team members.

Team Motivation and Attitudes

The first team-level predictor in our model is team motivation and attitudes – an omnibus concept that is like the team's personality. It encompasses several aspects of how the team feels about itself and its environment. In particular, teams that believe that they can succeed (i.e., have high levels of potency; Guzzo, 1986; Guzzo, Yost, Campbell, & Shea, 1993) are more likely to respond positively to changes in their environment. They are more likely to respond to setbacks or failures by trying again rather than by disengaging from the task at hand (Bandura, 1997; Locke & Latham, 1990), and tend to react to environments of uncertainty with "venturesomeness" rather than fear (Bandura, 1997). Further, teams whose members are committed to the team's goals more than their individual goals are more likely to put forth the extra effort required to achieve goals – even when setbacks are encountered or it is necessary to develop new and creative strategies (Chesney & Locke, 1991; Locke & Latham, 1990). In fact, West and Wallace (1991) reported that greater team commitment was linked to higher degrees of team innovation (an aspect of team adaptability). The potency and goal commitment aspects of the "team's personality" are relevant since both resilience to obstacles and handling environments of uncertainty are elements of team adaptability.

In addition, teams that have a shared attitude that team members should be able to speak their minds are more likely to be adaptable (Axtell, Holman, Unsworth, Wall, & Waterson, 2000; Edmondson, 1999; West & Wallace, 1991), as this is important for the generation of new and innovative ideas – a critical aspect of team adaptability. Additionally, the level of cooperativeness and emotional stability within the team are important for maintaining a positive team attitude. Both of these were discussed as predictors of individual adaptability, and are also important at the team level. When team members are able to work together effectively, the team can devote its resources to its task and handling a situation rather than to internal team functioning. Remaining calm and rational under pressure or stress – and staying focused on the task at hand – can be particularly important in emergency situations. If team members keep their wits about them, then the team should be able to move forward in accomplishing its mission and not be paralyzed by negative emotions. Furthermore, it may be that agreeable/cooperative individuals are more likely to demonstrate backing-up behaviors, while those low in emotional stability are less likely (Porter et al., 2001). To the extent that team members back each other up, instead of letting critical team functions go unfulfilled because "it's not my job," the team is more likely to be able to respond to a variety of situations and to respond quickly under pressure.

Adaptive Mental Models

In addition to team motivation and attitudes, adaptive mental models are hypothesized to directly predict team adaptive performance. Cannon-Bowers,

Salas, and Converse (1993) hold that team members must share common or overlapping cognitive representations of task requirements, procedures, and role responsibilities to perform effectively – or shared "mental models." Holding shared mental models for team functioning allows team members to anticipate the moves of their fellow team members more easily, thus enhancing the ability of the team to adjust and react "automatically" when necessary. It allows teams to coordinate their actions implicitly, which is typically more effective than overtly communicating who needs to be doing what (Entin & Serfaty, 1999; Kleinman & Serfaty, 1989). This is likely due to team members' responding to each other more quickly and performing backing-up behaviors more readily (Cannon-Bowers, Tannenbaum, Salas, & Volpe, 1995).

For adaptive team performance, it is important that team members share similar representations of how the team will adapt under various conditions. This will allow team members to all be "on the same page" when it comes to interpreting adaptive situations, determining responses to the situations, coordinating their actions, and so forth. Thus, by adaptive mental models, we are referring to the shared knowledge that team members have concerning team adaptability.

Continuing through our model (see Fig. 1), we now turn to those variables that are hypothesized to affect team adaptive performance indirectly through adaptive mental models and team motivation and attitudes. Beginning with predictors of adaptive mental models, we have focused our attention on team experience, team leadership, and team heterogeneity. Team motivation and attitudes is hypothesized to be affected by team experience and team leadership. Each of these is defined and discussed below.

Team Experience

Adaptive mental models develop in part through previous experience with having to adapt. In particular, teams likely learn which strategies are effective and ineffective in different conditions as they react to various adaptive situations. This knowledge becomes integrated into the mental models of team members, such that they develop a shared understanding of the most appropriate responses to changing conditions. A similar suggestion has been made by Klein and Pierce (2001) who proposed that adaptive teams have more experience in solving problems and as such have built up "routines" to carry out adaptive processes. To emphasize the dynamic nature of these shared mental models, note the path in Fig. 1 from team adaptive performance back to team experience. This path captures the idea that the revision and updating of a team's shared mental models for adaptation is an ongoing feedback process in response to previous experiences with adapting.

A team's experiences can also affect its motivation and attitudes toward adaptive situations. For example, as a team accumulates more and more instances of successful adaptation, the team's confidence in its ability to handle future situations likely rises. That is, a team's level of potency is heavily impacted by past experiences (Shea & Guzzo, 1987). It might also be the case that experience together as a team increases levels of cooperativeness among team members; if experience in past situations has indicated that other team members can be trusted and cooperation results in successful adaptation, cooperativeness may well increase with experience. As a third example, emotional stability might be impacted by the team's experience with adaptation, such that the team approaches adaptive situations more calmly as they gain experience with certain types of situations.

Team Heterogeneity

As hypothesized in our model (see Fig. 1), the heterogeneity or diversity of a team is also likely to be important in the development of adaptive mental models. Most work in the area of team composition has focused on demographic characteristics of team members, usually in terms of gender and race/ethnicity. However, heterogeneity also exists in terms of areas of expertise, organizational backgrounds/positions, etc. In fact, Mohrman, Cohen, and Mohrman (1995) held that the function of team-based organizations is to bring people with different knowledge bases together in order to solve complex problems.

Often, heterogeneity is valued in teams because people's characteristics are seen as affecting the way they view the world, how they think about problems, how they react to other people, etc. (e.g., Jackson, May, & Whitney, 1992). Thus, variation in people leads to variation in ideas that are brought to the table for solving problems and other activities. However, while different perspectives can be valuable (a point that will be discussed later), they can be a drawback to establishing shared mental models. Differences in perspectives can lead to difficulties in exchanges of information and interactions among team members, and, as discussed above, these are key aspects of developing shared mental models. Empirically, higher degrees of heterogeneity have been linked to less technical communication among team members (as reported in Shea & Guzzo, 1987), and also to poorer team performance under conditions of time pressure and stress – where efficient coordination and communication are important (Bettenhausen, 1991). Because of the difficulties associated with heterogeneity, the intent behind composing many teams is to create enough diversity to allow for the generation of new and innovative ideas, but not so much diversity that team members have difficulty interacting and establishing common ways of interpreting the environment.

The intent here is not to say that adaptable teams should not be diverse or heterogeneous. In fact, for activities like problem solving, diversity can be beneficial for team performance (Lau & Murninghan, 1998; Shea & Guzzo, 1987). Furthermore, we are not arguing that it is impossible for heterogeneous teams to establish shared mental models. In fact, even diverse team members likely share similarities that provide some common ground for establishing mental models – they typically work for the same organization, have similar work experiences, etc. Further, Chatman and Flynn (2001) found that the effects of heterogeneity in establishing group norms dissipated with time and interaction among team members; the same could very well hold true with respect to establishing shared mental models. Thus, elements of diversity mostly likely lengthen the amount of time it would take for a work team to establish mental models for team functioning, and diversity should therefore be recognized as a barrier.

Team Leadership

In the model presented in Fig. 1, team leadership refers to actions that guide the team toward effective adaptation. Such behaviors need not be exercised by a formal team leader, but rather can be performed by any member of the team. While some teams may have a single leader, it is not uncommon to find teams with several informal leaders instead of – or in conjunction with – a formal leader. As Sundstrom, De Meuse, and Futrell (1990, p. 124) noted, "A team can have a manager, administrator, leader, supervisor, facilitator, director, coordinator, spokesperson, or chairperson – or several of these." In the discussion below, team leader refers to any member of the team to whom others look for guidance, whether or not he/she has a formal leadership position.

One of the most important roles of a team leader is to serve as a role model, thereby influencing the tone and attitudes of the team. For example, those acting in a leadership capacity can model adaptive behaviors for the team. A team leader who willingly receives and provides back up is sending the message that such behavior is valued, thereby influencing the team members' attitudes toward backing-up behaviors. A leader can also provide feedback in such a way as to bolster team confidence (i.e., raise its level of potency).

Furthermore, team leaders can also impact teams' adaptive mental models. They can either tell their teams how particular situations will be handled (e.g., setting guidelines for problem solving, providing feedback on what is appropriate and inappropriate actions), or they can demonstrate how the team should behave through their own actions. Consider the above example of a team leader who receives and provides backing-up behaviors. This leader is not only displaying a willing attitude with respect to backing-up behaviors, but is also communicating that backing-up behaviors are appropriate in the situation being faced. Accordingly, receiving and providing back up becomes part of the team's mental models for addressing such a situation. The team's adaptive mental models are thus based in part on observing how team leaders perform in situations calling for the team to adapt.

Team Type

To this point in our discussion of team adaptability, we have treated the term "teams" as a fairly general concept. However, going beyond these basic characteristics, there are a number of different types of collectives that exist under the broad umbrella of "team." Team membership may be stable, or it may change frequently. A team might exist only to address a specific task, or it might be a permanent body that addresses issues as they arise. As such, there are key differences that characterize the various types of teams, and a number of researchers have defined team taxonomies (e.g., Sundstrom et al., 1990; Cohen & Bailey, 1997; Kozlowski et al., 1999).

The important point to note for our purposes is the degree to which different dimensions of adaptive performance are likely to be more or less relevant for different types of teams. This is similar to the idea that different jobs have different profiles of adaptability requirements (Pulakos et al., 2000). For example, teams like fire-fighting teams are likely respond to crises and emergencies more often than other teams. Teams like quality control circles, on the other hand, might be more focused on solving problems creatively. Thus, while some dimensions of team adaptive performance are likely important for all teams, we must consider that the importance of others may vary by team type.

SELECTING ADAPTABLE TEAMS

The team adaptability model presented in Fig. 1 illustrates that individual adaptability is only one component of creating an adaptable team. The different experiences and backgrounds of the team members are also important, contributing to both team experiences as well as team heterogeneity. Furthermore, selecting teams where the members trust each other and have confidence in each other may enhance the team's ability to adapt by contributing to positive motivation and attitudes. In addition, the nature of the team's leader is also critical and should be considered in selecting for, or assembling, an adaptable team. Leaders who encourage open communication, admit to mistakes, support backing-up behaviors, etc. are likely to have more adaptable teams than those who do not. Of course, in addition to selection, some of the predictors of team adaptability can also likely benefit from training (e.g., proceduralizing responses to certain situations, cross-training to understand others' roles and responsibilities). Training team members on following specified procedures as they interact with each other has been found to help teams coordinate their actions and respond to emergencies more quickly and effectively (Holt et al., 2001).

football.

SELECTION MEASURES

With respect to developing actual selection measures, paper-and-pencil measures of the constructs mentioned above could be developed at the individual level and, in fact, some already exist. Pulakos, Schmitt, Dorsey, Hedge, and Borman (2002) demonstrated incremental validity over traditional cognitive and noncognitive predictors for paper-and-pencil measures developed to tap adaptability constructs such as experience adapting in various situations. The Pulakos et al. (2002) measures demonstrated not only criterion-related validity, but also yielded dimensionality (in a confirmatory factor analysis) consistent with the original adaptability model proposed by Pulakos et al. (2000).

Evidence of the validity of experience-based measures of adaptability suggests other possible selection methods, such as structured interviews. For example, experience-based structured interviews (Motowidlo et al., 1992; Pulakos & Schmitt, 1995) targeted at key behavioral dimensions (e.g., dimensions of adaptive performance) may increment the prediction afforded by more general cognitive and personality measures. In addition, structured interviews can be implemented with relative ease and efficiency, especially where concerns about speed of hiring or applicant reactions to extensive testing are of concern.

Beyond traditional paper-and-pencil and interview measures, the domain of assessment exercises and simulations is another area worthy of investigation in terms of predicting adaptive performance. Such exercises and simulations range from low-fidelity, situational judgment tests (SJTs) to full-scale work simulations. In terms of low-fidelity measures, recent research suggests a promising "construct-oriented" approach for developing SJTs (Ployhart & Ryan, 2002). This approach could possibly be used to target the set of dispositional and other characteristics linked to adaptive performance, while also incorporating a range of "adaptive" situations relevant to the job or jobs of interest (thus, potentially increasing content validity). In sampling adaptive situations to develop such situational judgment measures, team-based situations and settings are likely to be of particular importance to address some of the "multi-level" issues highlighted above.

With regard to higher fidelity measures, research using advanced simulations has demonstrated the capacity to capture aspects of adaptive performance. For example, Jodlowski, Brou, and Doane (2003) used a flight simulation task to show that expert performance among a sample of pilots dropped to approximately novice levels when faced with a scenario involving a novel, unannounced failure. The authors of this study proposed that such results have implications for assessing aspects of "adaptive expertise." Note that such simulations may also be adapted to tap team-oriented constructs and dimensions. For example, a flight simulation could be modified to simulate an entire cockpit, where aspects of crew coordination and team performance become paramount. This type of team-oriented assessment exercise could be relevant to selecting not only individuals but also entire teams. This latter issue, the selection of entire teams, has received limited attention in the personnel selection literature (Ployhart & Schneider, 2002b).

Finally, we suggested earlier that measures developed specifically to tap constructs related to adaptability could augment the prediction of adaptive performance. However, the demonstration of incremental validity becomes somewhat more complex when reflecting on possible multi-level approaches to measurement, which consider both individual and team-level predictors and criteria. As highlighted here, adaptive performance is certainly one domain that can be meaningfully considered at multiple levels. Ployhart and Schneider (2002a) highlighted the potential challenges in combining measures and criteria at different levels. As stated by these authors, "the old solution of combining all performance dimensions into a composite of overall performance may work at the individual level but will not work when the criteria are at multiple levels." We join these authors in encouraging research, such as Murphy and Shiarella's (1998) investigation into the multi-variate assessment of validity, which may hold answers to addressing the multi-level validity dilemma.

CONCLUSIONS

In the current chapter, we reviewed a number of constructs, levels of measurement, and selection methods applicable to selecting more adaptive workers. A number of the topics discussed here warrant further research. For example, we presented a model of individual adaptive performance that specified underlying KSAO constructs that were hypothesized to differentially predict the eight dimensions of adaptive performance identified in the Pulakos et al. (2000) research. Future research should empirically investigate the extent to which these individual differences constructs are actually useful for predicting the adaptive performance dimensions they are hypothesized to predict.

Second, we proposed a model of adaptive performance that was largely based on the Pulakos et al. (2000) model of individual adaptive performance and a review of the team literature. One research endeavor that would facilitate verifying the model of team adaptive performance would be to collect critical incidents of team performance across a wide variety of organizations and jobs. This type of research would help to clarify the extent to which the performance model proposed here is comprehensive and accurate in terms of defining team adaptive performance. Another area of research that should be pursued is examining whether the hypothesized predictors of team adaptive performance suggested in our proposed model, and their relationships with each other, can be confirmed.

Finally, we suggested a number of different types of methods that we feel may be most useful in selecting a workforce and teams that have the capacity to be adaptive when the situation requires them to do so. However, empirical research is needed to confirm that the types of selection methods suggested are indeed the most effective for predicting performance. As applied researchers address the above research topics and add to the knowledge base regarding adaptability, effective methods for capturing aspects of adaptive performance can be incorporated into the toolkit of selection practitioners. Consequently, selection practitioners will become increasingly better equipped to help organizations stay viable in everchanging and dynamic environments.

NOTES

1. In addressing team adaptive performance, it is important to keep in mind that we considered it to be a component of overall team performance. Another important piece of overall performance is technical performance, and we make the assumption that each individual team member is able to perform his/her technical tasks in contribution to the team's performance (McIntyre & Salas, 1995).

REFERENCES

Ackerman, P. L. (1988). Determinants of individual differences during skill acquisition: Cognitive abilities and information processing. *Journal of Experimental Psychology: General, 117*, 288–318.

Ashford, S. J. (1986). Feedback-seeking in individual adaptation: A resource perspective. *Academy of Management Journal, 29*(3), 465–487.

Axtell, C. M., Holman, D. J., Unsworth, K. L., Wall, T. D., & Waterson, P. E. (2000). Shopfloor innovation: Facilitating the suggestion and implementation of ideas. *Journal of Occupational and Organizational Psychology, 73*, 265–285.

Bandura, A. (1997). *Self-efficacy: The exercise of control.* New York: Freeman.

Barrick, M. R., & Mount, M. K. (1991). The big five personality dimensions and job performance: A meta analysis. *Personnel Psychology, 44*, 1–26.

Barrick, M. R., Mount, M. K., Neubert, M. J., & Stewart, G. L. (1998). Relating member ability and personality to work-team processes and team effectiveness. *Journal of Applied Psychology, 83*(3), 377–391.

Bettenhausen, K. L. (1991). Five years of group research: What we have learned and what needs to be addressed. *Journal of Management, 17*(2), 345–381.

Binning, J. F., & Barrett, G. V. (1989). Validity of personnel decisions: A conceptual analysis of the inferential and evidential bases. *Journal of Applied Psychology, 74*, 478–494.

Black, J. S. (1990). Locus of control, social support, stress, and adjustment in international transfers. *Asia-Pacific Journal of Management, 7*, 1–29.

Borman, W. C., McKee, A. S., & Schneider, R. J. (1996). Personality characteristics. In: N. Peterson & M. Mumford (Eds), *Development of prototype occupational information system: Content model and sampling of occupations.* Washington, DC: American Institutes of Research.

Campbell, J. P. (1999). The definition and measurement of performance in the new age. In: D. R. Ilgen & E. D. Pulakos (Eds), *The changing nature of performance: Implications for staffing, motivation, and development.* San Francisco: Jossey-Bass.

Campbell, J. P., McCloy, R. A., Oppler, S. H., & Sager, C. E. (1993). A theory of performance. In: N. Schmitt & W. C. Borman (Eds), *Personnel selection in organizations* (pp. 35–70). San Francisco: Jossey-Bass.

Campione, J. C., Brown, A. L., & Bryant, N. R. (1985). Individual differences in learning and memory. In: R. J. Sternberg (Ed.), *Human abilities: An information processing approach.* New York: Freeman.

Cannon-Bowers, J. A., Salas, E., & Converse, S. (1993). Shared mental models in expert team decision making. In: N. J. Castellan Jr. (Ed.), *Individual and group decision making: Current issues* (pp. 221–246). Hillsdale, NJ: Erlbaum.

Cannon-Bowers, J. A., Tannenbaum, S. I., Salas, E., & Volpe, C. E. (1995). Defining competencies and establishing team training requirements. In: R. A. Guzzo & E. Salas and Associates (Eds), *Team effectiveness and decision making in organizations* (pp. 333–380). San Francisco, CA: Jossey-Bass.

Cantor, N., & Kihlstrom, J. F. (1987). *Personality and social intelligence*. Englewood Cliffs, NJ: Prentice-Hall.

Chao, G. T., O'Leary-Kelly, A. M., Wolf, S., Klein, H. J., & Gardner, P. D. (1994). Organizational socialization: Its content and consequences. *Journal of Applied Psychology*, *79*(5), 730–743.

Chatman, J. A., & Flynn, F. J. (2001). The influence of demographic heterogeneity on the emergence and consequences of cooperative norms in work teams. *Academy of Management Journal*, *44*(5), 956–974.

Chesney, A. A., & Locke, E. A. (1991). Relationships among goal difficulty, business strategies, and performance on a complex management simulation task. *Academy of Management Journal*, *34*(2), 400–424.

Cohen, S. G., & Bailey, D. E. (1997). What makes teams work: Group effectiveness research from the shop floor to the executive suite. *Journal of Management*, *23*, 239–290.

Costa, P. T., & McCrae, R. R. (1992). *Revised NEO personality inventory (NEO-PI-R) and NEO five-factor inventory (NEO-FFI) professional manual*. Odessa, FL: Psychological Assessment Resources.

Dix, J. E., & Savickas, M. L. (1995). Establishing a career: Developmental tasks and coping responses. *Journal of Vocational Behavior*, *47*, 93–107.

Dobbins, G. H., Cardy, R. L., & Carson, K. P. (1991). Examining fundamental assumptions: A contrast of person and system approaches to human resources management. In: G. R. Ferris & K. M. Rowland (Eds), *Research in personnel and human resources management* (Vol. 9, pp. 1–38). Greenwich, CT: JAI Press.

Dweck, C. S. (1986). Motivational processes affecting learning. *American Psychologist*, *41*, 1040–1048.

Edmondson, A. (1999). Psychological safety and learning behavior in work teams. *Administrative Science Quarterly*, *44*, 350–383.

Edwards, J. E., & Morrison, R. F. (1994). Selecting and classifying future naval officers: The paradox of greater specialization in broader areas. In: M. G. Rumsey, C. B. Walker & J. H. Harris (Eds), *Personnel selection and classification*. Hillsdale, NJ: Erlbaum.

Entin, E. E., & Serfaty, D. (1999). Adaptive team coordination. *Human Factors*, *41*, 312–325.

Fiedler, F. E., & Fiedler, J. (1975). Port noise complaints: Verbal and behavioral reactions to airport related noise. *Journal of Applied Psychology*, *60*(4), 498–506.

Fleishman, J. A. (1984). Personality characteristics and coping patterns. *Journal of Health and Social Behavior*, *25*, 229–244.

Fleishman, J. A. (1992). *Fleishman-job analysis survey (F-JAS)*. Palo Alto, CA: Consulting Psychologists Press.

Fleishman, J. A., & Mumford, M. D. (1989). Abilities as causes of individual differences in skill acquisition. *Human Performance*, *2*(3), 201–223.

Gellatly, I. R., Paunonen, S. V., Myer, J. P., Jackson, D. N., & Goffin, R. D. (1991). Personality, vocational interest, and cognitive predictors of managerial job performance and satisfaction. *Personality and Individual Differences*, *12*, 221–231.

Goodman, J. (1994). Career adaptability in adults: A construct whose time has come. *The Career Development Quarterly*, *43*, 74–84.

Greenlaw, P. S. (1972). The achievement motive and PIDS. *Personnel Journal, 51*(September), 658–662.

Guzzo, R. A. (1986). Group decision making and group effectiveness in organizations. In: P. S. Goodman (Ed.), *Designing effective work groups* (pp. 34–71). San Francisco: Jossey-Bass.

Guzzo, R. A., Yost, P. R., Campbell, R. J., & Shea, G. P. (1993). Potency in groups: Articulating a construct. *British Journal of Social Psychology, 32*, 87–106.

Hall, D. T., & Mirvis, P. H. (1995). The new career contract: Developing the whole person at mid-life and beyond. *Journal of Vocational Behavior, 47*, 269–289.

Hatano, G., & Inagaki, K. (1986). Two courses of expertise. In: H. Stevenson, H. Azuma & K. Hakuta (Eds), *Child development and education in Japan*. Freeman: New York.

Hesketh, B., & Neal, A. (1999). Technology and performance. In: D. R. Ilgen & E. D. Pulakos (Eds), *The changing nature of performance: Implications for staffing, motivation, and development*. San Francisco: Jossey-Bass.

Hogan, R., & Hogan, J. (1992). *Manual for the Hogan personality inventory*. Tulsa, OK: Hogan Assessment Systems.

Holahan, C. J., & Moos, R. H. (1987). Personal and contextual determinants of coping strategies. *Journal of Personality and Social Psychology, 22*(5), 946–955.

Hollenbeck, J. R., LePine, J. A., & Ilgen, D. R. (1996). Adapting to roles in decision-making teams. In: K. R. Murphy (Ed.), *Individual differences and behavior in organizations*. San Francisco, CA: Jossey-Bass.

Holt, R. W., Boehm-Davis, D. A., Hansberger, J., Beaubein, J., Incalcaterra, K., & Seamster, T. (2001). *Evaluation of proceduralized CRM training at a regional airline*. Unpublished manuscript.

Holyoak, K. J. (1991). Symbolic connectionism: Toward third-generation theories of expertise. In: K. A. Ericsson & J. Smith (Eds), *Toward a general theory of expertise*. Cambridge: Cambridge University Press.

Hough, L. M. (1992). The "big five" personality variables – construct confusion: Description versus prediction. *Human Performance, 5*, 139–155.

Hunter, J. E., & Hunter, R. F. (1984). Validity and utility of alternative predictors of job performance. *Psychological Bulletin, 96*, 72–98.

Ilgen, D. R., & Pulakos, E. D. (1999). Employee performance in todays organizations. In: D. R. Ilgen & E. D. Pulakos (Eds), *The changing nature of work performance: Implications for staffing, motivation, and development*. San Francisco: Jossey-Bass.

Jackson, S. E., May, K. E., & Whitney, K. (1992). Understanding the dynamics of diversity in decision-making teams. In: R. A. Guzzo & E. Salas and Associates (Eds), *Team effectiveness and decision making in organizations* (pp. 204–261). San Francisco, CA: Jossey-Bass.

Jackson, S. E., & Schuler, R. S. (1995). Understanding human resource management in the context of organizations and their environments. *Annual Review of Psychology, 46*, 237–264.

Jodlowski, M., Brou, R., & Doane, S. M. (2003). Adaptive expertise during simulated flight. Paper presented at the 47th annual meeting of the Human Factors Society, Denver, CO, (October).

Judge, T. A., Thoresen, C. J., & Pucik, V. (1996). Managerial coping with organizational change: A dispositional perspective. Paper presented at the annual academy of management meetings, Cincinnati, OH, (August).

Kinicki, A. J., & Latack, J. C. (1990). Explication of the construct of coping with involuntary job loss. *Journal of Vocational Behavior, 36*, 339–360.

Klein, G., & Pierce, L. (2001). Adaptive teams. Paper presented at the 6th international command and control research and technology symposium, Annapolis, MD.
Kleinman, D., & Serfaty, D. (1989). Team performance assessment in distributed decision making. Paper presented at the simulation and training research symposium on interactive networked simulation for training, University of Central Florida, Orlando, (April).
Kobasa, S. C. (1979). Stressful life events, personality, and health: An inquiry into hardiness. *Journal of Personality and Social Psychology*, *37*, 1–11.
Kobasa, S. C., Maddi, S. R., & Kahn, S. (1981). Hardiness and health: A prospective study. *Journal of Personality and Social Psychology*, *42*, 168–172.
Koch, J. L., Tung, R., Gmelch, W., & Swent, B. (1982). Job stress among school administrators: Factorial dimensions and differential effects. *Journal of Applied Psychology*, *67*, 493–499.
Kozlowski, S. W. J., Gully, S. M., Nason, E. R., & Smith, E. M. (1999). Developing adaptive teams: A theory of compilation and performance across levels and time. In: D. R. Ilgen & E. D. Pulakos (Eds), *The changing nature of work performance: Implications for staffing, motivation, and development*. San Francisco: Jossey-Bass.
Kozlowski, S. W. J., Gully, S. M., Salas, E., & Cannon-Bowers, J. A. (1996). Team leadership and development: Theory, principles, and guidelines for training leaders and teams. In: M. Beyerlein, S. Beyerlein & D. Johnson (Eds), *Advances in interdisciplinary studies of work teams: Team leadership* (Vol. 3). Greenwich, CT: JAI Press.
Lau, D. C., & Murninghan, J. K. (1998). Demographic diversity and faultlines: The compositional dynamics of organizational groups. *Academy of Management Review*, *23*(2), 325–340.
Locke, E., & Latham, G. (1990). *A theory of goal setting and task performance*. Englewood Cliffs, NJ: Prentice-Hall.
London, M., & Mone, E. M. (1999). Continuous learning. In: D. R. Ilgen & E. D. Pulakos (Eds), *The changing nature of performance: Implications for staffing, motivation, and development*. San Francisco: Jossey-Bass.
Marks, M. A., Zaccaro, S. J., & Mathieu, J. E. (2000). Performance implications of leader briefings and team-interaction training for team adaptation to novel environments. *Journal of Applied Psychology*, *85*, 971–986.
Marlowe, H. A., Jr. (1986). Social intelligence: Evidence for multidimensionality and construct independence. *Journal of Educational Psychology*, *78*(1), 52–58.
McCrae, R. R., & Costa, P. T., Jr. (1989). The structure of interpersonal traits: Wiggins's circumplex and the five-factor model. *Journal of Personality and Social Psychology*, *56*, 586–595.
McCrae, R. R., & John, O. P. (1992). An introduction to the five-factor model and its applications. *Journal of Personality*, *60*, 175–215.
McIntyre, R. M., & Salas, E. (1995). Measuring and managing for team performance: Lessons from complex environments. In: R. A. Guzzo & E. Salas and Associates (Eds), *Team effectiveness and decision making in organizations* (pp. 9–45). San Francisco, CA: Jossey-Bass.
Milgram, N. A., Pinchas, C., & Ronen, Y. (1988). Prediction of performance in basic training of women soldiers. *Psychological Reports*, *62*(2), 359–370.
Mohrman, S. A., Cohen, S. G., & Mohrman, A. M. (1995). *Designing team-based organizations: New forms for knowledge work*. San Francisco, CA: Jossey-Bass.
Moss, G. E. (1973). *Illness, immunity, and social interaction*. New York: Wiley.

Motowidlo, S. J., Dunnette, M. D., Carter, G. W., Tippins, N., Werner, S., Burnett, J. R., & Vaughan, M. J. (1992). Studies of the structured behavioral interview. *Journal of Applied Psychology*, *77*(5), 571–587.

Motowidlo, S. J., Packard, J. S., & Manning, M. R. (1986). *Journal of Applied Psychology*, *71*(4), 618–629.

Murphy, K. (1989). Dimensions of job performance. In: R. Dillon & J. Pelligrino (Eds), *Testing: Applied and theoretical perspectives* (pp. 218–247). New York: Praeger.

Murphy, K. R., & Shiarella, A. H. (1998). Implications of the multidimensional nature of job performance for the validity of selection tests: Multivariate frameworks for studying test validity. *Personnel Psychology*, *51*, 823–854.

Murphy, P. R., & Jackson, S. E. (1999). Managing work role performance: Challenges for twenty-first century organizations and their employees. In: D. R. Ilgen & E. D. Pulakos (Eds), *The changing nature of performance: Implications for staffing, motivation, and development*. San Francisco: Jossey-Bass.

Noe, R., & Ford, K. J. (1992). Emerging issues and new directions for training research. *Research in Personnel and Human Resource Management*, *10*, 345–384.

Ostroff, C., & Bowen, D. E. (2000). Moving HR to a higher level: Hr practices and organizational effectiveness. In: K. Klein & S. W. J. Kozlowski (Eds), *Multilevel theory, research, and methods in organizations: Foundations, extensions, and new directions* (pp. 211–266). San Francisco: Jossey-Bass.

Parkes, K. R. (1984). Locus of control, cognitive appraisal, and coping in stressful situations. *Journal of Personality and Social Psychology*, *46*, 655–668.

Patrickson, M. (1987). Adaptation by employees to new technology. *Journal of Occupational Psychology*, *59*, 1–11.

Paulhus, D. L., & Martin, C. L. (1988). Functional flexibility: A new conception of interpersonal flexibility. *Journal of Personality and Social Psychology*, *55*(1), 88–101.

Peterson, N. G., Smith, D., Hoffman, R. G., Pulakos, E. D., Reynolds, D. H., Potts, B. C., Oppler, S. H., & Whetzel, D. L. (1993). *Expanding the concept of quality in personnel base period final report*. Washington, DC: American Institutes for Research.

Ployhart, R. E., & Bliese, P. D. (2005). Individual adaptability (I-ADAPT) theory: Conceptualizing the antecedents, consequences, and measurement of individual differences in adaptability. In: S. Burke, L. G. Pierce & E. Salas (Eds), *Understanding adaptability: A prerequisite for effective performance within complex environments. Advances in human performance and cognitive engineering research* (Vol. 6). Elsevier Ltd.

Ployhart, R. E., & Ryan, A. (2002). Situational judgment tests: Validity evidence for an alternative development method. Paper presented at the annual conference of the Society for Industrial and Organizational Psychology, Toronto, Canada.

Ployhart, R. E., & Schneider, B. (2002a). A multilevel perspective on personnel selection: Implications for selection system design, assessment, and construct validation. In: F. J. Dansereau & F. Yamarino (Eds), *Research in multi-level issues: The many faces of multi-level issues* (Vol. 1, pp. 95–140). Oxford, UK: Elsevier.

Ployhart, R. E., & Schneider, B. (2002b). A multilevel perspective on personnel selection: When will practice catch up? In: F. J. Dansereau & F. Yamarino (Eds), *Research in multi-level issues: The many faces of multi-level issues* (Vol. 1, pp. 165–175). Oxford, UK: Elsevier.

Porter, C. O. L. H., Hollenbeck, J. R., Ilgen, D. R., Ellis, A. P. J., West, B. J., & Moon, H. (2001). Backing up behaviors in teams: The role of personality and legitimacy of need.

Paper presented at the 16th annual conference of the Society for Industrial and Organizational Psychology, San Diego, CA.

Pulakos, E. D., Arad, S., Donovan, M. A., & Plamondon, K. E. (2000). Adaptability in the work place: Development of a taxonomy of adaptive performance. *Journal of Applied Psychology*, *85*, 612–624.

Pulakos, E. D., & Schmitt, N. (1995). Experienced-based and situational interview questions: Studies of validity. *Personnel Psychology*, *48*, 289–308.

Pulakos, E. D., Schmitt, N., Dorsey, D. W., Hedge, J. W., & Borman, W. C. (2002). Predicting adaptive performance: Further tests of a model of adaptability. *Human Performance*, *15*(4), 299–323.

Ree, M. J., Carretta, T. R., & Teachout, M. S. (1995). Role of ability and prior knowledge in complex training performance. *Journal of Applied Psychology*, *80*(6), 721–730.

Ree, M. J., Earles, J. A., & Teachout, M. S. (1994). Predicting job performance: Not much more than g. *Journal of Applied Psychology*, *79*(4), 518–524.

Schmeck, R. R. (1988). *Learning strategies and learning style*. New York: Plenum.

Schneider, R. J. (1992). *An individual-differences approach to understanding and predicting social competence*. Unpublished doctoral dissertation, University of Minnesota, Minneapolis.

Shea, G. P., & Guzzo, R. A. (1987). Groups as human resources. *Research in Personnel and Human Resource Management*, *5*, 323–356.

Showers, C. J., & Cantor, N. (1985). Social cognition: A look at motivated strategies. In: M. Rosenzweig & L. W. Porter (Eds), *Annual Review of Psychology* (Vol. 36, pp. 275–305). Palo Alto, CA: Annual Reviews.

Smith, E. M., Ford, J. K., & Kozlowski, S. W. J. (1997). Building adaptive expertise: Implications for training design. In: M. A. Quinones & A. Dudda (Eds), *Training for 21st century technology: Applications of psychological research*. Washington, DC: APA Books.

Snow, R. E., & Lohman, D. L. (1984). Toward a theory of cognitive aptitude for learning from instruction. *Journal of Educational Psychology*, *76*, 347–376.

Sundstrom, E., De Meuse, K. P., & Futrell, D. (1990). Work teams: Applications and effectiveness. *American Psychologist*, *45*, 120–133.

Tellegen, A. (1985). Structures of mood and personality and their relevance to assessing anxiety with an emphasis on self-report. In: A. Tuma & J. Maser (Eds), *Anxiety and the anxiety disorders* (pp. 681–706). Hillsdale, NJ: Erlbaum.

Thach, L., & Woodman, R. W. (1994). Organizational change and information technology: Managing on the edge of cyberspace. *Organizational Dynamics*, *23*(1), 30–46.

Wagner, R. K. (1986). The search for intraterrestrial intelligence. In: R. J. Sternberg & R. K. Wagner (Eds), *Practical intelligence: Nature and origins of competence in the everyday world*. Cambridge: Cambridge University Press.

Waller, M. J. (1999). The timing of adaptive group responses to nonroutine events. *Academy of Management Journal*, *42*, 127–137.

Weinstein, N. D. (1978). Individual differences in reactions to noise: A longitudinal study in a college dormitory. *Journal of Applied Psychology*, *63*(4), 458–466.

Weiss, S. J. (1984). The effects of transition modules on new graduate adaptation. *Research in Nursing and Health*, *7*, 51–59.

West, M. A., & Wallace, M. (1991). Innovation in health care teams. *European Journal of Social Psychology*, *21*, 303–315.

Whitbourne, S. K. (1986). Openness to experience, identity flexibility, and life changes in adults. *Journal of Personality and Social Psychology*, *50*, 163–168.

White, S. S., Dorsey, D. W., Pulakos, E. D., Smith, E. M., & Incalcaterra, K. (2002). *Measuring and developing adaptable analysts and teams: Literature review and preliminary model of team adaptive performance*. Technical Report no. 400, Washington, DC: Personnel Decisions Research Institutes.

Wing, H., Peterson, N. G., & Hoffman, R. G. (1984). Expert judgments of predictor–criterion validity relationships. Paper presented at the annual convention of the American Psychological Association, Toronto, Canada, (August).

VISUALIZATION TOOLS TO ADAPT TO COMPLEX MILITARY ENVIRONMENTS

Mike Barnes, John Warner, David Hillis, Liana Suantak, Jerzy Rozenblit and Patricia McDermott

ABSTRACT

This chapter addresses adaptation to dynamic, novel and uncertain military environments. These environments require a shift from a maneuver warfare paradigm to an asymmetric world where shifting alliances, questionable civilian loyalties, opaque cultures, and the requirement to maintain peace one day and combat the next makes for a particularly confusing situation. This new warfare paradigm requires adaptation to an uncertain, complex environment.

The initial section discusses a general cognitive model of visualization called RAVENS and its importance for adaptation developed specifically to address complex military environments. RAVENS posits that humans are inherently flexible decision makers and situation awareness depends on the ability of humans to create narrative visualizations that capture the overall context of complex military environments. Using the framework as a guideline, we will examine two important visualization research

Understanding Adaptability: A Prerequisite for Effective Performance within Complex Environments
Advances in Human Performance and Cognitive Engineering Research, Volume 6, 73–113

ISSN: 1479-3601/doi:10.1016/S1479-3601(05)06003-0

programs whose purpose is to allow military operators to rapidly adapt to volatile situations. The first program investigates cognitive effects such as the framing bias and their possible interactions with a variety of display concepts during a series of missile defense simulations. The experimenters presented risk as a spatial representation of uncertainty and target value that emphasized either expected population lost or expected population saved. The second program investigated the feasibility of using visualizations generated from Scheherazade (a coevolutionary algorithm) to aid MI analysts in predicting emergent tactics of terrorist groups during urban operations. Finally, we discuss the value of these approaches for providing coherent narrative understanding as called for in the RAVENS model.

1. INTRODUCTION

MG Robert Scales has published a sobering article on the nature of future conflicts entitled the *Adaptive Enemy* (Scales, 2000). What makes Scales' article particularly disturbing is that it was written before September 11th. He points out that the enemy does not need to defeat us on the battlefield. The enemy simply can outwait us, and take advantage of our vulnerabilities. The technology we possess is a two-edged sword; intelligent adversaries can use our requirements for information dominance to create deception and chaos because they can operate in smaller units and often attack unpredictably making our intelligence efforts difficult at best. Because they do not depend on a well-defined doctrine and order of battle, the simpler nature of their tactics and planning cycles makes their actions particularly difficult to predict.

This chapter addresses adaptation to this new military environment. The authors will cover a variety of visualization concepts and tools whose purpose is to improve the soldier's ability to understand and adjust rapidly to volatile, often unpredictable future military missions (Barnes, 2003; Warner, 2003). These environments require a shift from a maneuver warfare paradigm to an asymmetric world where shifting alliances, questionable civilian loyalties, opaque cultures, and the requirement to maintain peace one day and combat the next makes for a particularly confusing situation. Interestingly, this shift in paradigm parallels a shift in the scientific paradigm from mechanistic and deterministic perspectives to an emphasis on uncertain and complex processes.

This new warfare paradigm requires adaptation to an uncertain, complex environment. Over a long period of time, humans can adapt to the harshest and most inhospitable circumstances. However, the types of situations we will discuss are those that change so rapidly that any one strategy is bound to fail, especially in situations where there is no strictly predictable outcome. The term uncertainty indicates that there are *n* options with varying degrees of certitude whereas complexity refers to situations where the number of possible options is unknown or the situation is so volatile that there is no exact probability structure. It is the latter two paradigms that this chapter is particularly interested in addressing since emergent tactics and behaviors that occur in terrorist environments are precisely the events that pose the greatest challenge in the current world situation (Bar-Yam, 1997; Waldrop, 1993).

The initial section discusses a general cognitive model of visualization and its importance for adaptation developed specifically to address complex military environments (Warner, 2003). Visualization in this sense implies more than being able to image a particular situation. It also suggests a creative process where various options are considered and their consequences and likelihood are considered as well (Barnes, 2003). Experts can often visualize a correct solution to a familiar problem set quite rapidly. Unfortunately, there are many situations where such a process is not sufficient (Klein, 1998). The next section addresses cognitive biases and their impact on the human ability to visualize uncertain environments. The purpose of this ongoing research is to develop better visualization techniques for humans in uncertain – high-risk environments wherein the decision cycle is too rapid to even consider traditional decision theoretic analyses. The final section discusses Scheherazade, a visualization and simulation tool developed to aid intelligence analysts in anti-terrorist planning. Scheherazade (Barnes & Hillis, 2003) uses the complexity inherent in coevolutionary algorithms to allow the intelligence analysts to visualize unusual, difficult-to-predict behaviors that emerge out of the adaptation process. It represents a new generation of visualization tools whose purpose is not to predict but to impart insight and a better understanding of the complex cycle of adversarial behaviors.

Thus, in the course of this chapter, we will move from an overarching theoretical framework to specific problems the framework might address to a very specific (and detailed) tool that tries to develop in the analyst those skills encouraged by the framework. The central theme to the whole chapter is the idea that adaptation requires a coherent representation of key relationships in an otherwise complex and uncertain environment. People, we will claim, have a natural sense-making ability that helps them when these key relationships are identified; therefore, the important task for visualization is to help provide what the soldier needs to identify these key relationships and to provide richer mental models than cognitive limitations might otherwise make available.

2. RAVENS: A GENERAL COGNITIVE MODEL

In the modern battle space, the commanders and their staff face critical decisions in dynamic and uncertain environments characterized by a wide possible range of threats. Further, each operation may be quite different from other operations, even those with similar goals, making expertise hard to grow. These new environments often involve unfamiliar cultures in which some may be allies and some may be foes, low-density languages, and rapid deployment. This is a difficult combination for developing reliable intelligence. These environments are what we will call "data-rich but knowledge poor" in that there is a lot of complex information that can be gathered, but building useful knowledge out of all that data is not so simple. The military is getting very good at collecting and distributing large amounts of information. The more critical task of achieving situational awareness (SA), making sense out of that data for the decision maker, is much more challenging.

The goal of this section is to outline a framework for approaching the problems raised by SA for missions, such as the military now faces, that require both rapid knowledge building and previously uncommon levels of adaptiveness. An important aspect of this framework is to propose that the best sort of visualization will help decision makers maintain dynamic and adaptive models of the situation. For this reason, there will be an emphasis on storytelling (reflecting narrative cognition in the human) as a powerful human sense-making ability that needs to be cultivated in the human decision maker and supported by information automation.

The framework is referred to as the RAVENS, which stands for "Rapid Adaptive Visualization of Emergent and Novel Situations." The acronym itself refers to the goal of the framework as much as the application of it. It should be noted that "visualization" should be interpreted broadly as any means that helps one clearly represent and think about the battle space. Visualization in this sense encompasses any or all perceptual modalities or even semantic cognitive processes. Unfortunately, while the term "visualization" seems tied to the visual modality, there are no really good alternate terms. The name RAVENS is also symbolic, given the military intelligence flavor of this work, in that RAVENS is associated with military intelligence and with understanding the situation. In Norse mythology, Odin sends out two ravens, named Thought and Memory, to gather information from all corners of the world and report to him each day.

The framework being described here is based on a theory of problem solving for the intelligence domain developed by Warner and Burnstein (1996) that proposes there are four modes of thinking each of which results in different transformations to information to turn it into aggregated information, meaning, and pragmatics. These four modes are constructive, diagnostic, reactive, and explanatory. This framework stands on its own without reading Warner and Burnstein. However, the framework is based on the explanatory mode, which becomes very important in sense-making.

'adaptive visualization'

2.1. Adaptiveness and Situational Awareness

From the perspective of RAVENS, an adaptive commander or other planner is someone who can respond flexibly not only to changes in the dynamic situation, but can also adapt flexibly to knowledge about the situation. This necessarily entails more than having a handful of loosely associated facts, it requires being able to understand complex relationships in the situation and to be able to revise one's overall model of the battlespace when needed. Perception and understanding of dynamic and uncertain environments cannot be based on template solutions or fixed expectations. This calls for more than a picture of the situation. SA requires something like a dynamic, even evolving, model of the situation. These ideas have important implications for "adaptive visualization." The visualizations being used to help the decision maker must either be model-driven themselves or, at the very least, support the human in being able to think in terms of some kind of dynamic mental model. What is visualized must help the overall situation make sense to the decision maker so that the decision maker knows what aspects of the situation are relevant and most important. This point will be illustrated in the sections that follow. For example, experiments with visualizations that help soldiers overcome cognitive biases in assessing risk will be described. Still later, Scheherazade, a simulation-based visualization tool that allows the analyst to explore emergent consequences of complex interactions that might be difficult for the analyst to represent on their own will be described.

You will notice above the recurrence of terms that allude to "situational awareness." Endsley (1995, 2002) defined SA as:

> … the perception of the elements in the environment within a volume of time and space, the comprehension of their meaning, and the projection of their status in the near future.

Notice that this definition encompasses not just awareness of what is going on in the battlespace right now, answering questions like "who?", "what?", "how many?", "where?", and so on. SA includes the requisite comprehension of the big picture to make projections about the future, answering questions like "why", "what next?", "what if?", and other longer range planning questions. This scope is important because the key to being adaptive is to achieve coherent yet flexible understanding of the whole situation. What underlies achieving SA in novel environments is sense-making (Weick, 1995). While sense-making, figuring out how elements of the situation fit together so that the overall situation is coherent, is a uniquely human ability, information visualization can aid this activity.

2.2. Adaptive Sense-Making: The Value of a Good Story

The notion of "adaptive visualization" turns on the concept of helping the decision maker adapt as the situation changes. At a minimum, this requires that the support technology makes the decision maker aware that the situation has changed. However, the goal would be to support those cognitive processes in the human that drive the sense-making ability. For that reason, it is important to look at the cognitive processes, which RAVENS assumes underlie SA and sense-making.

The human decision maker must make sense out of any situation, especially when uncertainty is high. As humans, we are compelled to engage in "sense-making," to take any surprise, anomaly, or unexpected behavior, and make it fit smoothly with what we know. In traditional war, this is easier because the expectations and set of alternatives are much narrower. However, when key relationships are not always clear, particularly causal relationships, we resort to a cognitive process referred to here as *storytelling* or sometimes, more formally, as *narrative cognition.*

This framework takes a constructivist approach to SA. Constructivist approaches to psychology assume that we do not simply sense and perceive photographically veridical exemplars of "what is out there" and store them in memory, like photos in a filing cabinet. Rather, we extract essential features of reality and use them as a "good enough" version of the original (Fiske, 1993; Kintsch, 1998; Klein, 1998). This abstracted structure (sometimes referred to as a *schema*) is then imposed on reality where it acts as a filter for both perception and memory. In our attempts to maintain coherence, either perception or memory may be changed to get the "best fit" to the overall structure. Thus, both perception and memory, the things we think about, are constructed in real time, not just stored and retrieved. Storytelling is, in fact, the ultimate constructive process as the result is not just a representation, but also a constructive simulation. The advantage of a constructive cognitive system is that it is efficient – a lot can be done, given sufficient experience, with expectations about the world without verifying every pixel of reality.

Narrative cognition is a process by which humans flexibly and adaptively build knowledge about and make sense of the world, to transfer this understanding to others, and, in so doing, allow others to do a better job of reading our minds (that is, inferring our intentions). Storytelling can be a tool for sense-making in the face of less-than-perfect and incomplete data because it does not depend entirely on truth and logic. Rather, it fits the data to what you know and have experienced and even to your sense of self in the world. This can have some drawbacks, but it is not a flaw as some have suggested (most notably, Kahneman & Tversky, 1973). Brains are not limited to syllogistic and Boolean rationality as digital computational devices are and, as a result, people do not make their decisions on the basis of well-formed if–then statements and calculated probabilities. This, we would argue, is mostly (but not always) a good thing. It really depends on what your objective is and what data or information you have to work with. However, as you will see in Section 3, the brain will tend to fill gaps based on expectations and even biases that, though efficient, may lead us to counterproductive analyses.

The idea that human storytelling is a powerful and even preferred means of understanding situations and learning about the world is not new. It has been taken quite seriously by the humanities, including history, anthropology, law, education, management, artificial intelligence, human–computer interface design, and constructionist-based psychotherapy (Bruner, 1990, 2002; Harre & Gillett, 1994; Hirokawa, DeGooyer, & Valde, 2000; Klein, 1998; Murray, 1995; Pennington & Hastie, 1993; Rossiter, 1999; Shank, 1990; Snowden, 2000; Weick, 1995).

The RAVENS framework considers "story" or narrative to be a cognitive structure, like a schema, but model-like so that relationships between people and events are captured holistically. Stories, as knowledge structures, are rooted to a particular situation; they reflect time, place, intent, behavior, and goals. They also provide a point-of-view (POV) or experiencing self, which is as important to gathering intelligence as it is to any situated work of fiction. This is what makes storytelling pragmatic (Fiske, 1993; Warner & Burnstein, 1996). We will thus define this story representation as a thematically organized and coherent representation or model of actors, roles, behaviors, goals and their relationships to one's self or POV, and one's previous knowledge of the world.

We will first elaborate a few of the terms used in this definition so as to be as clear and concrete as possible. *Thematically* refers to an essential property of stories, that they have a central subject or "thing in the world" that they are modeling. It is this theme that gives the relations, particularly causal relationships, between the essential elements (actors, their roles, their actions in those roles) not only meaning but consequences in the model. *Coherent* refers to the result of what has come to be called sense-making. Sense-making is the ability to take unexpected events and normalize them with our already existing knowledge and experience. This may be done by altering the model or by changing our expectations. Finally, the terms *self* or *POV* (these are interchangeable) refer to the "narrative center of gravity" (Bruner, 1990) that drives the model, provides the emotion, defines the consequences as well as the goals, and provides this knowledge "structure" with its flexibility and dynamism.

Coherence or sense-making relies on this "best-fit" idea implied by constructive theories. As long as what is experienced fits within a tolerable range of variability to our expectations, it will be incorporated into our model of the situation. This means the situation will continue to be coherent and will not require a lot of extra cognitive resources to maintain coherence. However, in the types of missions currently being seen, where expectations are so different from outcomes, they can no longer be accommodated by the same model. It is here that storytelling is invoked to generate either new relationships or a new model. This is what allows the human to be adaptive.

Storytelling is a tool for and invoked by dealing with unexpected outcomes. It is no accident that stories as entertainment turn on conflict and difficulty. Narrative structure, because it is richly semantic (carries meaning) and pragmatic (relates that meaning to one's goals, POV, and emotions), allows one to make projections about the future (plans) and decisions. That is, narrative is an ideal way to discover and represent causal chains. When something unexpected occurs, one of two things can happen, depending on factors such as the importance of the event (pragmatically), how great the mismatch is with expectations, the consequences of the difference for achieving the goal, and other factors. One possibility is that the narrative structure imposes itself on the unexpected outcome or event and forces a fit in the model. This is always the least costly solution, in terms of cognitive resources, and thus is probably always the brain's default solution. The second possibility is that the narrative schema shifts dramatically. This is much harder – we usually have to sit down for a while after this happens and may even experience it with some amount of stress and alarm.

Stories are easily shared, if imperfectly. That is, to the degree that our models of the world overlap and are mutually coherent, stories can be passed from one person to another. The advantages of this are enormous. It means that one person can pass not just information but his/her understanding of that information to another. This is no small accomplishment. Because stories are constructed not only from actual perceptual information, but also from one's personal experience and POV, each person's story is somewhat idiosyncratic. This range of individual interpretation is somewhat bounded by culture and domain, but not as much as one might think. We often misunderstand each other, but it is in fact much more surprising how often misunderstandings do not happen. If someone narrates a situation for another and they share enough experience, culture, and domain in common, the person receiving that story should be able to go away with a "good enough" understanding of the situation as the narrator understands it and may even be able to "read" the narrator's mind. That is, the listener may be able to understand the intent of a request from the narrator even though the request lacks sufficient detail in its surface form (Klein, 1998). This is very hard to do with almost any other kind of information presentation.

However, this story sharing and mind reading is a double-edged sword for adaptability. We said that this depends on overlap between our models of the world and, thus, overlap in our perceptions and experience. If, however, we are involved with another culture where there is much less overlap in perception and experience but we assume they should see things the same way, we are not going to be adaptive at all. That is why the mental model needs to be constructed from data, not from experience alone.

2.3. Sense-Making: Building Understanding in the Decision Maker

Above, the case was made for storytelling as a unique human ability for the essential task of making sense of the world in order to achieve SA. It was suggested that passed-on culture and domain stories make it easier to accomplish this sense-making task. Nowhere is sense-making more vital than in military intelligence. However, this is the task that has become much harder when operations and their contexts change from mission to mission. Can decision support technology and human engineering be used to support storytelling in order to provide more rapid coherence and SA?

One fruitful area to consider is the idea of narrative information visualization (Gershon & Page, 2001). Most information in a database, which is where the visualized information is drawn from, tends to be typically organized in an object-oriented manner. This hierarchical inheritance structure is useful for the kinds of knowledge that can be agreed upon, objects and ideas that are well defined within the culture or domain, such as general knowledge and domain knowledge. However, it is not the structure that will help to construct a story. What is needed is a way of organizing information thematically. What is the current situation about, who are the major players, and what roles do they seem to be acting out given their behaviors?

The key to aiding the human is to provide him or her with visualizations that encourage building narrative out of the data, or at the very least providing key relationships in a way that the human will understand that they are important and build on them. This suggests that presenting data in a model-driven simulation, perhaps with game-play interaction, would be a beneficial way to represent the data one needs to incorporate the situation. These simulations would themselves be organized by assumptions about theme and roles of different actors and might be able to provide collaborative story comparison among staff or different levels of echelon. This kind of story-like external representation and simulation tool or tool suite could prove invaluable to the human decision maker, particularly for aiding generations of multiple hypotheses.

Simulation tools, which have recently become more of a focus for training and system design, are equally important as tools in the planning process in the battlespace, helping to make sense of the unfolding situation, and actually testing coherence. In planning a simulation during scenario design, generating stories helps one consider all the possible interactions between agents and actions. This has been realized for some time in user interface design with a movement sometimes referred to as *scenario-based design* (Carroll, 1999). For example, if one is trying to design a new information interface, he or she might consider the role the human is going to play, what information he or she, or some subject matter expert (SME), think is relevant and what use they are going to put it to. What kinds of things might actually happen when the user tries to use this interface? What other thing is the user trying to do or think about at the same time? Is trying to do certain things at certain times going to end up frustrating the user because of the different ways tasks are set up – that is, how does the user feel and what is the user's POV?

The same thing applies to a complex simulation. Simulations of human systems in dynamic environments are not always captured well by parameter lists and algorithmic weightings. They are also not captured in static scenarios. Simulations need stories as well, not unlike the writers' conference that might be done before creating a television series and its progress over the next season. In this case, a mixture of computer programmers, soldier SMEs, and even storytellers collaborate to evaluate and elaborate the nature of the thematic organization of this simulation. Simulations, like stories, need to be imbedded in a domain and a context (Snowden, 2000). General simulations are not likely to capture the kinds of interactions that we see as the context of each operation changes. When things change, the simulation has to adapt, just as the decision maker's thinking has to adapt. The simulation will never be able to provide the decisions, but it must be able to portray the changes those decisions are going to be based on.

However, there still seems to be some limitations to the dynamics of these solutions. To accomplish narrative visualization of an unfolding situation, you would like the model to evolve just as the real situation does and adapt to those changes. Evolutionary algorithms seem to show a great deal of promise here. These algorithms (see Section 4 for an example) might be utilized to model self-organizing social networks and dynamic probability spaces, creating much more adaptability than current network approaches that still rely too heavily on pre-determined rule sets.

Immersive simulation is a technique that has been explored for training situations for some time. Immersive simulations are simulations that utilize all the sensory modalities to create as realistic an experience as possible. Movies on a large screen in a dark theater with surround sound are an immersive simulation. In fact, the military has turned to movie studios, entertainment engineers, and video game developers to help them explore ways of building experience. This allows soldiers to explore possible outcomes and relative risk while experiencing the more pragmatic relationships in a way that would be hard to capture without that degree of immersion. Because of the inherent "storytelling" involved in setting up an immersive simulation, gaps in knowledge might be quickly identified.

The upshot is that there is a need to provide visualizations that can put the human in a narrative mode while planning, can provide model or story-based organizations of data, and can tell the decision maker something about what the data mean to them and to their mission. There is also a need to capture the dynamic nature of the situation as it evolves in the models. If the human and the decision aid share similar models, the human will be able to see much more easily what relationships fit and what relationships do not. That will make for an adaptive planner. The RAVENS framework provides an approach for exploring (research) and developing such tools and for further investigating how human narrative cognition is used in sense-making.

3. VISUALIZING RISK

In the previous section, a broad conceptual theory was presented that suggests there is a need to create coherent relationships between knowledge and information as a foundation for rapid adaptation that can reduce both uncertainty and complexity. In this section, a particular visualization problem and some empirical attempts to provide narrative coherence will be examined. The problem presented here is that of visualizing uncertainty and risk. Adapting to uncertainty requires a coherent mental representation of the situation. One of the key problems in presenting information about risk and uncertainty are the cognitive biases that decision makers bring to the task (Wickens & Hollands, 2000; McDermott et al., 2002). It is also true that experts can make effective decisions rapidly if they are familiar with their environment (Klein, 1998; Lopes, 1986). Unfortunately, as we have pointed out in the discussion of RAVENS, in part because each situation tends to be different, we will not always be able to have experts with long experience making decisions as might have been possible in the latter years of the Cold War. The question that this series of experiments addresses is how to display uncertainty and risk in order to enhance the soldier's understanding of the military situation so that the resulting decisions resemble the expert and not the biased decision maker. Doing so requires modeling complex relationships in a way that allows the soldier to understand not just what is happening now, but what is likely to happen in the future.

Johnson-Laird, Legrenzi, Girotto, Legrenzi, and Caverni (1999) posit that the reason for many of the observed deficiencies in decision making is an impoverished mental model of the decision space. Humans partition their decision space into a perceived number of options with weightings representing the certitude of each option. The problem according to these authors is that the decision maker often perceives fewer options than in fact exist in that space. For example, they examined the famous "Monty Hall" problem of a contestant choosing a prize behind one of the three doors. In this case, after Monty shows a contestant that the prize is not behind one of the two doors they did not choose, the contestant usually stayed with the original choice because they assumed it was equally likely that the prize was in either of the options left. However, analysis indicates that counterintuitively, there are six possible outcomes: 2/3 of which favors switching doors (the answer hinges on the number of cases in which the prize is not behind the chosen doors (see Johnson-Laird et al., 1999, p. 82). This example almost has an air of trickery about it but it does illustrate that as a probability space becomes more complex, humans tend to simplify the mental model necessary to visualize the uncertainty space. The purpose of visualization aids is to alleviate the computational and visualization requirements humans encounter when making decisions in complex environments.

The initial experiment in this study attempted to simplify the veridical visualization process for the operator while ensuring that the display was not subject to well-known decision biases. The experiment was set in a national missile defense (NMD) paradigm with a trained but non-expert subject pool (i.e., the actual system was not built and the Air Force operators had initial training in order to help design the evolving system). Based on the frequency visualization literature and discussion with engineers, the probabilities were recast as number of possible "leakers." This allowed the operators to visualize the probability of an enemy missile not being intercepted (leakers) as a concrete frequency (i.e., 20 possible leakers per 1,000 represented a 2% expected leaker rate). Unfortunately, this measure also involved the possibility of the operators being influenced by a well-known decision bias – the framing effect (Tversky & Kahneman, 1981). Framing theory predicted that the operator decision strategy would change depending on whether outcomes were presented in terms of possible losses as opposed to possible gains. We investigated the possibility of a framing effect and the efficacy of giving the operators leakers as opposed to probability of success representations by testing 16 operators during a game-like simulation of an ongoing missile attack. The operators made missile allocation decisions and answered SA probes in a time-constrained setting. The results did not indicate a framing effect on decision strategy; however, representing the efficacy of the allocation plan in terms of expected frequency of leakers did improve the operator's SA score. Presumably, operators were not influenced in their decision making by how the uncertainty information was represented (frequency of possible leakers versus probability of success display) but they were able to answer probe questions more accurately and more rapidly if they were presented as leakers as opposed to probability information (Barnes, Wickens, & Smith, 2000).

The follow-on experiments investigated format variables and in particular how they might interact with cognitive biases such as framing (Barnes, McDermott, Hutchins, Gillan, & Rothrock, 2003; McDermott, et al., 2003). In general, risk information is better displayed with a graphical format (Smith & Wickens, 1999). However, there are a number of experiments that attest to superiority of textual formats. The crucial factor seems to be whether the presented information captures the dynamics of the process being represented (Meyer, Shamo, & Gopher, 1999; Wickens & Hollands, 2000). Thus, the efficacy of the format depends on the specific decision environment and on task demands as well as type of format. The NMD situation is both an important military problem and a case in which the physics of the sensors and interceptors can be used to make fairly accurate predictions about threat probabilities, value of the intended targets, and the probability of successful interception. A simulation environment in which the operator's task is to ensure proper allocation of defensive missiles was created. The simulated display indicates both the state of uncertainty and the value of the defended targets (U.S. cities) during an ongoing missile attack. The problem space is volatile because probabilities change as events unfold and interceptors succeed or fail and additional threats are discovered by the defensive systems. The experimental constraints required the operator to respond within 10–15 s of receiving a probe emulating the rapid decision cycle of many military situations.

3.1. Simulation Tool

Before conducting the simulation experiment, the type of graphical format that would be most effective for this type of environment needed to be determined. Two types of presentation format, square or circular, and two presentation modes, risk information being separated or integrated (Gillan & Hutchins, 2002) were examined. The integrated displays were also configural in the sense that while the separable displays showed two dimensions: probability of interception and population of defended city, the combined displays area showed the emergent dimension of overall risk (expected population lost). The square display in particular was similar conceptually to the configural displays evaluated by Bennett, Toms, and Woods (1993) for nuclear power plants.

A pilot study was conducted with 24 college students to determine how the graphics should be presented. The goal was to determine which display elements were most easily understood and best supported SA. The pilot was a complete 2×2 within-subjects factorial design consisting of four trials. Each trial consisted of various presentations of the same style of display. Every display had six graphs of the same type, with each graph representing a city, A through F, respectively. Trial order was counterbalanced. Subjects were shown various city displays that varied in overall risk, population, and probability of being successfully attacked and were asked to respond to printed probes querying the subject on various attributes of the cities. Subjects responded by clicking an "answer" button on the display. Response times were recorded from the moment the "ready" button was clicked until the moment the "answer" button was clicked. Accuracy of the typed responses was also recorded. This procedure was repeated for each display combination. The results indicated that the combined (i.e., integral) displays resulted in both more accurate and faster performance. This was a speed–accuracy trade-off with square type of format. The square format resulted in slower, but more accurate performance. Because the difference in latency was fairly small and accuracy was considered the more important criterion, the square format was used to evaluate configural representations in the simulation experiment.

The purpose of the simulation experiment was to understand the interaction of cognitive and perceptual display factors on both the operators' missile allocation decisions and SA performance. The Barnes et al. (2000) experiment failed to show the well-documented framing effect (cf., Mayhorn, Fisk, & Whittle, 2002). One major difference between the two paradigms is that the students in the Tversky and Kahneman (1981) study made decisions based on overall risk whereas our study was concerned only with how uncertainty was represented. In military environments, overall risk is the parameter the commander uses to make decisions (i.e., the military value of making the correct or incorrect choice weighted by its probability). In the present experiment, overall risk was shown in two presentation modes, integral or separable, and two formats, alphanumeric or graphical. Also, risk was framed in two conditions: possible population saved or possible population loss in terms of the current allocation plan. Fig. 1 shows risk information in a separable display with gain information – values of a successful decision. The value of the target was defined in terms of the

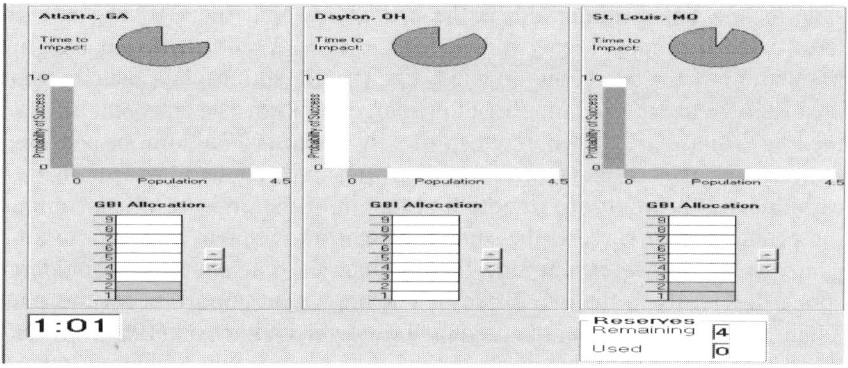

Fig. 1. Visualization Aid Showing Separable Information in Terms of Probability of Successful Interception and Value of the Target in Terms of Population.

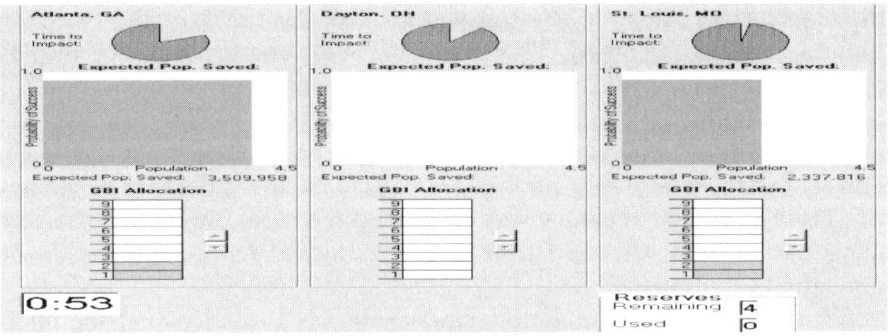

Fig. 2. Display Showing Overall Risk Area as Expected Number of Civilians Saved (Gain Information).

population of the city being targeted. The probability represented the probability that one of our missiles would intercept the incoming missile successfully. The ground-based interceptors (GBI) were inventory on hand and the remaining portion of the circle was time left to make an allocation decision.

Fig. 2 shows similar information; however, the expected value of this particular strategy is shown as the combined area of probability of success and population (overall risk). (Note that both displays are somewhat distorted to fit on the page.) In terms of experimental conditions, this display is graphic, integral (combined), and framed in terms of expected population saved.

The other framing condition shows the same information in terms of possible losses. The *Y* dimension is the probability that the GBI will not intercept the incoming enemy missile whereas the *X* information is still the population of the city being targeted. For the integral display, the emergent area is now the expected number of civilian casualties. The emergent areas in the loss displays are shown in red so that the subjects would not be confused between the two displays (green – number saved versus red – number of casualties). It is important to note that loss information is simply one minus the probability of success; the same information is imparted with a loss or gain display. However, framing theory suggests that operators should respond differently to the two displays. The prediction important for this paradigm (which differs from the original Tversky & Kahneman (1981) – in that there are no sure gain decisions) is that the operator will be biased toward avoiding losses versus the same decision framed to improve potential gains. This prediction follows from the steepness of the loss curve compared to the gain curves in Prospect theory as well as loss avoidance behaviors noted in other decision-making paradigms (Tversky & Kahneman, 1981; Shafir & Tversky, 1995). One prediction is straightforward when the information is given in terms of expected losses; the operator should take more missiles out of reserves than when the same information is given in terms of possible gains. The other is subtler; situations were set up where small cities were not covered with any interceptor missiles. In half of these conditions, the expected value for allocating a reserve interceptor (GBIs) to an uncovered small city was higher than to put the reserve GBI on one of the other cities. In the other half, the expected value was higher whenever the city was left uncovered (assign no missiles from reserves) and the operator used the reserve missile to protect one of the other (much larger) cities. The loss avoidance thesis would predict that the operator would leave fewer cities uncovered in both conditions when the displays emphasized possible losses versus the same decision situation when the information was given in terms of expected gains. It is important to remember that the expected utility was the same for both the loss and gain conditions and the subject's individual risk biases should not influence the results (they experienced both conditions – it was the relative decisions under the two frames that were being measured).

3.2. Simulation Study Methods

Research was conducted to investigate how the following display parameters affected SA and decision making:

- Presentation mode: Information about city population and probability of success was integrated into a value for expected population saved or kept separate.
- Format: Information presented in graphical or alphanumeric format.
- Frame: Information was conveyed in terms of gains (probability of success and expected population saved) or losses (probability of failure and expected population lost).

The experiment was a 2.2×2 mixed factorial design with presentation mode as a between variable. Format and frame were within variables and frame was blocked. The levels of format, presentation mode, and frame were combined in all possible ways to create eight displays. The within-subject variables were counterbalanced to avoid sequence effects.

Forty-eight students were recruited from introductory psychology classes at the New Mexico State University. Subjects participated on a volunteer basis. Participants sat in front of the computer monitor and entered their responses with a mouse. The NMD scenario software was developed at Micro Analysis & Design. Instructions were delivered via a self-paced PowerPoint® presentation. Some information and its format were common across the eight displays. The number of reserve GBIs used, the number of reserve GBIs remaining, and time elapsed in the scenario were numerically represented. Each target city had its own area of the display. Within that area, the following were presented (from top to bottom): time until the incoming missile impacts, probability of successfully intercepting the incoming missile, population of the target city, and GBI missile allocation along with up and down arrow buttons that allowed participants to increase or decrease the number of reserve GBIs allocated. The way the remaining information was represented depended on the specific display. The graphic displays have been described above.

Integral alphanumeric gain. Information about the GBIs allocated, time to impact, probability of success, and value as well as the value of expected population saved were numerical. The color green indicated the gain condition.

Integral alphanumeric loss. Information about the GBIs allocated, time to impact, probability of failure, and value as well as the value of expected population lost were numerical. The color red indicated the loss condition.

Sixteen scenarios were used in the experimental trials. There were four types of scenarios that dictated the number of cities attacked, the size of the cities, and the number of GBIs allocated. Scenarios were randomly matched to displays so that each display had four associated scenarios, one of each type. This was done for the separate (between) condition and repeated for the combined (between) condition.

The scenarios had several factors in common. Between three and five cities were attacked, three or four reserve GBIs were available, and between zero and three initial GBIs were assigned to each city. Each scenario was 2 min long and contained four SA probes and one reserve missile allocation probe. The SA probes were intended to engage the participants, increase workload, and determine how well the displays were understood. The scenario was frozen during SA probes and participants had 10 s to respond by clicking on the appropriate answer. Failure to respond was recorded as a "no answer." The SA probes asked about relationships such as, "Which city has the highest probability of success?" The information on the screen was occluded during the probe so participants had to rely on memory. The reserve allocation probes always occurred at the end of the scenario and lasted for 15 s. Participants were prompted to allocate missiles and the up and down arrows for each city became active. As participants allocated missiles, the information on the display (i.e., probability of success, population saved) was updated dynamically to show the impact of allocations. Participants could continue to change allocations for the full 15 s, which was displayed via a timer countdown.

The session began with a self-paced training presentation that described the participant's role, the displays, and the scenarios. The participant had the opportunity to ask questions. The order of practice and experimental trials was as follows: four practice scenarios (one of each display type), two practice scenarios in the frame that they were about to be tested in (i.e., gain or loss), eight experimental trials in the first frame, two practice scenarios in the second frame, and eight experimental scenarios in the second frame. The entire procedure took approximately 90 min. The practice and experimental trials were presented in random order blocked by frame. At the conclusion of each scenario, the participant clicked on the "OK" button to advance to the next scenario.

3.3. Results of Simulation Study

The dependent measures recorded by the simulation software were: reserve GBI allocation, SA probe accuracy, and SA probe response time. Decision making was assessed via GBI allocations. SA was measured by SA probe accuracy and response time. In addition, risk behavior was analyzed in relation to whether GBIs were allocated to small cities. Repeated measures ANOVA were performed on the decision score (i.e., reserve GBI allocation), accuracy, response time, and small city coverage.

Decision score. A decision score was used to measure deviation from normative GBI allocation. This score depended on how the participant allocated his or her reserves compared to an optimal solution.

The decision score equaled the participant's expected population loss minus the optimal expected value where the participant's expected population loss was the sum of the probability of failure multiplied by the population for every city in the scenario including the possibility of a future attack. The same information could have been given from the inverse (expected lives saved), but a common reference measure was used for all conditions. There was a significant interaction of frame by content, $F(1, 46) = 12.484$, $p \leqslant 0.0001$. In the integral displays, performance was better (fewer expected casualties) with the loss (200,000 versus 260,000) condition but in the separable displays, performance was better in the gain condition with no significant main effects.

SA accuracy. The SA accuracy measure was an average percent correct for the probe conditions. If the participant did not respond this was treated as an incorrect response. There was a significant interaction of frame by format, $F(1, 46) = 7.163$, $p \leqslant 0.010$. In the graphical displays there was almost no difference between gain and loss conditions but in the alphanumeric displays, SA accuracy was higher in the gain condition than in the loss condition. There was a main effect of frame, $F(1, 46) = 16.642$, $p \leqslant 0.0001$ and a main effect of format, $F(1, 46) = 9.371$, $p \leqslant 0.004$. SA accuracy was better in gain than loss (0.859 versus 0.807) and better in graphical than alphanumeric (0.854 versus 0.813).

SA response time. Response time was recorded in seconds. There were four instances in which a participant did not respond and these were coded as the maximum time (10 s). There was a significant interaction of frame by format, $F(1, 46) = 4.594$, $p < 0.037$. In the alphanumeric displays, response time on both gain and loss displays was roughly equivalent. However, in the graphical displays, performance on the gain and loss displays differed with response time being higher in the loss condition than in the gain condition.

Small cities analysis. In order to see if participants were risk seeking or risk averse in relation to small cities (i.e., did they have a bias to not leave any city uncovered and avoid a sure loss) and how this was impacted by display type, the coverage of small cities was analyzed. The experiment was designed so that in some of the scenarios the normative allocation involved leaving one small city uncovered. Since the distribution of "uncovered" small cities was not balanced across conditions, the scenarios were split into two types and analyzed separately: those in which the small cities should be covered and those in which a small city should be uncovered.

For the small cities that should have been covered (i.e., defended), there were three effects. There was a two-way interaction of frame by format, $F(1, 46) = 60.926$, $p < 0.0001$. The difference between gain and loss displays was relatively large in the graphical condition compared to the difference between gain and loss displays in the alphanumeric condition. There was a main effect of frame, $F(1, 46) = 124.305$, $p < 0.0001$ such that more small cities were appropriately covered in the loss displays than the gain displays (0.569 versus 0.369). There was also a main effect of format, $F(1, 46) = 24.306$, $p < 0.0001$ such that more small cities were appropriately covered in the alphanumeric displays than the graphical displays (0.507 versus 0.431).

For the cities that should have been left uncovered by the expected value rules, the same effects were found but the strengths of the effects were weaker.

There was a two-way interaction of frame by format, $F(1, 46) = 5.736$, $p < 0.021$. In the graphical condition, there were more cities appropriately left uncovered (0.20) for gain displays than for loss displays (0.10) while there was virtually no difference between gain and loss displays in the alphanumeric condition. There was a main effect of frame, $F(1, 46) = 5.618$, $p < 0.022$, with a higher percentage of subjects correctly leaving cities uncovered in the gain frame than in the loss frame (0.158 versus 0.108). There was a main effect of format, $F(1, 46) = 7.108$, $p < 0.011$, with a higher percentage of subjects correctly leaving cities uncovered in the graphical condition than in the alphanumeric condition (0.156 versus 0.109).

3.4. Discussion

The principal purpose of the study was to understand the relationship between visualization and the framing decision bias. Although the framing model makes specific predictions about risk seeking and risk aversion in particular situations, both processes are a reflection of the well-documented loss avoidance bias. Humans attempt to avoid sure losses even when the alternative decision would lead to a higher expected value for lives saved. Specifically, the psychological loss functions are steeper than gain functions and it is worse to lose money than to fail to show a gain of equal monetary value (Shafir & Tversky, 1995).

The latter inequality implies that if the same situation is framed in terms of losses, the results will be different from that framed in terms of possible gains. In the present experiment, participants were expected to take more missiles out of reserves to avoid losses compared to the same situation wherein the results were framed in terms of possible lives saved. This behavior was predicted even though the importance of keeping some missiles in reserve was emphasized in the instructions (i.e., it was not optimal to take too many missiles out of reserves). Although the framing trend was in the predicted direction, the prediction on reserve decisions was not significant because the participants tended to take out almost all their reserves in both framing conditions resulting in sub-optimal decisions. The average value for missiles left in reserve was less than one for both cases. This general trend agrees with previous research and is probably an extension of the loss avoidance principle. In the above-reported first experiment, NMD operators reported being more concerned about the present attack than about possible future attacks to the extent that they tended to underweigh the probabilities of the future attack (Barnes et al., 2000). Again, this makes sense if they are biased toward reducing losses in the present compared to possible future losses.

Conditions were also created where the expected value of covering all the target cities with GBIs would result in more expected losses than if the GBIs were allocated to protect the larger cities and some of the smaller cities were not protected (uncovered). This was an attempt to replicate the risk-seeking behavior that Tversky and Kahneman (1981) found in the original study (replicated recently by Mayhorn et al., 2002). The logic in the present experiment was that test subjects would avoid leaving a small city uncovered (because it is a sure loss) to a greater extent for loss display conditions than for gain conditions even in cases where larger cities were not given adequate protection based on expected value models. This prediction was supported by the data. Participants in the loss presentation condition covered more small cities under conditions where it was both appropriate (higher expected value by doing so) and inappropriate (lower expected value by doing so). Thus, subjects presented with loss displays were risk seeking in the sense of Tversky and Kahneman; they would rather risk a possible higher expected loss for larger cities than accept a sure loss for a smaller city. In general, both where it was appropriate and where it was inappropriate, information in terms of losses made the subjects more sensitive to protecting against the sure losses of smaller cities. An unexpected finding was that the loss avoidance effects were more pronounced for the graphical displays than for alphanumeric displays. This suggests that the graphical representations emphasized the impact of the loss of small cities indicating an important interaction between the visualization format and the framing bias.

Predictions were also made that improved visualization would lessen the loss avoidance biases. Observers' visualization parameters were varied in two manners. In the risk content conditions, probability (p) and population value (v) was presented for each city as either separate indices or as a combined expected value. This was important theoretically because the Tversky and Kahneman (1981) experiment presented this information as separate values. Thus, it is possible that their effects were due to the computational overhead that computing an expected value entailed. In the presentation conditions, information was presented as either combined information (expected risk) or as separate values (population and probability). For format, the graphical displays showed this as a configural area or as two bar graphs. We argued that the configural representations would make the implications of expected value solutions more obvious to the observer ameliorating their loss avoidance biases. The only significant effect was an interaction between frame and presentation. As predicted, combining information as an expected value improved decision score performance for the loss framing condition; however, the gain condition actually showed degraded performance when it was presented as a combined expected value. The formatting of the display had no significant effect suggesting it was not a perceptual artifact of the displays themselves. Thus, the framing bias was evinced by the type of reserve decisions operators made but framing showed no main effect on decision-making effectiveness. It appears that gain and loss information resulted in non-optimal decisions that canceled each other out in terms of overall effectiveness. We are in the process of investigating possible reasons for this in a follow-up study.

For NMD, operators' SA is a crucial part of their mission statement. During an actual missile attack, being aware of the parameter of the unfolding attack was not only important for missile allocation but the results were also critical to numerous other entities both for military and civil disaster planning. For that reason, an independent measure of SA was used. For probe performance, graphical configural displays were better than the numeric displays, a finding that agreed with most of the literature on the efficacy of graphical representations for uncertainty data (Smith & Wickens, 1999). More surprisingly, gain information was remembered better and responded to more rapidly than loss information. This contradicted the previous research on NMD performance, wherein the operators had better SA for "missile leakers" (based on probability of loss) than for probability of success information (Barnes et al., 2000). The present study offers a more complete picture of the unfolding NMD situation since it combines risk and uncertainty for the decision maker.

The results imply that the framing bias exists but affects decision effectiveness only tangentially. In general, the operator tended to use all reserves in both framing conditions. In follow-on experiments, we are investigating better feedback visualizations and training techniques to improve decision effectiveness. The operator must learn to use the visualization information to make more effective decisions to adapt to the changing NMD situation. It seems likely the import of reserve decisions was allusive to the operators in our experiments because they did not receive feedback on the effects of holding missiles in reserve. Future efforts will focus on the type and amount of feedback visualization necessary to make NMD operators aware of the implications of their allocation decisions. If our emerging hypothesis is correct, the utility of visualizations will be their ability to signal to the operator (based on past experience) the consequences of the risk factors on future as well as current missile attacks. The framing effect and its implications on SA are the basis of the study we completed recently and are in the process of analyzing (Rothrock et al., 2003). The purpose of that study was to understand more fully the somewhat contradictory results we obtained between the first and third studies.

In summary, this series of studies has shown important interactions between cognitive biases and visualization methods. The ongoing research is an attempt to mitigate these effects in order to develop visualization and training methods to improve decision making and SA under risk in volatile environments. Success would seem to depend on integrating coherent risk and uncertainty information into a richer mental model that provides SA for both the present situation and for future possibilities.

4. COEVOLUTIONARY ALGORITHMS FOR PEACEKEEPING SIMULATIONS: VISUALIZING EMERGENT SOLUTIONS

In the previous section, a series of empirical studies was used to examine the application of coherent visualizations to a specific problem set, decision making about risk in the face of present and future uncertainty. In this section, an example of a visualization tool that might be used to support narrative thinking about complex and uncertain situations is presented. Here we are not focused on empirical results or types of visualization. Rather, we are looking at the kinds of decision aids that might help the soldier maintain narrative SA. That is, what sort of tool can visualize key relationships and make them coherent, which the theory of Section 2 says is important, and also help decision makers include in their solution space a richer number of possible solutions, which was seen as important in the decision-making experiments of Section 3.

This is a specific research tool, a prototype, intended to allow an analyst to be able to see and explore emergent relationships that might not normally be explored. The tool visualizes their interactions as a narrative (3D animation), but then provides a rich data set for filling in one's mental model where experience (or lack of it) and cognitive biases might leave gaps. As a prototype, the specific visualizations used are not being presented as the most optimal solutions, but rather are presenting the conceptual tool as an available approach that can help the analyst both understand and adapt to complex and uncertain situations. It does so by pushing the analyst into a scenario-driven narrative mode for making complex patterns and relationships coherent. Thus, this section should show how some of the more conceptual goals of the theory in Section 2 might be actually implemented in decision support architecture.

The domain of this simulation-based analysis system is the less-conventional set of military missions classified under the label of stability and support operations (SASO), including peacekeeping, disaster relief, anti-terrorist security operations, and other non-force-on-force combat scenarios. The military defines the purpose of stability operations as being "to promote and sustain regional and global stability" and the primary role of stability operations is "to meet the immediate needs of designated groups, for a limited time, until civil authorities can accomplish these tasks without military assistance" (Department of the Army, 2003). SASO operations may also have the goals of keeping armed conflicts contained and quieting domestic disturbances. The resulting scenarios are very similar to situations that troops in Iraq face daily.

This section introduces a system that provides multi-sided coevolution for military peacekeeping missions. Because of the complex environment, the interactions of sides are captured in a simulation in which all sides compete (i.e., adapt) to the changing situations with analytical visualization methods being used to display results in a format intuitive to the analyst.

Many applications currently exist to support commanders' decision making in conventional warfare scenarios. FOX (Schlabach, Hayes, & Goldberg, 1999) notably used genetic algorithms to create conventional warfare courses-of-action (COA). One of the major drawbacks of FOX was that it only allowed evolution of the blue side (U.S. forces) against several static COAs of the red (enemy) side. Hillis and Winkler (2001) developed a coevolutionary approach to the FOX simulation that allowed the red and blue sides to adapt to each other's tactics. However, the conventionality of the tactics and the simplicity of the paradigm did not allow Military Intelligence (MI) analysts to gain insights into more complex environments such as Iraq. The principal advantage of Scheherazade visualizations is in their ability to portray emergent solutions as the different entities compete to obtain conflicting goals in complex SASO environments (Schlabach & Hillis, 2003). In this sense, it captures the dynamics of entities that adapt to a volatile environment in contrast to rule-based solutions, which have a more constrained set of outcomes.

4.1. Overview

A four-part approach has been developed: creating the SASO environment, the coevolution of COAs by several agents, the SASO simulation named

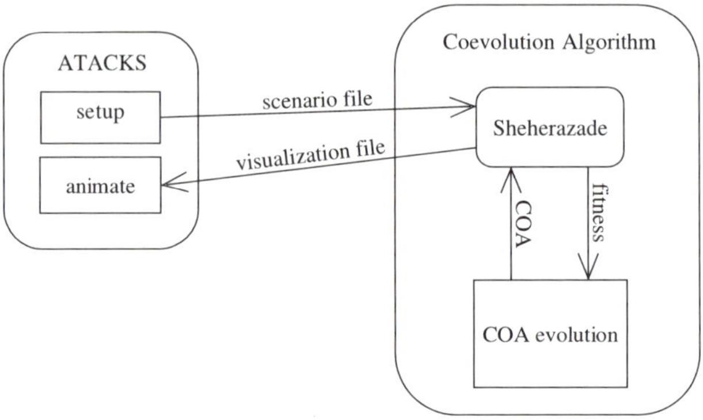

Fig. 3. System Overview.

Scheherazade (Schlabach & Hillis, 2003), and the analysis of the results with evolution and scenario visualizations. These parts work together as shown in Fig. 3.

4.2. Creating the SASO Environment

The SASO environment was developed in a cooperative enterprise between Ft. Huachuca researchers and ARL (Schlabach & Hillis, 2003). The scenario contains entities, factions, and locales (see Fig. 4). The entities could be terrorists, refugees, media, non-government organizations, or peacekeeping forces. Each entity has relative combat, intelligence, and other strengths and belongs to an allegiance or faction. Each faction has a starting animosity or friendliness to every other faction. The locales contain percentages of the population of each faction, and each locale has a starting attitude or calmness. The military expert defines all the values for the entities, factions, and locales to start modeling a situation he or she wants to investigate by having the system generate COAs for each of the entities.

After establishing the environment, the military expert also assigns each entity to an agent. A simple assignment consists of each agent's entities belonging to one faction. The assignment of entities to agents is important in defining the fitness functions or goals of each agent. For example, if all entities of agent 3 belong to the faction named "Eastern Alliance," then the fitness function of that agent could be to cause local unrest. Another fitness

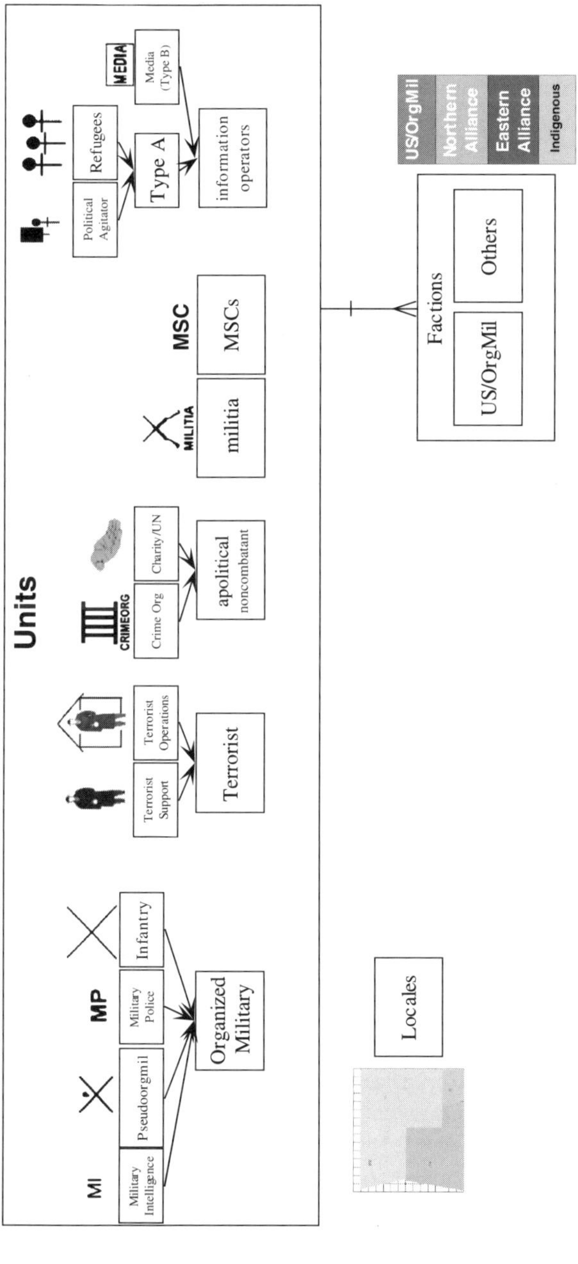

Fig. 4. Entities and their Relationships.

criterion could be to inflict as much damage as possible on another faction or it could be a weighted combination of several of these factors.

4.3. Coevolution of COAs

Once the scenario parameters have been defined, the system can begin evolving movements and targets for each of the agents through a genetic algorithm (GA). The GA allows each agent to take its turn evolving. As each agent changes the movements and target factions of its entities, each of the other agents tries to find a better set of movements and target factions for its own entities to reach a better fitness score.

For many entities, the chromosomes for the GA consist of a list of scheduled movements and targets, if the entity type engages in combat. For the organized military entities that make up the blue or friendly faction, the chromosomes are a set of assignments of units to military subordinate commands, which are, in turn assigned to locales.

The GA takes these chromosomes and passes them to the SASO simulation, which returns with several scores that make up the fitness function. (The scores are actually averages of many runs of the same chromosomes due to the stochastic nature of the simulation.) The GA uses the fitness function to select, crossover, and mutate new COAs, which are again played, scored, and selected. The agents take their respective turns evolving against the other agents' COAs, changing their strategies in reaction to the other agents' changes.

4.4. Scheherazade: The SASO Simulation

As mentioned previously, the coevolution algorithm uses the SASO simulation, named Scheherazade, after the famous character of "1,001 Arabian Nights," as values for its fitness function. The basic concepts of entities, factions, and locales will be introduced in Section 4.4.1. A more detailed description of the environment, entities, events, and explanation of respective COAs in the simulation algorithm follows.

4.4.1. Environment

The basic environment consists of factions and locales. Factions are deliberately vague groupings of people assumed to be nominally united by common affiliations and that tend to be thought of as a group, such as "NATO" or "the ethnic Serbs." They are not necessarily politically or organizationally united.

A faction's "animosity" toward another faction represents its "feelings" for that faction. Every provocation (incident, violation, terrorist hit, military attack, etc.) causes the victim's faction to increase its animosity level toward the perpetrator's faction.

Locales are geographical regions, which can be thought of as neighborhoods within a city or states/provinces within a nation. Locales have several properties including geographic size, population size, and which other locales are neighbors. The local population of a locale is also divided among the factions. An important property that affects many events in the simulation is the locale's "attitude."

"Attitude" for each locale influences the probability that one faction will attack a target of another faction, given the chance. The attitude score cumulatively reflects the effects of the recent incidents in the locale, emotional value of locale, population over/under density, developmental factors, etc. Attitude is also usually an important factor in the fitness functions of the agents.

4.4.2. Entities and COAs

Entity types describe the options available to a player set. Different entity types have different COA mechanisms such as a list of movements, times, and targets or a division of power among locales.

For each simulation turn, or clock tick, every entity is located within one of the locales. Entities within the same locale have a probability of interacting, depending upon a number of factors, which include entity characteristics as well as the locales' properties listed earlier.

The entity types Scheherazade offers the scenario designer are organized military, militia, terrorists, information operators, and apolitical noncombatants, as shown in Fig. 4. Each entity type has different properties and behaviors some of which contribute to calming effects, while others contribute to agitating effects. There are certain properties and behaviors which all entities share. An entity's calming or agitating effects are amplified proportionally to the relative size of the local populace in its faction. Every attack and incident drives the attitude up in proportion to its severity.

4.4.3. Events

In Scheherazade the entities interact with the environment to model certain real-world events such as:

Clock ticks represent temporal dimensions defined by the analyst. They regulate the order of play for agent actions. Within a clock tick, entities within each locale consult the locale conditions (current attitudes, population demographics, other entities in the locale) to determine its action for that clock tick. Incidents describe a class of interactions between entities or an entity and the local population. Incidents have an associated "severity" rating to determine the appropriate adjustment to make to attitude levels. When an incident occurs that includes combat, Scheherazade consults the weighted combat values of the contributing entities and assesses combat attrition.

4.5. Visualization

Our research in this area concentrates on the visualization of the novel symbologies of the entities and their behaviors. We provide visualizations of specific actions, as well as abstracted, conceptual displays of the relationships of entities and regions. We use the Advanced Tactical Architecture for Combat Knowledge System (ATACKS), previously described in Suantak, Momen, Rozenblit, Barnes, and Fichtl (2001), to show the movements and graphs of a simulation run.

ATACKS is a three-dimensional (3-D) visualization tool that facilitates rapid, flexible development of high-level battlespace representations as well as execution and assessment of war-gaming scenarios. It expands standard battlefield symbology by providing abstract symbols on 3-D abstract battle space terrains. It extends normal spatial visualization through process-centered displays that seek to enhance the commander's understanding of the situation by presenting qualitative data in novel formats.

The visualizations of a simulation run play an important role in our development and analysis of Scheherazade. ATACKS provides a graphical user interface to set up a scenario and then provides several displays to show important events and values for a scenario.

4.6. SASO Simulation Analysis

Once a military expert has used ATACKS to define a scenario, the resulting file is used to run the coevolution algorithm. As the coevolution algorithm is running, it passes COAs to Scheherazade in order to get back the fitness scores. Scheherazade produces an output visualization file of each of the best COAs for each agent per generation. These data files can then be read by ATACKS to create an animation and several displays that show the COAs, movements, incidents, attitudes, damage (attrition), and animosities for that run. Most importantly, these displays show relationships, such as the effect of movement and incidents on locale attitudes, and relative changes of animosities between factions.

A set of easily recognizable icons for each type of entity was created. Fig. 4 shows the entities and their relationships, as well as example colors for locales and factions. The entity icons were then placed on 3-D units that move between locales, as shown in Fig. 5.

Each icon is filled in with its faction color. The colored bar graph in the center of the locale indicates the percentages of population that belong to each faction in that locale. For each clock tick, entities move in and out of locales in the 3-D environment of ATACKS. However, an overall view of the movements and events has proven more helpful in understanding scenarios, as the RAVENS framework would lead one to expect.

Using consistent colors and icons, a movement graph showing the in and out movements of each entity appears in Fig. 6. The background colors

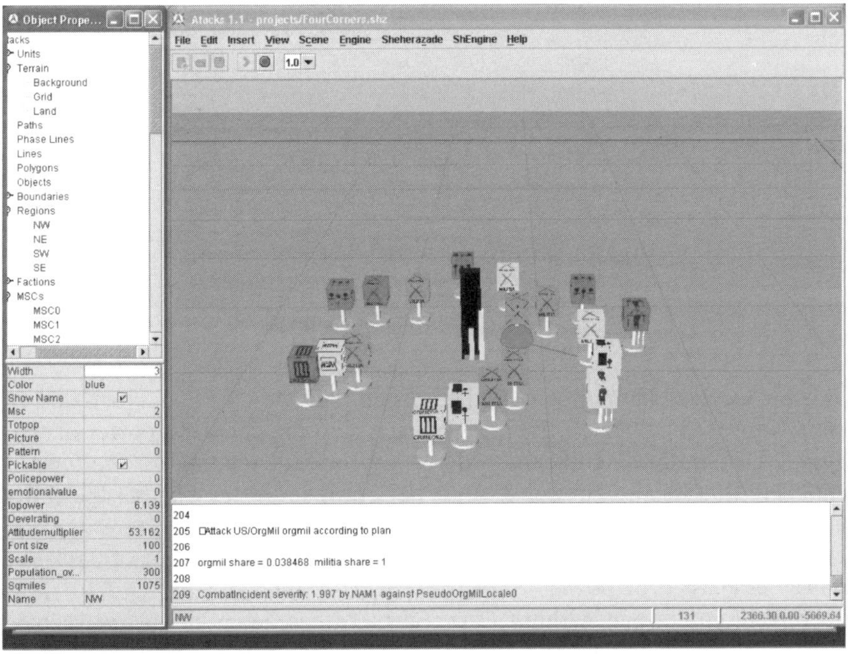

Fig. 5. ATACKS Snapshot Showing Sherherazade Entities.

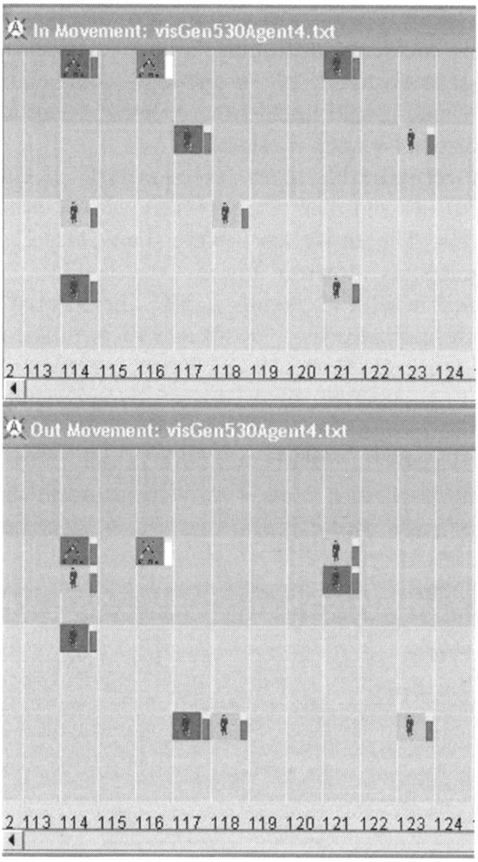

Fig. 6. Movement Graphs.

indicate locales; the numbers on the bottom indicate on which clock tick an entity moves. The bar on the right of each icon indicates the power of that entity, a value that significantly affects attitude (depending on the type of entity) of that locale. The color of the bar graph indicates whether the entity is calming (white) or agitating (red). Thus, this display conveys entity type, entity allegiance, clock tick moved, locale moved to (and out of), relative power, and type of power. Similar types of graphs can be used to show movement and targets within COAs. Further, these icons can be interactive. Right clicking on an icon can allow you to reassign targets within a COA on the fly.

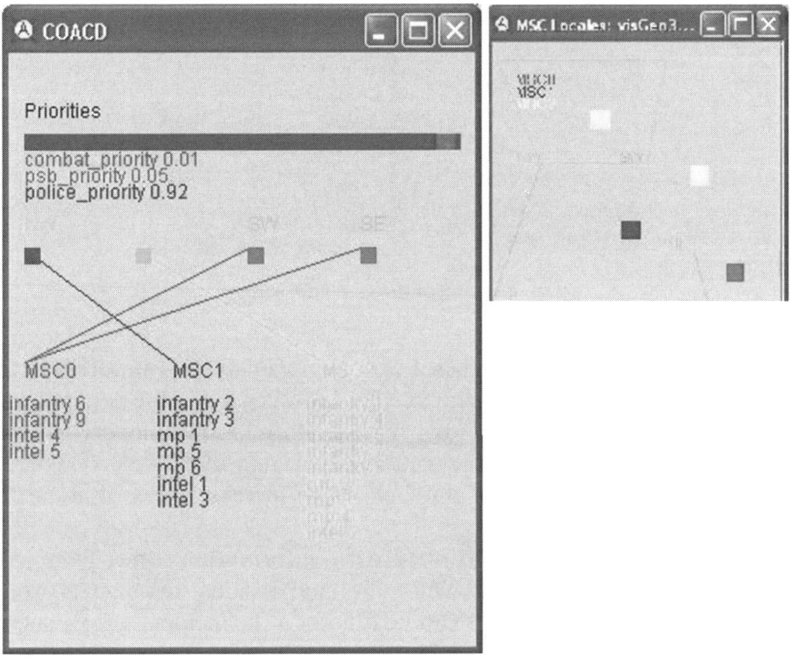

Fig. 7. Organized Military COA.

The COA of the organized military unit has a different structure. Therefore, it requires a different kind of visualization as seen in Fig. 7, which shows which entities have been assigned to which Military Support Command (MSC) and which MSCs are assigned to each locale. As Fig. 9 shows, an MSC can be responsible for more than one locale.

Other factors, such as faction animosities and locale attitudes are important influences on the SASO simulation that may be a part of the fitness functions. The animosities are graphed on a starplot (Wong & Bergeron, 1997). For example, the first graph in Fig. 8 shows the animosities for and against the U.S. faction. Each radial corresponds to a faction, consistent with the colors of the entities. The further away from the center, the more animosity the U.S. has for the corresponding faction. The middle of the radial denotes a neutral attitude.

Standard line graphs, with some annotation, show changes in attitudes, accumulations of damage per faction, and any other factors of interest to the user. The line graph shown in Fig. 9 graphs the attitudes of the four locales over clock ticks, color-coded again to the locale colors.

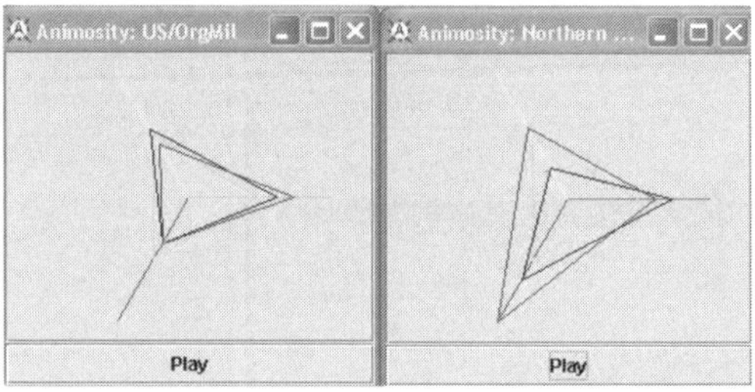

Fig. 8. Starplots of Animosities.

Each line for each locale is labeled with the incidents that occurred at that clock tick. The graph in Fig. 9 shows calm attitudes in the locales, and more and more incidents as time goes by. A large jump in incidents occurs in the SW locale toward the end of the scenario, agitating that locale. This graph illustrates a strategy by one of the factions to increase the attitude in that locale.

Currently, the most clear and meaningful information comes from looking at the attitude line graph. Once the analyst identifies a trend, more information about the incidents can be found on the incident graph, such as that shown in Fig. 10. This display shows the two units involved in the incident. The perpetrator is shown on top, the locale in which it occurred is the background color, the clock tick is on the x-axis, the type of incident is written as an abbreviation underneath the two icons, and the bar graph on the right indicates the severity of the incident. For example, a yellow militia unit attacked a blue organized military unit at clock tick 95, causing an incident of noticeable severity (severities tend to be quite low).

Therefore, to analyze an SASO simulation battle, a user can examine the various displays, from attitudes to animosities, and movements and incidents. This ability has been invaluable in trying to understand the dynamics of the system as a whole.

4.7. Coevolution Analysis

Applying coevolution to this problem is a natural choice because it should be more likely to produce robust plans and also give some indication of possible dangerous counterplans from the other players. There are other, more important advantages as well. Observing the coevolutionary run as it plays out can yield surprising insights into the nature of the war-game

Fig. 9. Locale Attitudes and Incidents.

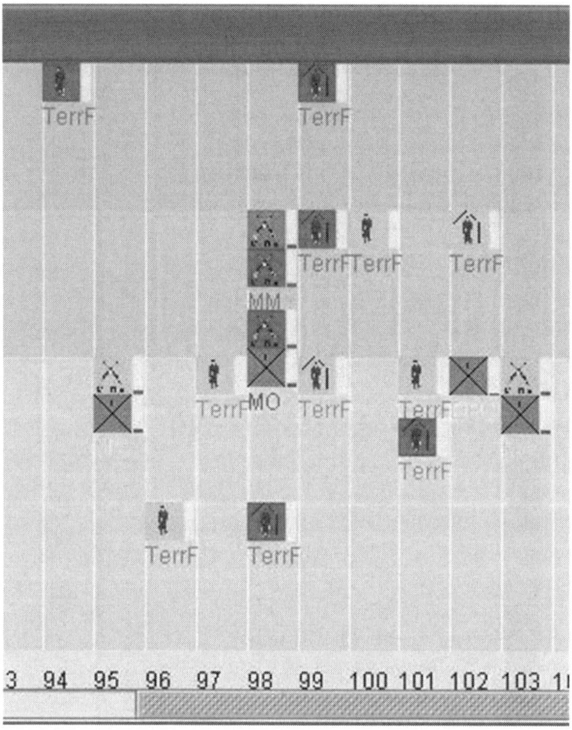

Fig. 10. Incidents.

simulator and potentially about the real-world situation it is intended to model.

In our experience, coevolutionary war gaming rarely leads to stable states where each player settles on one strategy. Instead, the system tends to drift between quasi-stable cycles where, like the game (scissors, paper, stone), a changed plan by one player leads to natural and obvious reactions from the other players. Obviousness, however, lies in the eyes of the beholder. The utility of the technique comes from the fact that the GA frequently exploits aspects of the system of which the human designers and operators were unaware.

Our objective is to harness this effect in order to show an operator important facts about the simulation (and hopefully about the mission itself) that might otherwise be overlooked. Currently, finding meaning from a coevolutionary run is more art than science. One watches coevolution as it unfolds, following plan and counterplan as the players continually adapt. By definition, we do not know for what we are searching until, in a Zen-like flash of enlightenment, it seems obvious. The purpose of our visualization research is to portray results in such a manner that these insights are obvious to the trained analyst (and not only to the experienced expert).

The coevolutionary process requires visualizations of the simulation in order to compare successful COAs. The GA explores the search space by finding COAs that produce better outcomes for the respective player. However, it does not explain why one COA may be better than another COA. By comparing the simulation runs, an analyst can use the visualizations to determine what actual strategy resulted in a better score and more importantly, why.

Each agent evolves against the current best set of COAs of the other agents, known as the "hill," and only gets a chance to update the hill with its own best strategy every 10 cycles. This allows all of the agents enough time to evolve more mature strategies. Therefore, at generation 1, agent 1 may obtain the best score. For the next nine generations, each of the other agents evolves against the current best score. Finally, at generation 10, agent 2 is allowed to place its best set of movements, targets, etc. as the new best score (i.e., the new king of the hill). This system has the effect that each agent's strategy can potentially change radically every 10 generations.

These kinds of analyses have led to many insights into our system. Using visualization to show trends in this complex environment has led to a much better understanding of how the separate rules and the coevolution interact. There is still research to be done before the system is going to be useful for an analyst. In conjunction with military experts, we are currently developing a user-friendly interface that will permit the analyst to define Scheherazade's parameters. Eventually, the interface will allow the operator to play the role of any of the *n* factions in the gaming environment and visualize the adaptations that other factions use to improve their scores.

Developing the optimal mix of set rules and coevolution will require interacting with actual analysts during field exercises or even actual operations to define the proper type of visualizations and the underlying intelligent software. More rigorous evaluations and in situ testing will be required before its military utility is established. However, the concept is promising because it is designed to impart insight using a narrative format. Scheherazade does not so much predict the future as it highlights which of the "1,001 possible stories" are not only most likely but also those that are most potentially dangerous and counterintuitive. In effect, the analyst is able to visualize adaptation in process.

5. CONCLUSION

This chapter was based on the RAVENS framework that elucidated the cognitive aspects of battlefield visualization. RAVENS posits that humans are inherently flexible decision makers and SA depends on the ability of humans to create narrative visualizations that capture the overall context of complex military environments. Using the framework as a guideline, we discussed two important visualization research programs whose purpose is to allow military operators to rapidly adapt to volatile situations. The first program investigated cognitive effects such as the framing bias and their possible interactions with a variety of display concepts during a series of missile defense simulations. The experimenters presented risk as a spatial representation of uncertainty and target value that emphasized either expected population lost or expected population saved. The second program investigated the feasibility of using visualizations generated from Scheherazade (a coevolutionary algorithm) to aid MI analysts in predicting emergent tactics of terrorist groups during urban operations. The underpinnings of Scheherazade consist of a user interface to define a peacekeeping environment, a simple simulation tool, a coevolutionary algorithm for iterative adaptations, and a visualization module. We conclude, based on our analysis of future combat environments, research results, and the reviewed literature:

- Adaptations to future military missions will be particularly difficult because of the complexity and uncertainty inherent in asymmetric and anti-terrorist warfare.
- Visualization aids must promote insight and flexibility rather than doctrinal rule-based solutions suggested by past decision aiding research.
- RAVENS is a cognitive framework for military adaptation that posits that the best tool the human has for understanding dynamic and uncertain situations, and to make pragmatic decisions, is their own narrative cognitive abilities.
- Risk management and uncertainty judgments are involved in most important military decisions in adaptive environments. Visualizations need to be developed that impart SA but the designer must consider human cognitive biases as well as the perceptual characteristics of the display. These visualizations need to provide a rich and coherent mental model of possible outcomes.
- The initial research indicates that developing risk displays for missile defense is not straightforward. Our results show that humans process loss

and gain information differently but the framing biases tend to cancel each other out in terms of making optimal decisions.

- For SA, positive (gain) information was processed more effectively than negative (loss) information in most but not in all experimental conditions. Graphical formats that showed risk as an emergent property of area were in general more effective than other displays examined for SA.
- The general conclusion was that the operators did not necessarily understand the consequences of their missile defense decisions. Future research will examine the interaction of visualization cues with feedback and training parameters.
- A narrative model of visualization is inherently flexible in that it allows a common motif to be shared among multiple players with multiple variations possible as circumstances change.
- Scheherazade is an example of a new generation of visualization tools that use narrative formats and adaptive algorithms to interact with intelligence analysts.
- The goal of Scheherazade is to provide a means of representing and modeling dynamic and uncertain environments richly enough to give an analyst a coherent understanding of the consequences of possible tactical adaptations made by themselves and their adversaries.

REFERENCES

Barnes, M. J. (2003). *The human dimension of battlespace visualization: Research and design issues (ARL-TR-2855)*. Aberdeen Proving Ground, MD: U.S. Army Research Laboratory.

Barnes, M. J., & Hillis, D. (2003). *Dynamic visualization of co-evolving adversaries in small-scale contingencies*. ARL Compendium FY02 DRI Final Reports (pp. 43–57). U.S. Army Research Laboratory, Adelphi, MD.

Barnes, M., McDermott, P., Hutchins, S., Gillan, D., & Rothrock, L. (2003). *The presentation of risk and uncertainty in the context of National Missile Defense simulations*. Poster session presented at the proceedings of Collaborative Technologies Alliance (CTA) Symposium, College Park, MD.

Barnes, M. J., Wickens, C. D., & Smith, M. (2000). Visualizing uncertainty in an automated National Missile Defense simulation environment. *Proceedings of the 4th annual FedLab symposium: Advanced displays and interactive displays*, U.S. Army Research Laboratory, Adelphi, MD (pp. 107–111).

Bar-Yam, Y. (1997). *Dynamics of complex systems*. Reading, MA: Perseus Books.

Bennett, K. B., Toms, M. L., & Woods, D. D. (1993). Emergent features and graphical elements: Designing more effective configural displays. *Human Factors*, *35*(1), 71–97.

Bruner, J. (1990). *Acts of meaning*. Cambridge, MA: Harvard University Press.

Bruner, J. S. (2002). *Making stories: Law, literature, life.* New York, NY: Farrar, Straus, & Giroux.

Carroll, J. (1999). Five reasons for scenario-based design. *Proceedings of the 32nd Hawaii international conference on system sciences – 1999*, IEEE.

Department of the Army. (2003). *Stability and support operations* (FM 3–07). Washington, DC.

Endsley, M. R. (1995). Toward a theory of situation awareness in dynamic systems. *Human Factors, 37*, 32–64.

Endsley, M. R. (2002). Theoretical underpinnings of situation awareness: A critical review. In: M. R. Endsley & D. J. Garland (Eds), *Situation awareness analysis and measurement.* Mahwah, NJ: Lawrence Erlbaum Associates.

Fiske, S. T. (1993). Social cognition and social perception. *Annual Review of Psychology, 44*, 155–194.

Gershon, N., & Page, W. (2001). What storytelling can do for information visualization. *Communications of the ACM, 44*, 31–37.

Gillan, D., & Hutchins, S. (2002). *Display situation awareness: A study into information integration and presentation.* Unpublished manuscript. New Mexico State University, Las Cruces, NM.

Harre, R., & Gillett, G. (1994). *The discursive mind.* Thousand Oaks, CA: Sage.

Hillis, D., & Winkler R. (2001). The fox and the hare: A co-evolutionary approach to course of action generation. *Proceedings of the 5th annual Fed Lab symposium: Advanced displays and interactive displays consortium*, College Park, Maryland, USA.

Hirokawa, R., DeGooyer, D., & Valde, K. (2000). Using narratives to study task group effectiveness. *Small Group Research, 31*, 573–591.

Johnson-Laird, P. N., Legrenzi, P., Girotto, V., Legrenzi, M. S., & Caverni, J. (1999). Naïve probability: A mental model of extensional reasoning. *Psychological Review, 106*(1), 62–88.

Kahneman, D., & Tversky, A. (1973). On the psychology of prediction. *Psychological Review, 80*, 237–251.

Kintsch, W. (1998). *Comprehension: A paradigm for cognition.* New York, NY: Cambridge University Press.

Klein, G. (1998). *Sources of power: How people make decisions.* Cambridge, MA: MIT Press.

Lopes, L. (1986). Aesthetics and decision science. *IEEE Transactions on Systems, Man and Cybernetics, SMC-16*(3), 434–437.

Mayhorn, C. B., Fisk, A. D., & Whittle, J. D. (2002). Decisions, decisions: Analysis of age, cohort and time of testing of risky decisions options. *Human Factors, 44*(4), 515–521.

McDermott, P., Hutchins, S., Barnes, M., Könecke, C., Gillan, D., & Rothrock, L. (2002). The presentation of risk and uncertainty in the context of national missile defense simulations. *Proceedings of the human factors and ergonomics society 46th annual meeting*, Baltimore, Maryland, USA.

Meyer, J., Shamo, M. K., & Gopher, D. (1999). Information structure and the relative efficacy of tables and graphs. *Human Factors, 41*, 570–587.

Murray, K. (1995). Narrative partitioning: The ins and outs of identity construction. Posted at http://home.mira.net/~kmurray/psych/in&out.html, abridged from a published book chapter.

Pennington, N., & Hastie, R. (1993). Reasoning in explanation-based decision making. *Cognition, 49*, 123–163.

Rossiter, M. (1999). A narrative approach to development: Implications for adult education. *Adult Education Quarterly*, *50*, 56–71.

Rothrock, L., Sungsoon, P., Barnes, M. J., McDermott, P., Hutchins, S., & Gillan, D. (2003). Systematic analysis of risk visualization strategies for homeland defense. *Proceedings of the 2003 IEEE international conference on systems, man & cybernetics*, Washington, DC.

Scales, R. J. (2000). Adaptive enemy: Achieving victory by avoiding defeat. *Joint Force Quarterly (JFQ)*, 7–14.

Schlabach, J. L., Hayes, C. C., & Goldberg, D. E. (1999). FOX-GA: A genetic algorithm for generating and analyzing battlefield courses of action. *Evolutionary Computation*, *7*(1), 45–68.

Schlabach, J., & Hillis, D. (2003). *Sheherazade: A research platform for decision support in military stability and support operations*. BCBL-H Tech Report 2003–01. Battle Command Battle Lab, Ft. Huachuca, AZ.

Shafir, E., & Tversky, A. (1995). Decision making. In: E. E. Smith & E. E. D. Osherson (Eds), *Thinking* (pp. 77–100). Cambridge, MA: MIT.

Shank, R. (1990). *Tell me a story*. Evanston, IL: Northwestern University Press.

Smith, M., & Wickens, C. D. (1999). *The effects of highlighting and event history on operator decision making in a national missile defense system application*. Tech. Rep. No. ARL-99–4. Aviation Research Laboratory, University of Illinois, Savoy, IL.

Snowden, D. (2000). New wine in old wineskins: From organic to complex knowledge management through the use of story. *Emergence*, *2*, 50–64.

Suantak, L., Momen, F., Rozenblit, J., Barnes, M., & Fichtl, T. (2001). Intelligent decision support of support and stability operations (SASO) through symbolic visualization. *IEEE International Conference on Systems, Man, and Cybernetics*, *5*, 2927–2931.

Tversky, A., & Kahneman, D. (1981). The framing of decisions and the psychology of choice. *Science*, *211*, 453–458.

Waldrop, W. M. (1993). *Complexity: The emerging science at the edge of order and chaos*. New York: Simon Schuster.

Warner, J. (2003). RAVENS: A framework for rapid adaptive visualization of emergent and novel situations. *Proceedings of the RTO Systems Concepts and Integration (SCI-129) Panel*, Prague, Czech Republic.

Warner, J., & Burnstein, D. (1996). *Situation, domain and coherence: Towards a pragmatic psychology of understanding (ARL-CR-306)*. Aberdeen Proving Ground, MD: U.S. Army Research Laboratory.

Weick, K. (1995). *Sense making in organizations*. Thousand Oaks, CA: Sage Publications.

Wickens, C. D., & Hollands, J. G. (2000). *Engineering psychology and human performance*. Upper Saddle River, NJ: Prentice-Hall.

Wong, P. C., & Bergeron, R. D. (1997). 30 Years of multidimensional multivariate visualization. In: G. M. Nielson, H. Hagen & H. Müller (Eds), *Scientific visualization – overview, methodologies, techniques* (pp. 3–29). Los Alamitos, CA: IEEE Computer Society Press.

SECTION II: TEAM LEVEL

TEAM ADAPTATION: REALIZING TEAM SYNERGY

Kevin C. Stagl, C. Shawn Burke, Eduardo Salas and Linda Pierce

TEAM ADAPTATION: REALIZING TEAM SYNERGY

As operational environments become increasingly fluid, organizations are turning to teams as a proven performance arrangement to structure complex work. Teams are ubiquitous in modern organizations because they can be used to create synergies, streamline workflow, deliver innovative services, satisfy incumbent needs, maximize the benefits of technology connecting distributed employees, and seize market opportunities in a global village. Teams are also increasingly used because coordinating the "…activities of individuals in large organizations is like building a sand castle using single grains of sand" (West, Borrill, & Unsworth, 1998, p. 6).

Organizations also rely upon teams because they are by nature adaptive entities. Teams are well positioned to adapt because they have a deeper reservoir of social capital, capacities, competencies, experiences, and networks to draw upon when engaging in change (Zaccaro & Bader, 2003). Moreover, as teams are increasingly distributed, organizations can retain the talents of the best people available around the globe regardless of their location. By appropriately leveraging a wider range of localized social networks teams can inherently be more adaptable to local events and changes

Understanding Adaptability: A Prerequisite for Effective Performance within Complex Environments
Advances in Human Performance and Cognitive Engineering Research, Volume 6, 117–141

ISSN: 1479-3601/doi:10.1016/S1479-3601(05)06004-2

and thereby dynamically reallocate resources in a more timely, cost effective, productive, and efficient manner.

While teams are by nature primed to adapt, they also mandate higher levels of adaptation in order to sustain team effectiveness. If a team is going to fulfill stakeholder expectations, its members must act as compensatory systems for their teammates by providing backup behavior during coordinated action. Adaptive coordination, in turn, facilitates team performance and enhances stakeholder judgments about team effectiveness. Thus, teams are intertwined with adaptation; both as a naturally adaptive means of structuring work and because interdependent collectives necessitate adaptation in order to ultimately achieve synergies and team effectiveness.

Although teams are often utilized to navigate ambiguous, complex context, teams of experts often fail to adapt. This is especially problematic given an accelerating rate of change is one of the few constants of current operational context. In fact, this axiom holds true on a number of levels as adaptation is critical for individuals (see Campbell, 1999; Hollenbeck, LePine, & Ilgen, 1996; Howard, 1995; Hulin, 1991; Ilgen & Pulakos, 1999; LePine, Colquitt, & Erez, 2000; Ployhart, Saltz, Mayer, & Bliese, 2002; Pulakos, Arad, Donovan, & Plamondon, 2000; Pulakos et al., 2002; Takeuchi, Yum, & Tesluk, 2002; Zaccaro, Gilbert, Thor, & Mumford, 1991), teams (see Ancona & Chong, 1999; Burke, Fiore, & Salas, 2002; Entin & Serfaty, 1999; Gersick, 1988; Han, 2003; Klein & Pierce, 2001; Kozlowski, 1998; LePine, 2003; Marks, Zaccaro, & Mathieu, 2000; McGrath, Arrow, & Berdahl, 2000; Salas, Stagl, & Burke, 2004; Waller, 1999; Zaccaro & Bader, 2003), and organizations (see Conner & Hoopes, 1997; Dutton & Dukerich, 1991; Fox-Wolfgramm, Boal, & Hunt, 1998; Porras & Robertson, 1992; Tushman & Rosenkoph, 1996).

Despite the importance of adaptation to individual, team, and organizational effectiveness, few if any initiatives have attempted to delineate the nature of this construct or illuminate its nomological network (Campbell & Kuncel, 2001). In fact, up to this point in time, adaptation has not been the subject of much investigation in the behavioral sciences. In light of this situation, this chapter provides a multidisciplinary, multilevel, multiphasic conceptualization of adaptation at the team level. Drawing upon cognitive, human factors, and industrial-organizational psychology literature, team adaptation and the emergent nature of adaptive team performance are defined and centered in an Input Throughput Output (ITO) framework. The framework illustrates the core processes and emergent states that unfold and compile over time to emerge as adaptive team performance and result in team adaptation (see Fig. 1).

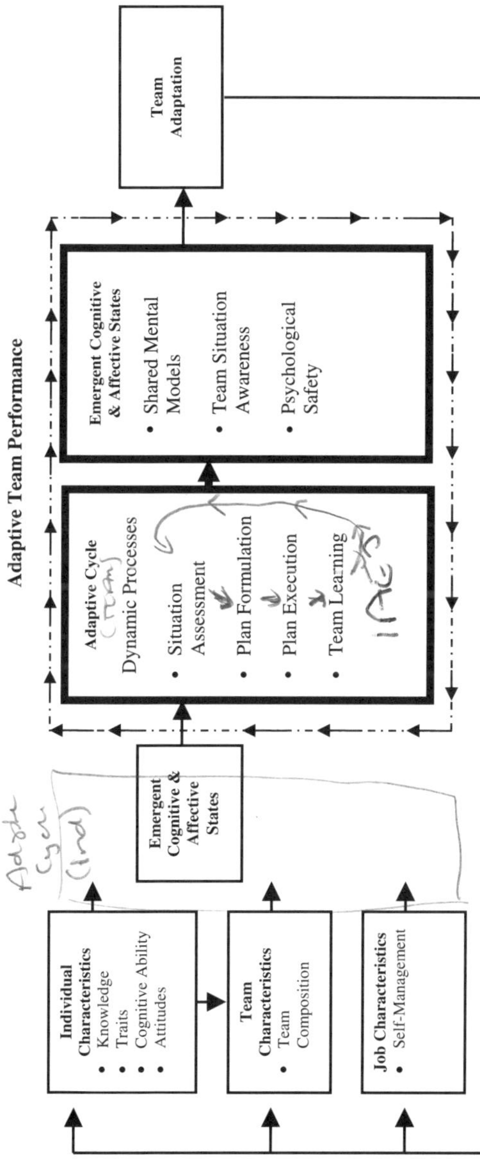

Fig. 1. Heuristic Framework of Team Adaptation.

TEAMS & TEAM CONTEXT

Teams are defined herein as complex entities characterized by: (1) two or more individuals, (2) who interact socially, (3) dynamically, (4) recursively, (5) adaptively, (6) have shared or common valued goals, (7) hold meaningful and high levels of task, feedback, and goal interdependencies, (8) are often hierarchically structured, (9) have a limited life-span, (10) whose expertise and roles are distributed, and (11) are embedded within an organizational/environmental context which influences and is influenced by enacted competencies and processes, emergent cognitive and affective states, performance outcomes, and stakeholder judgments of team member and team effectiveness (Salas, Stagl, Burke, & Goodwin, in press). The dynamic environments in which teams operate are typified by: (1) rapidly evolving ambiguous situations, (2) imperfect solutions, (3) information overload, (4) intense time pressure, and (5) where there are severe consequences of error (Orasanu & Salas, 1993).

TEAM ADAPTATION

The few endeavors which have been undertaken to date to conceptualize team adaptation have somewhat neglected the assertions of corresponding initiatives. This lack of inter-effort coordination is concerning, as differentiation without integration ultimately results in chaos. In order to arrive at the definition of team adaptation advanced in this chapter, existing organizational theory (e.g., general systems theory, open systems theory, sociotechnical systems theory) and prior definitions of adaptation at the team level were integrated (see Table 1).

Drawing from military psychology, Cannon-Bowers, Tannenbaum, Salas, and Volpe (1995) defined team adaptability as "the process by which a team is able to use information gathered from the task environment to adjust strategies through the use of compensatory behaviors and reallocation of intra-team resources" (p. 344). An examination of the field of human factors psychology reveals a second conceptualization advanced by Klein and Pierce (2001) who defined adaptive teams as "teams that are able to make the necessary modifications in order to meet new challenges" (p. 3). Merriam-Webster's Online Dictionary (2005) defined adaptation as (1) the act or process of adapting and (2) the state of being adapted.

A review of the industrial-organizational psychology literature reveals four more conceptualizations. Fleming, Wood, Dudley, Bader, and Zaccaro

Table 1. Successive Definitions of Team Adaptability and Team Adaptation.

Date of Origin	Authors	Definition
1995	Cannon-Bowers, Tannenbaum, Salas, and Volpe	The process by which a team is able to use information gathered from the task environment to adjust strategies through the use of compensatory behaviors and reallocation of intra-team resources
1999	Kozlowski, Gully, Nason, and Smith	Capability of the team to maintain coordinated interdependence and performance by selecting an appropriate network from its repertoire or by inventing a new configuration. Thus, adaptability refers to a metamorphic shift in the team network in the short-term to deal with the performance demands of a non-routine task
2001	Klein and Pierce	Teams that are able to make the necessary modifications in order to meet new challenges
2001	Kozlowski, Toney, Mullins, Weissbein, Brown, and Bell	The generalization of trained knowledge and skills to new, more difficult, and more complex task situations
2003	Fleming, Wood, Dudley, Bader, and Zaccaro	Functional change in response to altered environmental contingencies and a higher-order process that emerges from an integrated set of individual attributes
2003	LePine	Reactive and nonscripted adjustments to a team's system of member roles that contribute to team effectiveness
2004	Merriam-Webster's Online Dictionary	The act or process of adapting or the state of being adapted

(2003) suggested adaptability is a "functional change in response to altered environmental contingencies" and a "higher-order process that emerges from an integrated set of individual attributes" (p. 3). Kozlowski, Gully, Nason, and Smith (1999) defined team adaptability as the "capability of the team to maintain coordinated interdependence and performance by selecting an appropriate network from its repertoire or by inventing a new configuration" (p. 273). Adopting a slightly different approach, Kozlowski et al. (2001) defined adaptability in terms of the distal outcomes that result from integrated-embedded training delivered in context. Specifically, adaptability is defined by these researchers as "the generalization of trained knowledge and skills to new, more difficult, and more complex task situations" (Kozlowski et al., 2001, p. 107). LePine (2003) conceptualized team adaptation in terms of role structure changes defining this process as "reactive and nonscripted adjustments to a team's system of member roles that contribute to team effectiveness" (p. 28).

The above perspectives served as a platform upon which to build our definition of team adaptation. Synthesizing the above efforts, team adaptation is defined herein as: a change in team performance, in response to a salient cue or cue stream, which leads to a functional outcome for the entire team. Team adaptation is witnessed in the functional innovation of new, or modification of existing, structures, capacities, or cognitive and behavioral goal directed actions.

At its core, the definition of team adaptation advanced above is about change. Therefore, understanding, measuring, and tracking change over time is essential to gauging whether a team has adapted. Unfortunately, however, change is a complex, multi-faceted phenomenon that is both qualitative and quantitative in nature (Golembiewski, Billingsley, & Yeager, 1976). Put succinctly, understanding, structuring and "…measuring change is a very difficult problem" (Nunnally & Bernstein, 1994, p. 247). Fortunately, the above definition implies a straightforward approach to gauging team adaptation or team performance change. The two primary indicators of team adaptation are: (1) the realignment of team performance to levels of performance that were acceptable prior to the change event(s) and (2) the growth of the team and its members.

Prior efforts have similarly conceptualized team adaptation as a longitudinal process whereby a misalignment between outputs and demands is reduced (see Chan, 2000; Chen & Ployhart, 2004; Kozlowski et al., 1999). Specifically, when plotting team performance over time, the performance trend of adaptive teams is nonlinear; because an initially acceptable level of performance is followed by a transition period within which performance declines due to a misalignment, which in turn is followed by a performance increase, realignment, or adaptation (Chen & Ployhart, 2004). Specifically, teams adapt by compensating for a decrease in performance, which has resulted from a contextual change(s).

While the above noted initiatives have made significant strides in defining and gauging team adaptation, the current chapter supplements these efforts by more fully illuminating the nature of the 'longitudinal process' via which teams adapt. The next section introduces the concept of adaptive team performance, which comprises the core of this longitudinal process. Following this, both team adaptation and the emergent nature of adaptive team performance are centered in an ITO framework (see Fig. 1).

ADAPTIVE TEAM PERFORMANCE

From the foregoing discussion it can be inferred that fostering team adaptation is an essential, but complex process. Thus, it is advantageous to consider the constructs associated with team adaptation. Team adaptation is conceptualized in this chapter as the dependent variable of concern. There are a number of proximal and distal antecedents to team adaptation. The immediate temporal antecedents of team adaptation are several constructs that comprise adaptive team performance. Adaptive team performance is defined herein as: an emergent phenomenon which compiles over time from the unfolding of a recursive cycle whereby one or more team members utilize their resources to functionally change structures, capacities, and or cognitive and behavioral goal directed actions to meet expected or unexpected demands.

Adaptive team performance can be conceptualized as either a global property of the team or as a configural construct (Kozlowski et al., 1999). The definition of adaptive team performance advanced above implies a configural compilation emergence process. Therefore, as it is conceptualized herein, adaptive team performance is a multilevel phenomenon which compiles over time as team members and teams simultaneously, dynamically, and recursively enact behavioral processes and draw upon emergent cognitive states to engage in change. When treated as a configural property, adaptive team performance compiles bottom-up across levels.

Compilation assumes discontinuity, or the configuration of unique lower level properties to result in a higher-level property (Kozlowski & Klein, 2000). Constructs that compile are qualitatively different across levels. Thus, it is the pattern of lower level team member and dyadic actions that compile to characterize adaptive team performance. The exact process via which adaptive team performance emerges is contingent upon organizational context, work-flow interdependencies, and other situational factors (Klein & Kozlowski, 2000).

FRAMING TEAM ADAPTATION & ADAPTIVE TEAM PERFORMANCE

In order to illuminate the nomological network of team adaptation, a heuristic framework was developed (see Fig. 1). Fig. 1 presents an organizing ITO framework, which illustrates our initial thinking about some of the most relevant broad construct categories and specific variables central to facilitating team adaptation. Although basic, the framework depicts a wide range of construct categories including: (1) individual characteristics, (2) team characteristics, (3) job design characteristics, (4) individual and teams processes, and (5) emergent cognitive and affective states. These construct categories are comprised of a number of more specific construct categories and variables which serve as distal and proximal antecedents to team adaptation. Of note, however, Fig. 1 is advanced as a heuristic framework not as a testable model.

This section discusses the multiphasic process, which unfolds across time and levels to result in team adaptation (see Fig. 1). This section begins with two distinct subsections that discuss the constructs that collectively comprise adaptive team performance. Specifically, in the first subsection the four phase adaptive cycle and its constituent dynamic processes are addressed. Following this, a subsection detailing the emergent states, which flow from, and serve as proximal inputs into, this dynamic cycle is presented. As noted, the adaptive cycle is multiphasic, and as the first of its core processes is enacted, this action serves to revise emergent states. Moreover, as the next phase of the adaptive cycle is enacted teams draw upon these emergent states before and during action and update them continuously. Thus, our decision to discuss the adaptive cycle in a separate subsection than emergent states was made to frame the issues at hand more clearly for the reader rather than truly reflecting our thinking about the recursive, cyclical nature of adaptive team performance. Following this discussion, are subsections addressing individual, team, and job design characteristics.

Adaptive Cycle of Dynamic Processes

In this subsection, the nature of the four phase adaptive cycle, which is at the heart of adaptive team performance and ultimately team adaptation is addressed. The adaptive cycle is comprised of four core processes that are displayed dynamically and recursively. Processes are a variety of verbal and behavioral activities team members and teams interdependently engage in to achieve team goals (Marks, Mathieu, & Zaccaro, 2001). The four processes comprising the adaptive cycle are situation assessment, plan formulation, plan execution, and team learning. Our primary objective is to facilitate a closer inspection of this dynamic cycle so it can be understood in further depth, modeled, empirically examined in future research initiatives, and integrated with other conceptualizations of adaptation at the individual, team, and organizational levels.

Situation Assessment

The process depicted in Fig. 1 begins with an adaptive cycle of cognitive and behavioral action. Kicking off this cycle is the situation assessment process, primarily conducted at an individual level by team members. Situation assessment is comprised of "the human processes of gathering information (e.g., attention, pattern recognition, communication)" (Gutwin & Greenberg, 2004, p. 181).

Situation assessment is comprised of two sub-processes, cue recognition and meaning ascription. Specifically, at least one team member must draw upon their resources (e.g., cognitive abilities) to engage in situation assessment and via that process noticc the environmental cue or cue pattern that could potentially affect, or has already affected, the success of the team's mission. In fact, research suggests the speed with which environmental changes are recognized and appropriate responses are enacted is related to team adaptation (Waller, 1999).

After recognizing the cue, team members draw upon long-term memory to interpret and categorize a cue or cue pattern based upon existing knowledge structures (Endsley & Smith, 1996). Thus, the second step in situation assessment involves assigning meaning to the cue or cue pattern to determine its relevance to the team and task at hand. When possible, this information is communicated to the remaining team members, thereby serving to create or revise team situational awareness as well as shared mental models.

Plan Formulation

The second phase of the adaptive cycle illustrated in Fig. 1 is plan formulation. Planning involves: (1) choosing a course of action, (2) setting goals, (3) clarifying member roles, responsibilities, and performance expectations within the context of a course of action, (4) identifying relevant environmental characteristics and constraints, (5) prioritizing tasks, and (6) sharing information related to task requirements (Stout & Salas, 1993).

Essentially, the shared cognition created when team members become aware of the need to adapt provides a basis for the creation of a plan to surmount the surfaced obstacle that is creating a performance decrement. In other words, teams draw upon their shared situation awareness and shared mental models as cognitive reservoirs to formulate a plan for realigning team performance. It should be noted that plan formulation can occur on the fly in response to dynamically changing events or in a more systematic, proactive fashion.

Plan Execution

The third phase of the adaptive cycle is plan execution. Plans are executed via as an assortment of individual and team level processes that are enacted dynamically, simultaneously, and recursively. During the execution process individual level team member behaviors such as mutual performance monitoring, backup behavior, communication, and leadership assist in promoting the team level coordination needed to achieve team adaptation. Each of these processes is described in terms of their contribution to adaptive team performance next.

Mutual performance monitoring (MPM) has been defined as the capability to "keep track of fellow team member's work while carrying out their own…to ensure that everything is running as expected and to ensure that they are following procedures correctly" (McIntyre & Salas, 1995, p. 23). MPM contributes to adaptive team performance in part because monitoring fellow teammates allows teams to detect errors and performance decrements and ultimately provide assistance in a timelier manner. MPM also allows team members to become entrained to one another's tempo and pacing, thereby enhancing coordination when executing a plan. Finally, MPM contributes to the development of common ground or team situation awareness which teams draw upon during plan execution (McIntyre & Salas, 1995).

Backup behavior has been defined as "The discretionary provision of resources and task-related effort to another member of one's team that is intended to help that team member obtain the goals as defined by his or her role when it is apparent that the team member is failing to reach those goals" (Porter et al., 2003, pp. 391–392). Backup behavior provides the behavioral assistance, feedback, and or coaching that keeps the team running smoothly when a team member's resources are depleted or novel circumstances are encountered. In turn, this compensatory behavior is vital to adaptation in fluid environments.

Communication has been defined as "the process by which information is clearly and accurately exchanged between two or more team members in the prescribed manner with proper terminology; the ability to clarify or acknowledge the receipt of information" (Cannon-Bowers et al., 1995, p. 345). Communication is essential to exchanging information accumulated during MPM such as when providing backup behavior. Moreover, communication serves to revise shared cognitive and affective states, which are called upon during adaptive team performance.

Leadership has been defined as a process of influencing: (1) the task objectives and strategies of a group or organization, (2) people in the organization to implement the strategies and achieve the objectives, (3) group maintenance and identification, and (4) the culture of the organization (Yukl & Van Fleet, 1992). Prior research has suggested that leaders can facilitate adaptation by reviewing and revising procedures and methods (e.g., Gersick & Hackman, 1990; Hackman & Wageman, 2005).

Coordination concerns the organization, sequencing, and timing of a team's actions (Marks et al., 2001). Coordination is needed when team members synergistically address performance decrements during adaptation. Prior research suggests that in addition to explicit coordination, implicit coordination also serves to enhance adaptation (Entin & Serfaty, 1999). Moreover, coordination serves to update preexisting shared knowledge structures and affective states, which also contribute to team adaptation.

Team Learning

The final phase in the four phase adaptive cycle is team learning. Learning has been defined at the group level as "an ongoing process of reflection and action, characterized by asking questions, seeking feedback, experimenting, reflecting on results, and discussing errors or unexpected outcomes of actions" (Edmondson, 1999, p. 354). Learning is a process whereby knowledge is accumulated via testing assumptions, discussing differences, adjusting strategies in response to novel conditions, and forming new routines (Edmondson, Bohmer, & Pisano, 2001). Learning contributes to adaptation because members use accumulated knowledge when scanning their environment for changes, assigning meaning to changes, and adjusting accordingly.

As the situation assessment, plan formulation, plan execution, and team learning phases unfold within the adaptive cycle, team members' shared situation awareness, shared mental models, and level of psychological safety are revised. The role of these three emergent states in promoting adaptive team performance and team adaptation is discussed next.

Emergent States

As noted above, as the adaptive cycle is dynamically and recursively enacted emergent cognitive and affective states are updated; serving to provide the cognitive frameworks to guide current and future team action. Emergent states are: "constructs that characterize properties of the team that are typically dynamic in nature and vary as a function of team context, inputs, processes, and outcomes" (Marks et al., 2001, p. 357). In contrast, process variables describe team member and team level behavioral interaction, whereas emergent states characterize the cognitive, motivational, and affective state of the team (Marks et al., 2001).

There are three emergent states discussed in this section. Two of the three are cognitive in nature (i.e., shared mental models, shared situation awareness) while the third is psychological safety, a team level affective state which impacts the amount of learning that occurs both during and post-execution. Each time a phase of the adaptive cycle is conducted emergent states are updated and serve to form a foundation of proximal inputs to the start of the next phase and ultimately into the next cycle. The timing and exact number of adaptive team performance episodes needed to obtain the functional outcome of team adaptation are dependent on several individual and task characteristics, as well as, the nature of the challenge confronted. This process serves to revise emergent states, which, in turn, serve as inputs into another round of the adaptive cycle. Each of the three emergent states is discussed next.

Shared Mental Models

One construct central to both routine and adaptive team performance is shared mental models. Shared mental models have been described as the degree to which team members' long-term memory structures are in agreement or are compatible (Burke et al., 2002). Researchers have noted shared mental models address three general areas of content: (1) declarative, (2) procedural, and (3) strategic (Converse & Kahler, 1992). All three types of model content can facilitate adaptive team performance in novel circumstances. Researchers have also identified five types of shared mental models including: (1) equipment, (2) task, (3) team, (4) team interaction, and (5) problem/situation (Cannon-Bowers, Salas, & Converse, 1993; Rouse & Morris, 1986). These five models are arranged hierarchically from most static to malleable.

The value of mental models as an explanatory construct at the individual level has long been recognized, but only more recently has the concept of shared mental models received attention. Mounting evidence suggests shared mental models are critical for adaptive team performance. For example, it has been repeatedly asserted shared mental models can partially ameliorate the negative effects of time pressure and stress by facilitating implicit coordination and communication (Kleinman & Serfaty, 1989; Salas, Cannon-Bowers, & Johnston, 1997). Moreover, empirical evidence suggests both the sharedness and quality of team member shared mental models are important antecedents to team processes and task performance (Mathieu, Heffner, Goodwin, Salas, & Cannon-Bowers, 2000). Team members operating from a shared mental model have either a common or overlapping conceptual framework which enables them perceive, interpret, and respond to dynamic environments in a synchronized adaptive fashion.

Team Situation Awareness

Team situation awareness (TSA) has been defined as a shared understanding of a given situation at a given point in time (Salas, Prince, Baker, & Shrestha, 1995). TSA has been conceptualized as being comprised of three separate levels which are ordered in terms of complexity: (1) the perception of contextual features in relation to time and space, (2) an understanding of which of these features are important to the team's goals, and (3) the capability to forecast future events in light of the current situation (Endsley, 1995). TSA provides the shared understanding of current context and the events within it that signal the need for change. Therefore, TSA allows teams members to assign appropriate meaning to a cue or cue pattern, mentally simulate possible courses of action during plan formulation, and execute a plan that is most likely to remedy a performance decrement.

Psychological Safety

Team psychological safety has been conceptualized as a shared belief that the team is safe for interpersonal risk taking (Edmondson, 1999). Team psychological safety is an extension of research examining the characteristics of an organization's climate which serve to foster mutual respect and interpersonal trust (Schein & Bennis, 1965). When a team's climate is characterized by psychological safety, team members feel comfortable speaking up and taking interpersonal risks in terms of offering suggestions, critiques, expertise, and advice. When team members feel comfortable advancing ideas, regardless of whether their suggestion is ultimately functional for team adaptation, a wider range of perspectives will be advanced when formulating plans. Therefore, it is likely that the team psychological safety contributes to the plan formulation phase of the adaptive cycle in terms of team member monitoring, speaking-up to offer suggestions, and ultimately in the quality of plans advanced, accepted, and executed.

Individual Characteristics

As noted above, teams are comprised of two or more members, and therefore team member individual differences serve as both direct and indirect determinants of adaptive team performance. Direct determinants of adaptive team performance include job relevant knowledge, skill, and volitional choice behavior (see Campbell & Kuncell, 2001). Direct determinants are, in turn, a function of indirect determinants such as cognitive and psychomotor abilities, personality traits, perceptions, cognitive styles, attitudes, cultural assumptions, and experience (see Campbell, McCloy, Oppler, & Sager, 1993). This suggests the impact of indirect determinants such as team member personality traits, abilities, and attitudes on adaptive team performance is mediated and or moderated by the effort group members exert on a task, the knowledge and skills group members can apply to a task, and the task performance strategies used to accomplish a task (Driskell, Hogan, & Salas, 1987).

The framework of team adaptation illustrated in Fig. 1 includes one category of direct determinants (i.e., team member knowledge) and three categories of indirect determinants (i.e., team member traits, abilities, attitudes). The specific variables that comprise these categories are proposed to directly and interactively affect the core processes of adaptive team performance. Although team members draw upon their knowledge, skills, abilities, and other characteristics (KSAOs) during each phase of the adaptive cycle, illuminating the dozens of possible linkages between team member characteristics and adaptive team performance is beyond the scope of the current initiative. Rather, a sample of the theoretical and empirical evidence supporting the myriad of relationships between team member individual differences and both adaptive team performance and team adaptation is presented below. This literature is organized around the five individual difference categories illustrated in Fig. 1.

Knowledge

When viewed in light of Campbell and colleagues' above noted assertions about the direct and indirect determinants of task performance, there are two types of team member knowledge (i.e., declarative knowledge, procedural knowledge) that likely contribute to adaptive team performance.

Declarative knowledge is knowledge about performance relevant tasks and behaviors (Campbell, 1990). Exemplars of declarative knowledge include knowledge of principles, facts, goals, and self (Campbell et al., 1993). Essentially, declarative knowledge is knowing what to do. Procedural knowledge results when knowing what to do is combined with knowing how to do it (Campbell et al., 1993).

In regards to their contribution to adaptive team performance, both declarative and procedural knowledge can be attained about two domains, the team's tasks and the team's members. A team member's knowledge of the team's task provides the insight needed to both compare current performance against performance standards and enact a plan to remedy a performance decrement if adaptation is required. For example, a team member who has declarative knowledge about the team's task may recognize material resources are not being applied correctly during the process of situation assessment. If this team member's knowledge is procedural in nature, she/he may dynamically reallocate resources in order to adapt.

Team member declarative and procedural knowledge of teammates serves a similar purpose in contributing to adaptive team performance. For example, a team member may draw upon his or her declarative knowledge when explaining to a fellow teammate what they should be doing in order to meet performance expectations. If, however, the first team member possesses procedural knowledge, she/he can apply this knowledge to model the actual behaviors his or her teammate needs to enact in order to adapt to some recent change in the environment.

Traits

There are a plethora of current theories of personality. For example, personality has been conceptualized as both individual differences and the organization of these differences into a dynamic, holistic, cognitively grounded system that is a sum greater than the parts comprising it (Pervin, 1990). The individual differences comprising the personality system consist of a class of phenomena including traits, states, goals, attitudes, needs, interests, and dispositional tendencies (Milgram, 1991). The first of these phenomena, traits, are pertinent to this subsection.

Personality traits are constructs that are used to represent consistencies in thoughts, feelings, and actions. Thus, traits are enduring patterns of cognition, affect, and behavior across situations and over time. The personality traits which have most often been discussed in relation to adaptive team performance and team adaptation fall under the personality domain of Openness to Experience. Openness to Experience is a descriptive label given to one of the five factors comprising the Five Factor Model of personality (Costa & McCrae, 1985). A high level of Openness to Experience is denoted by a number of adjectives or trait descriptors including: imaginative, curios, open-minded, and original (Costa & McCrae, 1985).

A reasonable argument can be made curious team members are more likely to scan their environments for changes signaling the need for adaptation. Likewise, team members who are original will be beneficial to plan formulation during adaptive team performance. Moreover, team members who are open-minded will be more inclined to seek and accept a wider range of suggestions which are likely to be advanced during plan formulation when a team's climate is characterized by psychological safety. Accumulating research indirectly supports these assertions (see Barrick, Stewart, Neubert, & Mount, 1998; Barry & Stewart, 1997; Neuman, Wagner, & Christiansen, 1999). In fact, research suggests Openness to Experience is related to both team member (LePine et al., 2000) and team level (LePine, 2003) adaptation.

Cognitive Ability

Cognitive ability has been defined as intelligence or general mental ability (Schmidt & Hunter, 1998). While there are a number of ability taxonomies, most include both a general (i.e., *g*) and specific factors. These specific abilities include the "abilities to perceive, process, evaluate, compare, create, understand, manipulate, or generally think about information and ideas" (Guion, 1998, p. 124). For example, creativity has been conceptualized as an ability to see opportunities in unplanned events (Guion, 1998).

Cognitive ability tests are the most useful predictors of both future job performance and learning (Hunter & Hunter, 1984; Schmidt & Hunter, 1998). Therefore, it seems plausible that a team member's intellectual capacity would contribute to the effectiveness with which she/he engaged in the dynamic processes comprising adaptive team performance including: situation assessment, plan formulation, plan execution, and learning. For example, Guion's (1998) definition of creativity as the ability to see opportunities in unplanned events seems like the kind of capacity that is needed to recognize and assign appropriate meaning to cues during situation assessment.

Recent research has begun to indirectly assess the validity of the above assertions by investigating the relationships between cognitive ability and team adaptation. Because novel circumstances are characterized by increased complexity, team member cognitive ability can be more important for performance in novel than routine environments (Hunter & Hunter,

1984). Further, evidence supporting this assertion suggests team member's cognitive ability is related to adaptive decision-making performance (LePine et al., 2000). In fact, research evidence suggests cognitive ability is more strongly related to performance after a changed event (LePine et al., 2000).

Attitudes

Attitudes have been defined as "a favorable or unfavorable evaluative reaction toward something or someone, exhibited in one's beliefs, feelings, or behavior" (Myers, 2002, p. 130). Although a number of specific attitudes have been proposed as essential to teamwork, one that has particular implications for adaptive team performance and team adaptation is team orientation. Team orientation has been defined as the set of attitudes and beliefs that enable (or prevent) a team member to work effectively in interdependent teams (O'Shea, Driskell, Goodwin, Zbylut, & Weiss, 2004). A team orientation is conceptualized as having both cognitive (i.e., beliefs) and affective (i.e., attitudinal) components (O'Shea et al., 2004).

Team member expertise and other such knowledge structures are necessary but insufficient for team adaptation because teammates must often put aside their own goals and share their capabilities in order to achieve the collectives' goals (see DeShon, Kozlowski, Schmidt, Milner, & Wiechmann, 2005; Rutkowski, Steelman, & Griffith, 2004). For example, team members engaging in adaptive team performance often accept the responsibilities of their fellow team members in order to provide backup behavior during plan execution. The provision of backup behavior during plan execution may temporarily lower the individual task performance of the providing team member, but if that action is functional in terms of effectively executing plans carried out to remedy a performance decrement, then adaptation will likely ensue.

Indirectly supporting the above assertions, evidence suggests team performance is related to the frequency with which team members enact cooperative behaviors such as receiving and accepting input and suggestions from teammates (Driskell & Salas, 1992). Moreover, team cooperation has been found to mediate the relationship between team orientation and team performance (Eby & Dobbins, 1997).

Team Characteristics

The above subsections addressed the importance of team member knowledge, personality traits, cognitive abilities, and attitudes for the effective execution of the dynamic processes which comprise adaptive team performance and contribute to team adaptation. This discussion framed these individual level characteristics as direct and interactive antecedents to the specific processes comprising the adaptive cycle. In addition to this individual level conceptualization, operationalizations of these variables in aggregate can also affect adaptive team performance and team adaptation. For example, the mean level of cognitive ability within a team is likely to affect team level processes such as coordination. Also, the pattern or variance of shared mental models in a team may affect the latency of team adaptation.

Accumulating theoretical and empirical evidence supports the above assertions. In fact, it has been suggested that holding all other factors constant, teams composed of high-ability individuals will outperform teams made up of individuals with low abilities (Tannenbaum, Beard, & Salas, 1992). Empirical evidence suggests teams composed of high cognitive ability members are more adaptive than teams composed of members with low cognitive ability (LePine, 2003). Research evidence also suggests teams composed of members with a team orientation experience higher levels of satisfaction (Shaw, Duffy, & Stark, 2000) and display more cooperative behaviors (Wagner, 1995; Eby & Dobbins, 1997).

Job Characteristics

Team self-management has been conceptualized as a degree of freedom or control which a team possesses to determine how and when to coordinate inputs, make decisions, and schedule work (Campion, Medsker, & Higgs, 1993). Team self-management is the group level conceptualization of individual level team member autonomy (Campion et al., 1993). Self-management is similar in nature to other constructs such as autonomy (Hackman & Oldham, 1980), behavioral discretion (Cannon-Bowers, Salas, & Blickensderfer, 1998), and empowerment (Mohrman, Cohen, & Mohrman, 1995).

Self-management creates a sense of responsibility within the team for engaging in the behaviors vital to achieving work outcomes (Hackman & Oldham, 1980). Moreover, once a sense of responsibility is instilled, self-management allows teams the discretional latitude to maneuver financial and human capital resources to redress performance decrements in a timely manner. For example, a team that can control its resources can allocate them during plan execution without the need to seek approval via the usual bureaucratic channels. In this example, the latency with which a team can respond to changing circumstances is reduced and thereby team adaptation is enhanced. Accumulating empirical evidence indirectly supports this assertion, as studies suggest there is a positive relationship between team self-management and team effectiveness (Campion et al., 1993; Campion, Papper, & Medsker, 1996).

CONCLUSION

This chapter defined team adaptation and the emergent nature of adaptive team performance and centered these constructs in a heuristic framework (see Fig. 1). This initial organizing framework contains several key points about team adaptation. Specifically, team adaptation is: (1) the endogenous construct of interest, (2) operationalized as a change in team performance, (3) accomplished via the execution of adaptive team performance, (4) recursive in nature, and (5) inherently functional for the attainment of shared goals. The advanced framework also depicts the cyclical nature of adaptive team performance and thereby answers repeated calls for attention to temporal issues within team theory building and research (see McGrath, 1964; Ilgen, Hollenbeck, Johnson, & Jundt, 2005). The advanced framework also outlines the core constructs, which compile across levels and time to emerge as adaptive team performance. Finally, the advanced framework centers this longitudinal and cyclical process within a nomological network of lawful relations via an ITO framework.

The heuristic framework advanced herein also speaks to a number of practical implications. By illuminating the nature of team adaptation and the variables, which impinge upon it, this research paves a path for those stakeholders charged with facilitating team adaptation to follow. Specifically, the framework highlights the key constructs, which must be operationalized in terms of measures, tracked over time, and altered accordingly via intervention. In regards to this last point, the framework provides guidance to staffing, development, and retention efforts conducted to harness the adaptive capacity of a team and its members. Underscoring the importance of proactively managing a team and its members to foster change, Francis Bacon once remarked, "Things alter for the worse spontaneously, if they be not altered for the better designedly." The authors hope the advanced heuristic framework of team adaptation begins to provide the foundation needed for those architects of change.

ACKNOWLEDGMENTS

The views expressed in this work are those of the authors and do not necessarily reflect official Army policy. This work was supported by funding from the Army Research Laboratory's Advanced Decision Architecture Collaborative Technology Alliance (Cooperative Agreement DAAD19-01-2-0009).

REFERENCES

Ancona, D., & Chong, C. L. (1999). Cycles and synchrony: The temporal role of context in team behavior. In: R. Wageman (Ed.), *Research on managing groups and teams: Groups in context*. Stamford, CT: JAI Press.

Barrick, M. R., Stewart, G. L., Neubert, M. J., & Mount, M. K. (1998). Relating member ability and personality to work-team processes and team effectiveness. *Journal of Applied Psychology*, *83*, 377–391.

Barry, B., & Stewart, G. L. (1997). Composition, process and performance in self-managed groups: The role of personality. *Journal of Applied Psychology*, *1*, 62–78.

Burke, C. S., Fiore, S. M., & Salas, E. (2002). The role of shared cognition in enabling shared leadership and team adaptation. In: C. L. Pearce & J. A. Conger (Eds), *Shared leadership: Reframing the hows and whys of leadership* (pp. 103–122). Thousand Oaks, CA: Sage.

Campbell, J. P. (1990). Modeling the performance prediction problem in industrial and organizational psychology. In: M. D. Dunnette & L. M. Hough (Eds), *Handbook of industrial and organizational psychology* (pp. 687–732). Palo Alto, CA: Consulting Psychologists Press.

Campbell, J. P. (1999). The definition and measurement of performance in the new age. In: D. R. Ilgen & E. D. Pulakos (Eds), *The changing mature of performance: Implications for staffing, motivation, and development*. San Francisco, CA: Jossey-Bass.

Campbell, J. P., & Kuncel, N. R. (2001). Individual and team training. In: N. Anderson, D. S. Ones, H. K. Sinangil & C. Viswesvaran (Eds), *Handbook of industrial, work and organizational psychology* (pp. 272–312). London, England: Sage.

Campbell, J. P., McCloy, R. A., Oppler, S. H., & Sager, C. E. (1993). A theory of performance. In: N. Schmitt & W. C. Borman (Eds), *Personnel selection in organizations* (pp. 35–70). San Francisco, CA: Jossey-Bass.

Campion, M. A., Medsker, G. J., & Higgs, A. C. (1993). Relations between work group characteristics and effectiveness: Implications for designing effective work groups. *Personnel Psychology*, *46*, 823–850.

Campion, M. A., Papper, E. M., & Medsker, G. J. (1996). Relations between work team characteristics and effectiveness: A replication and extension. *Personnel Psychology*, *49*, 429–452.

Cannon-Bowers, J., Salas, E., & Blickensderfer, B. (1998, April). Making fine distinctions among team constructs: Worthy endeavor or "crewel" and unusual punishment? In:

R. Klimoski (Chair), *When is a work team a crew and does it matter?* Symposium conducted at the 13th Annual Conferences of the Society for Industrial and Organizational Psychology, Dallas, TX.

Cannon-Bowers, J., Salas, E., & Converse, S. (1993). Shared mental models in expert team decision making. In: N. J. Castellan Jr. (Ed.), *Individual and group decision making: Current issues* (pp. 221–246). Hillsdale, NJ: Lawrence Erlbaum Associates.

Cannon-Bowers, J. A., Tannenbaum, S. I., Salas, E., & Volpe, C. E. (1995). Defining competencies and establishing team training requirements. In: R. Guzzo & E. Salas (Eds), *Team effectiveness and decision making in organizations* (pp. 333–380). San Francisco, CA: Jossey-Bass.

Chan, D. (2000). Understanding adaptation to change in the work environment: Integrating individual difference and learning perspectives. *Research in Organizational Behavior, 18*, 1–42.

Chen, G., & Ployhart, R. E. (2004). Time for a change: Towards a theory of performance change. Paper presented at the 19th annual meeting for the society for industrial organizational psychology, Chicago, IL.

Conner, D. L., & Hoopes, L. L. (1997). Elements of human due diligence: Supporting the nimble organization. *Consulting Psychology Journal: Practice & Research, 49*, 17–24.

Converse, S. A., & Kahler, S. E. (1992, August). Shared mental models, team performance, and knowledge acquisition. Paper presented at the annual meeting of the American Psychological Association, Washington, DC.

Costa, P. T., & McCrae, R. R. (1985). *The NEO personality inventory manual4*. Odessa, FL: Psychological Assessment Resources.

DeShon, R. P., Kozlowski, S. W. J., Schmidt, A. M., Milner, K. R., & Wiechmann, D. (2005). A multiple-goal, multilevel model of feedback effects on the regulation of individual and team performance. *Journal of Applied Psychology, 6*, 1035–1056.

Driskell, J. E., Hogan, R., & Salas, E. (1987). Personality and group performance. *Review of Personality and Social Psychology, 9*, 91–112.

Driskell, J. E., & Salas, E. (1992). Collective behavior and team performance. *Human Factors, 34*, 277–288.

Dutton, J. E., & Dukerich, J. M. (1991). Keeping an eye on the mirror: Image and identity in organizational adaptation. *Academy of Management Journal, 14*, 517–554.

Eby, L. T., & Dobbins, G. H. (1997). Collectivistic orientation in teams: An individual and group-level analysis. *Journal of Organizational Behavior, 18*, 275–295.

Edmondson, A. (1999). Psychological safety and learning behavior in work teams. *Administrative Science Quarterly, 44*, 350–383.

Edmondson, A. C., Bohmer, R. M., & Pisano, G. P. (2001). Disrupted routines: Team learning and new technology implementation in hospitals. *Administrative Science Quarterly, 46*, 685–716.

Endsley, M. R. (1995). Toward a theory of situation awareness in dynamic systems. *Human Factors, 37*, 32–64.

Endsley, M. R., & Smith, R. P. (1996). Attention distribution and decision making in tactical air combat. *Human Factors, 38*, 232–250.

Entin, E. E., & Serfaty, D. (1999). Adaptive team coordination. *Human Factors, 41*, 312–325.

Fleming, P. J., Wood, G. M., Dudley, N. M., Bader, P. K., & Zaccaro, S. J. (2003, April). An adaptation training program for military leaders and teams. In: E. D. Pulakos

(Chair), *Mission critical: Developing adaptive performance in US Army Special Forces.* Symposium conducted at the 18th annual meeting for the Society for Industrial and Organizational Psychology, Orlando, FL.

Fox-Wolfgramm, S. J., Boal, K. B., & Hunt, J. G. (1998). Organizational adaptation to institutional change: A comparative study of first order change in prospector and defender banks. *Administrative Science Quarterly, 43*, 97–127.

Gersick, C. G. (1988). Time and transition in work teams: Toward a new model of group development. *Academy of Management Journal, 31*, 9–41.

Gersick, C. J. G., & Hackman, J. R. (1990). Habitual routines in task performing groups. *Organizational Behavior and Human Decision Processes, 47*, 65–97.

Golembiewski, R. T., Billingsley, K., & Yeager, S. (1976). Measuring change and persistence in human affairs: Types of change generated by OD designs. *Journal of Applied Behavioral Science, 12*, 133–157.

Guion, R. M. (1998). *Assessment, measurement, and prediction for personnel decisions.* Mahwah, NJ: Lawrence Erlbaum Associates.

Gutwin, C., & Greenberg, S. (2004). The importance of awareness for team cognition in distributed collaboration. In: E. Salas & S. Fiore (Eds), *Team cognition: Understanding the factors that drive process and performance.* Washington, DC: American Psychological Association.

Hackman, J. R., & Oldham, G. R. (1980). *Work redesign.* Reading, MA: Addison-Wesley.

Hackman, J. R., & Wageman, R. (2005). A theory of team coaching. *The Academy of Management Review, 30*, 269–287.

Han, T. Y. (2003). *Multilevel approach to individual and team adaptive performance.* Unpublished Ph.D. dissertation. University at Albany, New York.

Hollenbeck, J. R., LePine, J., & Ilgen, D. R. (1996). Adapting to roles in decision making teams. In: K. R. Murphy (Ed.), *Individual differences and behavior in organizations* (pp. 300–333). San Francisco, CA: Jossey-Bass.

Howard, A. (1995). A framework for work change. In: A. Howard (Ed.), *The changing nature of work* (pp. 3–44). San Francisco, CA: Jossey-Bass.

Hulin, C. (1991). Adaptation, persistence, and commitment in organizations. In: M. D. Dunnette & L. M. Hough (Eds), *Handbook of Industrial & Organizational Psychology.* Palo Alto, CA: Consulting Psychologists Press.

Hunter, J. E., & Hunter, R. F. (1984). Validity and utility of alternative predictors of job performance. *Psychological Bulletin, 96*, 72–98.

Ilgen, D. R., Hollenbeck, J. R., Johnson, M., & Jundt, D. (2005). Teams in organizations: From input-process-output models to IMOI models. *Annual Review of Psychology, 56*, 1–19.

Ilgen, D. R., & Pulakos, E. D. (Eds) (1999). *The changing nature of performance: Implications for staffing, motivation, and development.* San Francisco, CA: Jossey-Bass.

Klein, K., & Kozlowski, S. W. J. (Eds) (2000). *Multilevel theory, research, and methods in organizations: Foundations, extensions, and new directions.* San Francisco, CA: Jossey-Bass.

Klein, G., & Pierce, L. (2001). Adaptive teams. Paper presented at the 6th international command and control research and technology symposium. *Proceedings of the 2001 6th international command and control research and technology symposium*, Department of Defense Cooperative Research Program, Anapolis, MD.

Kleinman, D. L., & Serfaty, D. (1989). Team Performance assessment in distributed decision-making. *Proceedings of the symposium on interactive networked simulation for training*, Orlando, FL.

Kozlowski, S. W. J. (1998). Training and developing adaptive teams: Theory, principles, and research. In: J. A. Cannon Bowers & E. Salas (Eds), *Making decisions under stress: Implications for individual and team training* (pp. 15–153). Washington, DC: American Psychological Association.

Kozlowski, S. W. J., Gully, S. M., Nason, E. R., & Smith, E. M. (1999). Developing adaptive teams: A theory of compilation and performance across levels and time. In: D. R. Ilgen & E. D. Pulakos (Eds), *The changing nature of work and performance: Implications for staffing, personnel actions, and development* (pp. 240–292). San Francisco, CA: Jossey-Bass.

Kozlowski, S. W. J., & Klein, K. (2000). A multilevel approach to theory and research in organizations: Contextual, temporal, and emergent processes. In: K. J. Klein & S. W. J. Kozlowski (Eds), *Multilevel theory, research, and methods in organizations: Foundations, extensions, and new directions* (pp. 3–90). San Francisco: Jossey-Bass, Inc.

Kozlowski, S. W. J., Toney, R. J., Mullins, M. E., Weissbein, D. A., Brown, K. G., & Bell, B. S. (2001). Developing adaptation: A theory for the design of integrated-embedded training systems. *Advances in Human Performance and Cognitive Engineering Research, 1*, 59–122.

LePine, J. A. (2003). Team adaptation and postchange performance: Effects of team composition in terms of members' cognitive ability and personality. *Journal of Applied Psychology, 88*, 27–39.

LePine, J. A., Colquitt, J. A., & Erez, A. (2000). Adaptation to changing task contexts: Effects of general cognitive ability, conscientiousness, and openness to experience. *Personnel Psychology, 53*, 563–593.

Marks, M. A., Mathieu, J. E., & Zaccaro, S. J. (2001). A temporally based framework and taxonomy of team processes. *Academy of Management Review, 26*, 356–376.

Marks, M. A., Zaccaro, S. J., & Mathieu, J. E. (2000). Performance implications of leader briefings and team-interaction training for team adaptation to novel environments. *Journal of Applied Psychology, 6*, 971–986.

Mathieu, J. E., Heffner, T. S., Goodwin, G. F., Salas, E., & Cannon-Bowers, J. A. (2000). The influence of shared mental models on team process and performance. *Journal of Applied Psychology, 85*, 273–283.

McGrath, J. E. (1964). *Social psychology: A brief introduction.* New York: Holt, Rinehart & Winston.

McGrath, J. E., Arrow, H., & Berdahl, J. L. (2000). *A theory of groups as complex, adaptive, dynamic systems.* Newbury Park, CA: Sage.

McIntyre, R. M., & Salas, E. (1995). Measuring and managing for team performance: Emerging principles from complex environments. In: R. Guzzo & E. Salas (Eds), *Team effectiveness and decision making in organizations* (pp. 149–203). San Francisco, CA: Jossey-Bass.

Milgram, N. A. (1991). Personality factors in military psychology. In: R. Gal & A. D. Mangelsdorff (Eds), *Handbook of military psychology* (pp. 559–572). London: Wiley.

Mohrman, S. A. M., Cohen, S. G., & Mohrman, A. M. (1995). *Designing team-based organizations: New forms for knowledge work.* San Francisco, CA: Jossey-Bass.

Myers, D. G. (2002). *Social psychology.* New York: McGraw-Hill.

Neuman, G., Wagner, S. H., & Christiansen, N. D. (1999). The relationship between work-team personality composition and the job performance of teams. *Group and Organization Management, 1*, 28–45.

Nunnally, J., & Bernstein, I. (1994). *Psychometric theory.* New York: McGraw-Hill.

Orasanu, J., & Salas, E. (1993). Team decision making in complex environment. In: G. Klein, J. Orasanu, R. Calderwood & C. E. Zsambok (Eds), *Decision making in action: Models and methods* (pp. 327–345). Norwood, NJ: Ablex.

O'Shea, P. G., Driskell, J. E., Goodwin, G. F., Zbylut, M. L., & Weiss, S. M. (2004). *Development of a conditional reasoning measure of team orientation.* ARI Research Note. Department of the Army, Arlington, VA.

Pervin, L. A. (1990). A brief history of modern personality theory. In: L. A. Pervin (Ed.), *Handbook of personality theory and research.* New York: Guilford Press.

Ployhart, R. E., Saltz, J. L., Mayer, D. M., & Bliese, P. D. (2002). Individual adaptability: Measurement, construct validity, and relations to leadership performance. Paper presented at the Annual conference of the international personnel Management Association Assessment Council, New Orleans, LA.

Porras, J. I., & Robertson, P. J. (1992). Organizational development: Theory, practice, and research. In: M. D. Dunnette & L. M. Hough (Eds), *Handbook of industrial and organizational psychology* (2nd ed., Vol. 3, pp. 719–822). Palo Alto, CA: Consulting Psychologists Press.

Porter, C., Hollenbeck, J. R., Ilgen, D. R., Ellis, P. J., West, B., & Moon, H. (2003). Backing up behaviors in teams: The role of personality and legitimacy of need. *Journal of Applied Psychology, 3*, 391–403.

Pulakos, E. D., Arad, S., Donovan, M. A., & Plamondon, K. E. (2000). Adaptation in the workplace: Development of a taxonomy of adaptive performance. *Journal of Applied Psychology, 85*, 612–624.

Pulakos, E. D., Schmitt, N., Dorsey, D. W., Arad, S., Hedge, J. W., & Borman, W. C. (2002). Predicting adaptive performance: Further tests of a model of adaptability. *Human Performance, 4*, 299–323.

Rouse, W. B., & Morris, N. M. (1986). On looking into the black box: Prospects and limits in the search for mental models. *Psychological Bulletin, 100*, 349–363.

Rutkowski, K. A., Steelman, L. A., & Griffith, R. L. (2004). An empirical examination of accountability for performance development. Paper presented at the 19th Annual conference of the society for industrial organizational psychology, Chicago, IL.

Salas, E., Cannon-Bowers, J. A., & Johnston, J. H. (1997). How can you turn a team of experts into an expert team?: Emerging training strategies. In: C. E. Zsambok & G. Klein (Eds), *Naturalistic decision making* (pp. 359–370). Mahwah, NJ: Lawrence Erlbaum Associates.

Salas, E., Prince, C., Baker, D. P., & Shrestha, L. (1995). Situation awareness in team performance: Implications for measurement and training. *Human Factors, 37*, 123–136.

Salas, E., Stagl, K. C., & Burke, C. S. (2004). 25 years of team effectiveness in organizations: Research themes and emerging needs. In: C. L. Cooper & I. T. Robertson (Eds), *International review of industrial and organizational psychology* (Vol. 19, pp. 47–91). New York: Wiley.

Salas, E., Stagl, K. C., Burke, C. S., & Goodwin, G. F. (in press). Fostering team effectiveness in organizations: Toward an integrative theoretical framework of team performance. In: J. W. Shuart, W. Spaulding & J. Poland (Eds), *Modeling complex systems: Motivation, cognition and social processes, Nebraska symposium on motivation* (Vol. 51). Lincoln, NE: University of Nebraska Press.

Schein, E. H., & Bennis, W. G. (1965). *Personal and organizational change through group methods: The laboratory approach.* New York: Wiley.

Schmidt, F. L., & Hunter, J. E. (1998). The validity and utility of selection methods in personnel psychology: Practical and theoretical implications of 85 years of research findings. *Psychological Bulletin*, *124*, 262–274.

Shaw, J. D., Duffy, M. K., & Stark, E. M. (2000). Interdependence and preference for group work: Main and congruence effect son the satisfaction and performance of group members. *Journal of Management*, *26*, 259–279.

Stout, R. J., & Salas, E. (1993). The role of planning in coordinated team decision making: Implications for training. *Proceedings of the 37th annual meeting of the Human Factors and Ergonomics Society*, Santa Monica, CA (pp. 1238–1242).

Takeuchi, R., Yum, S., & Tesluk, P. E. (2002). An examination of crossover and spillover effects of spousal and expatriate cross-cultural adjustment on expatriate outcomes. *Journal of Applied Psychology*, *87*, 655–666.

Tannenbaum, S. I., Beard, R. L., & Salas, E. (1992). Team building and its influence on team effectiveness: An examination of conceptual and empirical developments. In: K. Kelly (Ed.), *Issues, theory, and research in industrial and organizational psychology* (pp. 117–153). New York: Elsevier Science.

Tushman, M. L., & Rosenkoph, L. (1996). Executive succession, strategic reorientation and performance growth: A longitudinal study in the US cement industry. *Management Science*, *42*, 939–954.

Wagner, J. A., III. (1995). Studies of individualism-collectivism: Effects of cooperation in groups. *Academy of Management Journal*, *38*, 152–172.

Waller, M. J. (1999). The timing of adaptive group responses to nonroutine events. *Academy of Management Journal*, *42*, 127–137.

West, M. A., Borrill, C. S., & Unsworth, K. L. (1998). Team effectiveness in organizations. In: C. L. Cooper & I. T. Robertson (Eds), *International review of industrial organizational psychology*. Chichester: Wiley.

Yukl, G., & Van Fleet, D. D. (1992). Theory and research on leadership in organizations. In: M. D. Dunnette & L. M. Hough (Eds), *Handbook of industrial and organizational psychology* (pp. 147–197). Palo Alto, CA: Consulting Psychologists Press.

Zaccaro, S. J., & Bader, P. (2003). E-leadership and the challenges of leading E-teams: Minimizing the bad and maximizing the good. *Organizational Dynamics*, *31*, 377–387.

Zaccaro, S. J., Gilbert, J., Thor, K. K., & Mumford, M. D. (1991). Leadership and social intelligence: Linking social perceptiveness and behavioral flexibility to leader effectiveness. *Leadership Quarterly*, *2*, 317–331.

CULTURAL ADAPTABILITY[☆]

Janet L. Sutton, Linda G. Pierce, C. Shawn Burke and Eduardo Salas

The U.S. military is transforming how it will do business and that transformation is being driven by diversity, a hallmark of future operations. General Charles C. Krulak, former Commandant of the U.S. Marine Corps, described the future operational environment as the three-block war. "In one moment in time, our service members will be feeding and clothing displaced refugees – providing humanitarian assistance. In the next moment, they will be holding two warring tribes apart conducting peacekeeping operations. Finally, they will be fighting a highly lethal mid-intensity battle. All on the same day, all within three city blocks" (Krulak, 1997). Operational diversity will be complicated by team diversity with future military operations regularly consisting of Joint, Interagency, and Multinational (JIM) teams. In the three-block war, operational and team diversity will fluctuate within missions making the ability to adjust strategies appropriately based on the environment a necessity. We call this ability "adaptability" and

[☆] The intent of this chapter was to provide a common body of basic knowledge of the effect of culture on teamwork and to encourage development of a broad perspective on culturally based influences as a background for understanding cultural adaptability. The subject of religion was not addressed as, even though it can be a very visible aspect of culture (i.e., religion often prescribes specific behavioral practices and influences codes of ethics and moral behavior), its impact is on culture, not multicultural teamwork directly.

Understanding Adaptability: A Prerequisite for Effective Performance within Complex Environments
Advances in Human Performance and Cognitive Engineering Research, Volume 6, 143–173

ISSN: 1479-3601/doi:10.1016/S1479-3601(05)06005-4

propose that successful military transformation will require individual and team adaptability. Team adaptability in multicultural environments will require "cultural adaptability."

Cultural adaptability refers to the ability to understand one's own and others' cognitive biases and to adapt, as necessary, to ensure successful team performance. This skill is comprised of three components: cultural competence, teamwork, and cultural adaptability. The foundation of cultural adaptability is cultural competence. Cultural competence is the ability to recognize that influences of thoughts and predisposition to action frequently have deep cultural roots. It is an understanding of the dominant values and orientations of each culture, keeping in mind that those values and orientations are not predictive of behavior but do provide a guiding model.

The second component of cultural adaptability is teamwork. Whether multinational or not, we propose that there are fundamental aspects of performance that are consistent across teams. For example, team performance is determined by individual competence, team competence, individual and team accountability, and team reward. Based on Fleishman and Zacarro's (1992) taxonomy of team functions, McGlynn, Sutton, Sprague, Demski, and Pierce (1997) posited that team competence is determined by the ability of the team to exchange information, coordinate actions, assign roles and responsibilities, error check, and act as a source of motivation. While there are other conceptualizations of teams and team competencies, the McGlynn et al. taxonomy (see Table 1) synthesizes elements of others' research (e.g., Fleishman & Quaintance, 1984; Salas, Dickinson, Converse, & Tannenbaum, 1992) in a way that is useful for understanding team performance, thus simplifying

Table 1. McGlynn et al. Taxonomy of Team Functions.

Information exchange	Includes information regarding member resources and constraints, team tasks and goals or mission, environmental characteristics and constraints, or priority assignment among subtasks
Coordination	Includes coordinating responses with task timing requirements or with responses of other members, including activity pacing, response sequencing, and time and position coordination
Assigning roles and responsibilities	Includes the need for role interchange and is the matching of member resources, skills, abilities, prior knowledge, task information, numbers, etc., to subtask requirements
Error checking	Includes the process of monitoring individual and team activity, identifying problems, and adjusting team and member activities in response to errors and omissions or the attainment or lack of attainment of standards of performance

the presentation of pertinent information. Army Research Laboratory (ARL) Human Research and Engineering Directorate (HRED) researchers used this taxonomy to build a model for understanding cultural diversity in teamwork. While acknowledging the important role that motivation plays in team performance, at the time of this research, it was decided not to explore motivational aspects of teamwork. The model is presented later in this chapter.

There are two facets to adaptability, the third component of cultural adaptability. After recognizing culturally based behaviors (i.e., cultural competence) and understanding the implication of those behaviors (i.e., teamwork), truly adaptable individuals (1) have knowledge about how to adapt their own behavior when working with others whose culture is not their own, and (2) make a personal choice to adapt their behavior, as needed, to enable effective teamwork.

Over the years, researchers have attempted to classify behaviors rooted in cultural values or cultural orientation that could affect social interactions, including that of multicultural teams. Most agree that there is a tendency for individuals of the same nationality to have similar behavior patterns and that those behaviors vary by degree depending on where an individual's values fall along a theoretical continuum. In other words, individuals can have significantly different culturally based biases that influence their behavior. In concert with biases of others, the resulting behaviors can either enhance or hinder team performance (Sutton & Pierce, 2003). Following from this, the purpose of this chapter is threefold. First, perceptual, interpretive, and evaluative biases that may serve to hinder cultural adaptability will be briefly described. Second, behaviors manifested from culturally based values and the resulting impact of those behaviors on multicultural teamwork will be examined. Third, a 3 (Culturally based Dimension: Power Distance, Uncertainty Avoidance, Activity Orientation) × 4 (Team Function: Situation Assessment, Coordination, Assigning of Roles and Responsibilities, Support) matrix, developed by the researchers at ARL HRED is presented as a framework for researchers to use as a guide for understanding the impact of cultural diversity on teamwork. This framework can be used to highlight the behaviors needed to promote cultural adaptability.

BARRIERS TO CULTURAL ADAPTABILITY

Barriers to cultural adaptability include perceptual, interpretive, and evaluative biases. Differences in culturally based perceptual patterns can be problematic given that interpretation and evaluation of behavior is a critical element of teamwork. Altogether, perceptual patterns are "selective, learned, culturally determined, consistent, and inaccurate" (Adler, 1986, p. 54). Selective exposure, selective attention, and selective retention are all hallmarks of the process of perception. Bagby (1970) demonstrated how perceptual patterns become selective even in childhood. He had American and Mexican children watch a bullfight and a baseball game simultaneously using a tachistoscope. When asked what they had seen, the American children claimed to have watched a baseball game, and the Mexican children claimed to have watched a bullfight. Neither group was aware that they had been presented two stimuli simultaneously. Both groups of children selected stimuli that had meaning for their culture and ignored or forgot the stimuli that had no meaning for them. The children's culture predisposed them to notice some things and not others. Perceptual selectivity is a key barrier to cultural adaptability and influences both interpretation and evaluation.

Interpretation and evaluation of communications and events, a problem inherent in multicultural teamwork, is another barrier to cultural adaptability. People tend to categorize their experiences, make assumptions about those experiences, and then draw conclusions regarding those experiences. These structured categories help individuals identify the same phenomenon through time. People categorize so that they may respond quickly and appropriately when in similar situations (Korzenny, 1984). Categorized information is framed within one's own cultural context. Meaning is assigned to the categories and thinking, then, falls into embedded patterns. Therefore, assumptions about communications, people, and events may be inaccurate if the information was categorized incorrectly initially.

Stereotyping is a form of categorization that can be effective when one is aware of the stereotype, it is relatively accurate, and it is not evaluative (Adler, 1986). Stereotypes can be used to guide interpretation of communications, people, and events until such time as one has actual experience with the stereotyped object and can modify or adapt assumptions about the meaning of messages or the cause of behaviors. Stereotyping inhibits cultural adaptability when it is maintained in the face of contradictory experience and is used to evaluate others.

Ethnocentrism and parochialism are perhaps the most serious barriers to cultural adaptability. Ethnocentrism can be defined as assuming that the ways of one's own culture are the best ways of doing things. Parochialism can be defined as assuming that the ways of one's own culture are the only ways of doing things. Comparison of other cultures to one's own culture creates an evaluative stereotype that forms the basis of these constructs.

Using one's own cultural standards to evaluate the behaviors of other cultural groups occurs more frequently than misperception or misinterpretation of communications, people, situations, and events (Adler, 1986). Members of ethnocentric or parochial groups believe other cultural groups to be inferior. They think and behave in ways consistent with their perceived superiority. Members of these groups do recognize cultural differences on their team and, by doing so, claim to be "tolerant" and "open minded." However, the cultural differences are often minimized. These individuals have a tendency to dismiss as unimportant, or to simply ignore, cultural differences in order to avoid potential problems that may arise as a result of those differences.

Both ethnocentrism and parochialism significantly impact multicultural teamwork in three ways. First, because cultural differences are diminished, little thought is given by members of these groups as to how messages are encoded and might be decoded by members of other cultures. Communication is difficult and occasionally impossible. Second, because the "other" group is perceived to be inferior, ethnocentric or parochial group members make little or no effort to learn more about them. The result is that perceptual patterns of members of the ethnocentric or parochial group are not modified based on experience with members of the "other" group. Negative biases toward the "other" group persist and may even become stronger over time. Third, no one benefits from the richness of experiences that can be found in cultural differences. There is little growth in terms of interpersonal relationship development. Team performance may be negatively affected when members of an ethnocentric or parochial group do not consider input from members of the "other" group, in the appropriate cultural context.

CULTURAL VALUES AND ORIENTATIONS

It is important that readers have the same understanding of the term "culture" as used in this chapter. Culture is derived from collective experiences arising from a group's social, political, and physical surroundings. It is "the totality of socially transmitted behavior patterns, arts, beliefs, institutions, and all other products of human work and thought typical of a population or community at a given time" (Berube et al., 1999). Culture is the acquired knowledge that people use to interpret experience and generate social behavior. Cultural knowledge forms values (i.e., basic convictions that people have regarding what is right and wrong, good and bad, important and unimportant), creates attitudes, and influences behavior. Values are abstract and general, relatively stable and not subject to sudden shifts or impulses of the moment. They serve as standard for judging behavior. In other words, behavior reflects values. Whereas the term "culture" could refer to any collective group experience (e.g., military culture or organizational culture), our focus is on national culture within a military environment, or the values, beliefs, and cognitions that guide interpretation of unfolding events and social interactions on multinational teams. Assumptions about the nature of reality, values, and philosophies (i.e., culture's "programming") can create barriers to effective teamwork even in a military environment when more than one national culture is represented.

This chapter presents the theories of cross-cultural variability listed in Table 2. Some theories are presented in more depth than others for the purpose of highlighting themes that can affect multicultural teamwork. The list is not intended to be inclusive of all cultural research. Reference to older research was excluded as was research deemed not to be directly applicable to multicultural teamwork. For example, Morris' (1942, 1948, 1956) early work on philosophies of life that serve as intellectual guidelines for cognition and behavior is not addressed. Additionally, Parsons and Shils' (1951) early work on pattern variability theory is not reviewed here. The dimensions identified in that body of work have been re-examined by other scientists and incorporated into more recent theories. The reader is encouraged to review these and other works not addressed in this chapter (e.g., Beamer, 2000; Heuser, 2000; Javidan & House, 2001).

Salas, Burke, Fowlkes, and Wilson (2004) argue that the cross-cultural dimensions that appear in the literature are merely broad categorizations and should serve only as a starting point in understanding cross-cultural interactions. Another argument frequently heard is that differences in behavior typically attributed to culture are merely individual differences. This begs the question of whether or not cross-cultural researchers should take away cultural labels, look for behavioral cues, and then cluster those cues as they strive to understand how to leverage adaptation capability. If so, perhaps the meta-variable to cultural adaptability is "awareness of differences." With this in mind, following is a discussion of theoretical perspectives presented as representative of the literature on behavioral manifestations of culturally based biases. Those themes are Human Relations, Power Relations, Rules Orientation, Time Orientation, Allocation of Status, Nature Orientation, Cognitive Style and Thinking Orientation, Communication Style, Public and Private Space, Gender Role Orientation, and Activity Orientation.

Table 2. Cultural Dimensions Impacting Teamwork Presented in the Chapter.

Theme	Cultural Dimension Identifiers	Source
Human Relations	Individualism–Collectivism	Hofstede, 1980
	Collectivism–Individualism	Triandis, 1989
	Simplicity–Complexity	Triandis, 1989
	Individualism–Communitarianism	Trompanaars and Hampdon-Turner, 1997
	Tight–Loose	Triandis, 1989
	Group Orientation	Kluckhohn and Strodtbeck, 1961
	Conservatism–Autonomy	Schwartz, 1999
	Human Nature	Kluckhohn and Strodtbeck, 1961
		Manzevski and Peterson, 1997
Power Relations	Power Distance	Hofstede, 1980
	Hierarchy–Egalitarianism	Schwartz, 1999
	Vertical–Horizontal	Triandis, 1989
Rules Orientation	Uncertainty Avoidance	Hofstede, 1980
	Universalism–Particularism	Trompanaars and Hampdon-Turner, 1997
Time Orientation	Monochronic–Polychronic	Hall and Hall, 1990
	Past–Present–Future	Kluckhohn and Strodtbeck, 1961
	Long–Short Term	Hofstede, 1980
	Sequential–Synchronic	Trompanaars and Hampdon-Turner, 1997
Allocation of Status	Achievement–Ascription	Trompanaars and Hampdon-Turner, 1997
Cognitive Style and	Field Dependence–Independence	Witkin and Berry, 1975
Thinking Orientation	Analytic–Holistic	Choi and Nisbett, 2000; Nisbett, Peng, Choi, & Norenzayan, 2001.
	Hemisphericity	Bogan, De Zure, TenHouten and Marsh, 1972
		Markus and Kitayama, 1991;
	Hypothetical–Concrete	Norenzayan and Nisbet, 2000
Communication	High–Low Context	Hall and Hall, 1990
Space	Specific–Diffuse	Triandis, 1989
		Trompanaars and Hampdon-Turner, 1997
Gender Role Orientation	Masculinity–Femininity	Hofstede, 1980
		Snodgrass, 1990
Activity Orientation	Doing–Thinking–Being	Kluckhohn and Strodtbeck, 1961

Human Relations

Often considered the over-arching value orientation for all cultures is the Individualism–Collectivism continuum. Several dimensions identified in the literature seem to fall naturally together and, to some degree, tap into the construct of Hofstede's (1980) Individualism–Collectivism (e.g.,

Collectivism–Individualism, Triandis, 1989; Individualism–Communitarianism, Trompanaars & Hampdon-Turner, 1997). As researchers have focused on different aspects of this dimension, the label of Individualism–Collectivism varies, but the focus remains on the relationship, and causes for the relationship, between the individual and the group.

At one end of the theoretical continuum are highly Individualistic cultures where the individual is believed to be the most important unit. Individualistic cultures may emerge from complex societies where the strength of group norms are "loose," (i.e., deviation from norms is tolerated and behaviors are freely chosen by the individual) (Triandis, 1989). Individuals with an Individualistic orientation are comfortable working with broad goals and flexible team processes. Individualistic cultures promote an "I can take care of myself" attitude. Basing decisions on meeting one's own needs is encouraged. Individualistic cultures value autonomy and seek self-actualization. As such, individuals with this orientation are comfortable working alone. People with an Individualistic orientation speak out, sharing their thoughts and ideas openly, and find intellectual debate stimulating. They tend not to take disagreement with their ideas personally. They often question statements made by others to gain clarification and may be perceived by those who do not share the Individualistic orientation as being confrontational at times. Their manner of speaking can be direct, going straight to the point they want to make. These behaviors do not generally cause problems if team members all have Individualistic biases to some degree.

At the other end of the theoretical continuum are highly Collectivistic cultures. These cultures believe that the group is the most important unit and group needs come before individual needs. Collectivistic cultures may emerge from simple societies where "proper behavior" is closely monitored by the society and adherence to norms is strictly enforced. In these "tight" Collectivistic cultures, behavior that deviates from the norm is not tolerated, in most circumstances (Triandis, 1989). There is a tendency for individuals with a Collectivistic orientation to believe that there is one best way to solve a problem and that leaders should be subject matter experts on the problem at hand. Collectivistic team members may become disappointed with leaders who are open to entertaining several ideas as valid. Individuals with a Collectivistic orientation value belonging and seek group harmony. Principal loyalty to the group (e.g., family, team, organization, institution) is encouraged. Team members from Collectivistic cultures are more likely than team members from Individualistic cultures to want to learn about the history behind a request before taking action. The process of decision making in Collectivistic societies is based on what is best for the group, not what is best for individual group members. Team members with a Collectivistic orientation prefer to blend into the group, avoiding attention-getting behavior. Their communication style can be indirect rather than direct. An individual with an indirect communication style might say, for example, "Have you considered calling Mr. Smith for help?" whereas someone with a direct communication style would make the same request by saying, "Call Mr. Smith today. He will help." Team members with a Collectivistic orientation will likely behave in such a manner as to avoid conflict. Conflict-avoidance behavior may be proactive or reactive. A few examples are not attending team meetings where tensions may run high, not initiating action where the result may be negative and disappointing to teammates, and not sharing vital information that might create factions in the team. Any team activity that sparks debate could result in defensiveness. Individuals with a Collectivistic orientation may become uneasy when others openly express disagreement with the team leader.

Group Orientation is described by the terms "Individualistic," "Collective," and "Hierarchical" and refers to the relationship of human beings to one another (Kluckhohn & Strodtbeck, 1961). This dimension seems to bridge the themes of Human Nature and Power Relations. When relating to others, Individualist-oriented individuals tend to behave in an informal manner, whereas Hierarchical-oriented individuals prefer formality. People from Individualistic cultures tend to be members of many groups, yet have weak group identification with those groups. Strong group identification with relatively few groups is characteristic of people in Hierarchical cultures. Gender roles are very distinct in Hierarchical cultures, but the differentiation between gender roles in Individualistic cultures is minimal. To earn respect in Individualistic cultures, people must demonstrate an ability to handle their position or role in society (i.e., achieving the position). In Hierarchical cultures, people expect positions or roles to be assigned and respect comes with the position, not the person. The basis of social reciprocity in Individualistic cultures is autonomy (i.e., independence) from societal rules or group norms, whereas obligation is the basis of social reciprocity in Hierarchical cultures. Characteristics of the "Collective" relationship between human beings are similar to the characteristics described previously for Collectivism.

Group Orientation can have a considerable impact on team performance (see Manzevski & Peterson, 1997). Because people from Individualistic cultures focus on taking responsibility for themselves, they are quick to notice, and point out, team members who are not taking personal responsibility for their own actions. This behavior has the potential for creating defensive posturing by those accused of shirking their duty. One outcome, detrimental to team performance, might be that the accused abdicate themselves from their duties, thereby increasing the workload for the rest of the team. Another outcome, this with the potential for enhancing team performance, might be that the accused are motivated to perform at even higher levels than expected to demonstrate pride in their contribution to the group process and performance outcomes. People with Collectivistic and Hierarchical cultural orientations can positively impact team performance by supporting decisions made and actions taken by the team leader and senior members, out of respect for the leadership role or senior status in the group. However, because they believe that the leader and team members with higher status in the group have responsibility for making decisions and directing actions of the team, those with a Hierarchical orientation may neither take the initiative nor be proactive in helping the team meet its goal.

The term "Conservatism" describes an "emphasis on maintenance of the status quo, propriety, and restraint of actions or inclinations that might disrupt the solidarity of the group or the traditional order" (Schwartz, 1999, p. 27). The term "Autonomy" describes a cultural emphasis on the uniqueness of individuals that supports expression of internal attributes (e.g., traits, feelings, preferences). Intellectual autonomy is the extent to which individuals independently pursue their own ideas, while affective autonomy is the extent to which individuals independently pursue affectively positive experiences (Schwartz, 1999).

Another value orientation with potentially serious implications for multicultural teamwork is a culturally based belief that basic human nature is basically good or basically evil (Kluckhohn & Strodtbeck, 1961). Two variations on this orientation are that man's basic nature can be mixed (i.e., a mixture of good and evil) or neutral (i.e., neither good nor evil). Individuals, whose cultural orientation toward human nature is evil, assume that all mankind's basic nature is evil. Destructive acts are expected. Man's inhumanity to man is perceived to be normal behavior. Individuals with this orientation tend to focus on the laws, rules and regulations, or policies set in place to protect people from harm. Individuals whose cultural orientation toward human nature is good, on the other hand, do not think harmful behavior is normal. A key characteristic of individuals with this belief system is the tendency to look for external (i.e., situational) rather than internal (i.e., distributional) explanations for harmful events.

Culturally based perceptions of good and evil can positively or negatively impact teamwork (Manzevski & Peterson, 1997). When human nature is perceived to be evil, there is little trust of others. Not being trusted can be insulting to team members who are proud of their honesty and integrity. When human nature is perceived to be evil, people feel the need to "watch their back" and, therefore, constantly monitor the behavior of others. This type of behavior is not conducive to building a strong team. If this monitoring behavior can be channeled properly, these individuals may prevent unfair advantage being taken of the team by other groups or entities. Individuals who believe that basic human nature is good contribute to building a strong team by encouraging trust and information sharing among team members. They can help to diffuse conflict among members by redirecting blame for perceived failure or wrongdoing from distributional to situational causes. All team members should be aware, however, that the trusting nature of individuals with this orientation could potentially jeopardize the security of people, places, and information.

Power Relations

Power Distance is defined as the extent to which the less powerful expect and accept that power is distributed unequally (Hofstede, 1980). Cultures have been identified as oriented toward high Power Distance or low Power Distance. In a similar line of research, Triandis (1989) defined high and low Power Distance as vertical and horizontal, respectively. More recently, individuals with a high-Power Distance orientation have been referred to as having a Hierarchical relationship pattern, and individuals with a low-Power Distance orientation have been referred to as having an Egalitarian relationship pattern (Schwartz, 1999). Hierarchy in academia, industry, and the military is a fact of life globally, but how individuals from different cultures respond to hierarchy differs widely. Hierarchy involves "a cultural emphasis on the legitimacy of an unequal distribution of power, roles, and resources" (Schwartz, 1999, p. 27).

Individuals with a Hierarchical relationship pattern tend to blindly obey orders of superiors. They prefer a multilevel organizational structure that provides detailed Standard Operating Procedures (SOPs) for guiding their work. Typically, they only want to hear what the team leader has to say and do not particularly value what their peers have to say. Participative team process is counter-cultural in a Hierarchical society. If a team leader wants to generate dialog on a team where the dominant Power Distance orientation is Hierarchy, the leader needs to create structure for that dialog to happen, because it is not likely to happen spontaneously.

Egalitarianism involves an "emphasis on transcendence of selfish interests in favor of voluntary commitment to promoting the welfare of others" (Schwartz, 1999, p. 28). Individuals with an Egalitarian relationship pattern believe that no one is inherently entitled to lead, as everyone is alike in dignity and worth. This could result in a tendency to treat team leaders informally, offer unsolicited advice, and even publicly disagree with leaders' ideas. On the other hand, when insight to problem solving and contribution to decision making are crucial elements of the team process, an Egalitarian relationship pattern is likely to produce more adaptable behavior than a Hierarchical relationship pattern.

ARL HRED researchers found the culturally based dimension of Power Distance to significantly impact teamwork at a multinational military headquarters operation; therefore, this dimension is reviewed in greater detail later in the chapter.

Rules Orientation

There are two cultural dimensions that reflect a rules orientation, Uncertainty Avoidance (Hofstede, 1980) and Universalism–Particularism (Trompanaars & Hampdon-Turner, 1997). Uncertainty Avoidance is defined as the extent to which people feel threatened by ambiguous situations and take action to avoid uncertainty. High Uncertainty Avoidance results in behaviors reflective of a High Need for Certainty. Low Uncertainty Avoidance results in behaviors reflective of a Low Need for Certainty. Many barriers to cultural adaptability are directly attributable to diversity in Uncertainty Avoidance orientation. As with Power Distance, the culturally based dimension of Uncertainty Avoidance was found to significantly impact teamwork at a multinational military headquarters operation. It is also reviewed in more detail later in the chapter.

Universalism is the belief that one should not modify their ideas and practices just because situations change (Trompanaars & Hampdon-Turner, 1997). Universalism implies that a broad set of rules exist to guide one's actions. Team members with this orientation may appear stubborn, inflexible, and resistant to change, refusing to adapt their behavior when necessitated by unexpected circumstances. On the other hand, team members with this orientation can serve as monitors for consistency of team process and performance. Particularism is the belief that circumstances dictate how ideas and practices should be applied. It implies that unique aspects of the individual and the situation should guide behavior. Team members with this cultural orientation are comfortable changing the rules to suit each unique situation and changing their behavior with each new set of relationships. Teamwork can be disrupted if, for example, leaders with a Particularism orientation are perceived by team members with a Universalism orientation to change their mind on a whim. On the other hand, a Particularism orientation can enhance teamwork when the need to adapt one's behavior to the social codes inherent in other cultures is recognized and acted upon as new members join the team.

Time Orientation

Hall and Hall (1990) defined time orientation along a continuum with theoretical endpoints labeled Monochronic – Polychronic. Individuals with a Monochronic time orientation consider things one at a time, isolating events when they are considered. As such, these individuals may fail to grasp the context of related verbal communications that are presented over time. Time is experienced and used in a linear way, segmented and compartmentalized. Characteristic of individuals from Monochronic cultures is promptness and adherence to schedules. This view of time creates pressure for action and performance. Time is considered to be tangible, something to be saved, spent, and managed. Because of this, team members with a Monochronic orientation can keep the team focused on long-range goals. On the other hand, Polychronic cultures do not emphasize adhering to schedules. This way of thinking is based on an understanding that plans and focus are constantly changing and, therefore, so should schedules. With this orientation, the focus is on the present or short term rather than the future. Team members with a Polychronic orientation do not feel the same pressure for immediate action or performance as those with a Monochronic orientation.

Kluckhohn and Strodtbeck (1961) were two of the first researchers to label a time continuum as ranging from Past to Future, where the Present indicates a midpoint on that continuum. People focused in the Past think of time in terms of cycles and perceive time to be an unlimited resource. They perceive that time moves slowly. They tend to respect tradition and look for historical support for their current thoughts and behavior. People oriented to the Present have a short-term focus. They might be heard saying, "What happened yesterday is old news. Who knows what will happen in the future, so let's take care of the immediate problem." People with a Future time orientation see time as a scare commodity. They see time "flying by." This belief system emphasizes opportunities. Generally, Future-focused individuals look to the long-term future rather than the short-term future.

Hofstede's (1980) short-term vs. long-term definition of culturally based perceptions of time is similar to that presented for the Past–Present–Future time continuum. Cultures possessing a short-term orientation tend to foster virtues related to the past and present. These cultures foster respect for tradition, tolerance of others, and an emphasis on short-term results (e.g., bottom line, immediate gratification of needs, enjoyment of leisure time, social consumption). Given this orientation, preservation of face and being seen as a stable individual who fulfills social obligations is an important virtue. Conversely, cultures possessing a long-term orientation are characterized by deferred gratification of needs and a view that traditions can be adapted to changing circumstances. For individuals with a long-term orientation, relationships are ordered by status and long-term virtues such as the importance of frugality, education, and perseverance are seen as important and promoted.

Another culturally based approach toward time is the concept of time as Sequential or Synchronous. In cultures where time is perceived to be Sequential, people do one thing at a time, are strict about keeping appointments on time and follow plans to the letter. In cultures where time is perceived to be Synchronous, people do more than one thing at a time and appointment times are approximations. Time is viewed as a series of passing events in Sequential cultures. In Synchronic cultures, time is viewed as the synergism of past, present, and future where time actually shapes events.

Clearly, time orientation affects teamwork. Individuals with a short-time orientation might remind the team of consequences previously experienced when certain actions were taken. In other words, they can share lessons learned so that mistakes will not be repeated. A downside of thinking in terms of the past is that individuals with a Past orientation may hold the team back from taking the chance of experiencing success with untried tactics or solutions to problems. Present-oriented individuals can keep the team focused on short-term goals and create the sense of urgency sometimes needed to motivate a team to perform. However, their short-term focus might blind them to problems that taking immediate action may cause in the future. Future-oriented individuals can help the team recognize the long-term implications of actions they may take in the present. By recognizing future implications of current actions, they can incorporate forward thinking ideas into real-time action plans. Team members must be aware, however, when working with future-oriented individuals, these individuals will work toward sacrificing short-term benefits for long-term potential, even when a long-term perspective is not important to the task at hand.

Allocation of Status

Orientation toward status is another cultural dimension identified as affecting human behavior and refers to how people are judged in society (Trompanaars & Hampdon-Turner, 1997). "Achievement" is a cultural orientation where people are accorded status based on how well they perform their functions (e.g., subject matter expertise) and on what they have accomplished. "Ascription" is a cultural orientation where status is attributed based on who or what a person is (i.e., based on age, gender, or social connections). Young, go-getting, Achievement-oriented individuals who come to a team with the assumption that their voices will be heard and their ideas respected based on their previous outstanding performance will be frustrated by a lack of respect from Ascription-oriented team members who do not ascribe status or respect based on performance. By the same token, older, well-established Ascription-oriented individuals may be frustrated by the perceived lack of respect for their ideas from Achievement-oriented team members.

Cognitive Style and Thinking Orientation

There is considerable research in the area of cultural influences on cognitive style (e.g., Kaplan, 1989; Maruyama, 1994). One theory is presented to demonstrate how environmental factors (e.g., culture) contribute to differences in cognitive styles, which, in turn, can impact teamwork.

Witkin and Berry (1975) posited that Field-Independent is a cognitive style defined by the ability to think analytically, differentiate between stimuli presented in the same field of consciousness, and cognitively restructure symbolic representations into different forms when required by the task. Loose, Individualist, Egalitarian cultures that emphasize independence, self-reliance, and achievement are most likely to contribute to development of a Field-Independent cognitive style. Field-Dependent is a cognitive style defined by the tendency to pay attention to dominant properties of field rather than think through alternative ways of viewing the same properties. Tight, Collectivist, Hierarchical cultures that emphasize conforming to authority (e.g., religious, familial, political) as well as social norms and whose environment requires little abstract thinking (e.g., farming) are most likely to contribute to development of a Field-Dependent cognitive style. A Field-Independent style is more likely to be the style of team members who appear to be somewhat insensitive to social cues, are impersonal and prefer to work alone. Team members with this style may not appreciate authority or social pressure to conform to team norms. They may be perceived to be less concerned about people than they are about principles and ideas, and may try to psychologically distance themselves from their teammates. A Field-Dependent style is more likely to be found in individuals who enjoy and are competent with interpersonal activity. Team members with this style pay close, though selective, attention to social cues. For example, they may be better at remembering names than Field-Independent individuals, if names are the cue on which they focus. Field-Dependent-oriented individuals may prefer working with others instead of working alone, exhibit concern for team members, and get along well with others.

It is also possible that culture influences which brain hemisphere is dominant and, therefore, influences thinking orientation (Bogen, De Zure, TenHouten, & Marsh, 1972). Hemisphericity is the study of brain lateralization. Hemispheric specialization implies that each hemisphere of the brain, left and right, is responsible for different cognitive functions. With regard to one's thinking orientation, it is possible that the left hemisphere supports the ability to think analytically, as opposed to holistically, which is supported by the right hemisphere. The left hemisphere may support the ability to think hypothetically or symbolically, whereas the right hemisphere may support a concrete thinking orientation. Of course, the ability to use more than one thought process is a capability everyone has, but socialization into a specific culture may reinforce the use of one hemisphere over the other. For example, cultures that rely strongly on context to derive meaning from messages may tend to use properties of thought purported to originate in the right hemisphere. Cultures that derive meaning from messages explicitly may rely more on left hemisphere functioning of verbal, abstract, logical, and analytic processes. For more information on thinking styles mentioned about, (see Choi & Nisbett, 2000; Nisbett, Peng, Choi, & Norenzayan, 2001; Markus & Kitayama, 1991; Norenzayan & Nisbett, 2000).

Communication

Language is perhaps the most visible aspect of culture and, too often, lack of language skill is blamed for poor functioning of multicultural teams when, in actuality, it is culturally based communication style that is contributing to poor teamwork.

Cultures vary in the importance of context for communication. For example, in High-Context cultures, which are typically Collectivist and oriented toward tradition and the past, the majority of information is to be found implicit in the message context. This means that gestures and words have little meaning outside of the context in which the message was delivered. Team members with a High-Context orientation tend to have extensive information networks. Relationships with individuals in their networks are close and personal. In Low-Context cultures, which are typically Individualist and Present- or Future-oriented, the meaning of messages is clearly and explicitly spelled out in the delivered message. This means team members with this orientation rely on a narrow range of detailed, objective information, presented to them in unambiguous physical (e.g., gesture) or verbal form, to derive meaning from communication. They do not allow extraneous information (e.g., age or status of the speaker) to influence the meaning of spoken words. Their own communiqués with teammates could be either very wordy, as they carry a lot of information or are very precise, where every word is important and carries a specific meaning. This is in contrast to individuals who have a High-Context orientation who tend to consistently deliver wordy messages since words themselves have little value. Team members with a Low-Context orientation tend to compartmentalize various aspects of their lives and may be perceived by those with a High-Context orientation as insensitive.

Public and Private Space

Culturally based orientation to space can be defined as Specific or Diffuse (Trompanaars & Hampdon-Turner, 1997). Cultures in which individuals have a large public space they readily share with others and a small private space they guard closely and share with only close friends and associates are defined as having a Specific space orientation. Individuals with this orientation will limit relationships with team members strictly to that of the business at hand. They also have the ability to compartmentalize roles. In other words, their role in their personal life does not necessarily reflect their role in their professional life. Cultures in which both public and private space are similar in size have a Diffuse space orientation. They tend to guard their public space carefully, because entry into public space also affords entry into private space. Individuals with this orientation mix personal and professional roles and assume that team activities should engage the whole person, including hobbies, family, and interests.

Miscellaneous

Masculinity–Femininity Gender Role Orientation

Gender role orientation reflects the tendency of a culture to value stereotypical masculine or feminine traits (Hofstede, 1980). Snodgrass (1990) investigated the persistence of these stereotypes and found that the content had not changed since 1980. Examples of enduring stereotypical masculine traits were found to be "aggressive," "independent," "never gives up," and "stands up under pressure." Examples of enduring stereotypical feminine traits were found to be "helpful" and "aware of others' feelings." Furthermore, Snodgrass found that masculinity represented task and power-orientation (e.g., successful, good leader, respected), while femininity represented social-orientation (e.g., cooperative, friendly, submissive). In Masculine-oriented cultures, the dominant values in society are success, money, and things. There is a strong emphasis on earning and recognition, which may result in high personal stress. In Feminine-oriented cultures, the dominant values in society are caring for others and the quality of life. The emphasis is on security and personal freedom. Team members, who may or may not be male, with a Masculine gender role orientation tend to be competitive. Team members, who may or may not be female, with a Feminine gender role orientation tend to respond to others with interpersonal sensitivity.

Activity Orientation

Activity Orientation highlights the relationships between people and their preferred mode of activity (Kluckhohn & Strodtbeck, 1961). This cultural dimension was also found to significantly impact teamwork at a multinational military headquarters operation and will be discussed in more detail later in this chapter. The terms "doing," "thinking," and "being" define states associated with one's orientation to activity. Individuals with a Doing orientation are focused on achievement and define activity as striving; something that requires effort and energy. They evaluate activity based on techniques and procedures. They see work as an end in itself, separate from play. Work is thought to be challenging and a means of problem solving. These individuals are often perceived to be compulsive. On the other hand, Thinking-oriented individuals take a rational, developmental approach to activity. At the opposite end of the Activity Orientation continuum, are individuals with a Being orientation who define activity as fatalistic, something preordained over which they have little control. Being-oriented team members evaluate activity in terms of goals and ideals and see work as a means to an end. Work is often perceived to be burdensome and, therefore, integrated with play. These individuals tend to be easygoing.

The impact of Activity Orientation on teamwork is considerable (Manzevski & Peterson, 1997). A Doing orientation can positively impact team performance, as individuals with that orientation are the first to notice discrepancies between what is actually taking place compared to what was planned to take place. Sometimes, even the slightest deviation from the plan could be disastrous. Doing-oriented individuals can help the team set goals and see that those goals are achieved. Thinking-oriented individuals benefit team process by carefully thinking through plans. They are most likely to discover facts indicating the need to reconsider a plan of action. Their strength lies in the ability to look at a problem, solution, or plan from several viewpoints and provide the rationale behind an issue. However, because it takes time to think things through carefully, they may be slower to provide their input than the team requires in order to be effective. A strength that Being-oriented individuals bring to the team is awareness of their own and their teammates' feelings. This awareness allows them to recognize discord among team members before it is obvious to the rest of the team. They can then take steps to diffuse building tension before it negatively impacts team performance.

FRAMEWORK FOR UNDERSTANDING CULTURAL DIVERSITY IN TEAMWORK

The list of cultural variables that can potentially impact multicultural teamwork is extensive. But does culture affect all teams the same way? Based on the taxonomy of four team functions (information exchange, coordination, assigning roles and responsibilities, and support behaviors such as error checking; Table 1), we would answer in the affirmative. While it is understood that within each function team tasks will vary (McGrath, 1984), these four functions are proposed to be the fundamental aspects of performance that are consistent across all teams, multinational or not. To further examine this hypothesis, ARL HRED researchers initiated a program of multicultural research in 2000.

The initial focus of the research program was on U.S. forces transitioning from war fighting to peacekeeping operations where a lack of skill in multinational teamwork was specifically identified as a weakness (for a more detailed review see Klein & Pierce, 2001; Pierce, 2002; Pierce & Pomranky, 2001). Eventually, the program was expanded to investigate the impact of culture on teamwork in a multinational military peacekeeping operation, the Stabilization Force Headquarters (HQ SFOR), Camp Butmir, Sarajevo, Bosnia-Herzegovina (BiH). HQ SFOR was charged with conducting military peacekeeping operations to provide a safe and secure environment to allow the local government and international community to enforce the Dayton Peace Accords. In this headquarters, officers from more than 30 nations worked together to manage the peacekeeping mission. The operation was clearly multinational and provided an excellent test bed for studying multicultural teams.

Using subject matter experts (Brown, 2002), focus groups, and scenario-based structured interviews, ARL HRED researchers found that learning how to work within a multinational military headquarters as a member of a multicultural team often occurred on-the-job and that the rate at which learning occurred influenced the ability of the team to operate (for more details see Sutton & Pierce, 2003). They also found that three cultural dimensions, in particular, hindered or contributed to effective multicultural teamwork at HQ SFOR as defined by team members themselves. Those dimensions were Power Distance, Uncertainty Avoidance, and Activity Orientation. It is the relationships between these three dimensions and the four team performance functions that appeared to explain culturally based behaviors affecting teamwork. Understanding these relationships is key to facilitating cultural adaptability.

Fig. 1 shows a 3 (Cultural Dimension) $\times$ 4 (Team Function) matrix developed by ARL HRED researchers as a model of behavioral components of culturally based biases as they pertain to fundamental team performance functions (Sutton & Pierce, 2003). This framework was designed to guide the study of multicultural team performance as well as to facilitate development of methods and tools for rapid team development and adaptive performance. A review of the components of the model follows.

It is not realistic to identify every conceivable point on a theoretical continuum that is reflective of all possible behaviors associated with a given dimension. Therefore, for discussion's sake, the framework presents theoretical endpoints of the dimensions identified as having the most impact on teamwork at HQ SFOR. The behavioral range endpoints for Power Distance are labeled Hierarchical for high Power Distance behaviors and Egalitarian for low Power Distance behaviors. The endpoints for the Uncertainty Avoidance continuum are labeled High Need for Certainty for

National Cultural Dimension	Range	Situation Assessment	Coordination	Assigning Roles & Responsibilities	Support Behavior
Power Distance	Hierarchical	Vertical	Centralized	Rank	Leader
	Egalitarian	Horizontal	Decentralized	Expertise	Team
Uncertainty Avoidance	High need for Certainty	Detailed Info	Well defined	Highly Specialized	Formal
	Low need for Certainty	Ambiguous Info	Ad hoc	Multi-functional	Informal
Activity Orientation	Independent	Direct Comms	Doing	Skills & Abilities	Task
	Interdependent	Indirect Comms	Being	Connection	Relationship

(Table title: Framework for Understanding Cultural Diversity in Teamwork; column group: Team Performance Functions)

Fig. 1. Framework for Understanding Cultural Diversity in Cognition and Teamwork.

high Uncertainty Avoidance behaviors and Low Need for Certainty for low Uncertainty Avoidance behaviors. The endpoints of the Activity Orientation continuum are labeled Independent and Interdependent, indicating the extent to which independence from team members or interdependence with team members is emphasized. There are 24 cells in the matrix that represent the intersection of a specific dimension and a specific team function (e.g., high Power Distance and Situation Assessment). Each of these cells contains one word (e.g., vertical) or phrase descriptive of a critical behavior that can either help or hinder multicultural teamwork.

Power Distance

The word "vertical" in Fig. 1 represents an individual's preference for vertical communication channels and vertical information flow when participating in a situation assessment activity. "Vertical" is a descriptor of behavior typically demonstrated by an individual whose behavioral tendencies are consistent with values associated with the high end of the Power Distance continuum (i.e., Hierarchical relationship pattern). The following statement made by a military officer at HQ SFOR provides an example of high Power Distance orientation and its potential impact on situation assessment: "As team leader, I think it is important for information to flow through me, or my second, to the team. A single point of contact leads to efficiency and accuracy of information distributed." From this perspective, information exchange is constrained by rank, perceived status, even nationality. At the other end of the Power Distance continuum, the word "horizontal" in Fig. 1 at the intersection of low Power Distance and situation assessment represents behavior typical of individuals with an Egalitarian relationship pattern. A statement reflective of low Power Distance for a team leader talking about situation assessment might be, "I don't have a problem with team members sharing information before I see it, as long as they keep me informed." From this perspective, information exchange on multicultural military teams is unconstrained by rank, perceived status on the team, or nationality. Table 3 contains statements made by officers at HQ SFOR to ARL HRED researchers that are clearly indicative of their relationship pattern preference.

With regard to Power Distance and coordination activities, individuals with a Hierarchical relationship pattern prefer "centralized" decision

Table 3. Statements by HQ SFOR Staff that are Reflective of Power Distance Orientation.

Hierarchical relationship pattern

- "I would have a clear idea of what I wanted to achieve before I presented a plan to the team. If we gain experience as we go along, then we'll make changes. But I certainly wouldn't leave it open to discussion at the beginning, because that would lead to questioning my leadership."
- "I would assume that the Chief of Staff would give me some guidance as to what he wants his program to consist of, but I don't think I would just have these guys come up with a plan. I would supply them with that."
- "It is essential that it [information flow] is centralized to me, and then, once a week, I can share the information with the team."
- "I am the Chief of the branch. How many times can I ask a subordinate for help?"

Egalitarian relationship pattern

- "As team leader, I don't have to make all the decisions."
- "At the first meeting, I would get a feel for what their [team members'] experiences are. I wouldn't actually assign them tasks to the different areas until I know a little bit more about them. But then once I have that information, they will be assigned tasks based on their knowledge and experience. I wouldn't be looking at rank, because Corporals, Sergeants, Majors, Colonels, and even the General bring different perspectives."
- "I would provide some guidelines, not very strict, to give them freedom to work in their own way of thinking, because that's why I probably choose them. I would choose people from five very different cultures, because there would be five different ways to solve the problem. I would give the main guidelines, but I would give them the freedom to solve the issue however they want to do it."
- "I have confidence in my team to bring the new Commander up to speed."

making (see Fig. 1). Team members expect the leader to be autocratic and controlling and they expect the leader to initiate most coordination activity. These individuals, when in a leadership position, tend to give detailed instruction. Individuals with an Egalitarian orientation toward coordination are comfortable with "decentralized" decision making and appreciate leaders who give intent-based guidelines rather than detailed instruction. While leaders are expected to be resourceful and democratic, they are not expected to take all coordination initiatives.

When assigning roles and responsibilities, rank and perceived status are more important to those with a Hierarchical relationship pattern than those with an Egalitarian relationship pattern as indicated by the term "rank" at the intersection of high Power Distance and assigning of roles and responsibilities in Fig. 1. These individuals expect roles to be assigned by rank or status. Subordinates expect to be told what to do and leaders expect obedience. Subordinates show respect for rank and position with little regard for level of expertise held by team leaders. The term "expertise" defines thoughts and behaviors associated with an Egalitarian relationship pattern in the assignment of roles and responsibilities. Roles are assigned based on the expertise of the individuals under consideration regardless of rank, status in the group, or nationality. Subordinates expect to be consulted on who should be assigned what responsibility and why. Leaders and subordinates with an Egalitarian relationship pattern believe everyone on the team to be equals, on a personal level.

As shown in Fig. 1 for support behavior, individuals with a Hierarchical relationship pattern believe it is the responsibility of the team's "leader" to monitor progress toward the team's goal and to correct errors found as a result of that monitoring. Individuals with an Egalitarian relationship pattern think it is the responsibility of "team" members, not the team leader, to monitor team performance and perform error-checking activities.

Uncertainty Avoidance

There are significantly different behaviors associated with the relationship between Uncertainty Avoidance and team performance functions than those associated with the relationship between Power Distance and team performance functions. Examples of behaviors associated with the construct of Uncertainty Avoidance can be seen in comments made to ARL HRED researchers by HQ SFOR staff presented in Table 4.

Table 4. Statements by HQ SFOR staff that are reflective of Uncertainty Avoidance Orientation.

High need for certainty

- "I'd like to see a meeting on Mondays, Wednesdays, and Fridays. On Mondays, we'd outline some goals and some tasks that should be accomplished during the week. On Wednesdays, we could do a review and find out if there's a problem that just wasn't working or tasks that were not able to be accomplished, for whatever reason. Then on Fridays, we'd do an end of the week wrap up of what was accomplished that week."
- "I would have the team come together for the morning meeting, then go back to their normal places of work to work on this project. They would then come together for formal meetings to discuss specific issues."
- "I would want a good amount of detail in project status reports. I'd definitely want a thorough understanding of what they're [team members] working on and where the team product is headed."
- "The most important thing to know is procedures."

Low need for certainty

- "If we didn't have a square peg to sit in a square hole, which I think would probably be the case, then we'd have to have a few circular ones and be partly multi-functional in certain areas."
- "I think to begin with everybody would kind of just contribute in a general way. Then once we saw what the problems were, we could decide what we wanted to work on. You know, break it down from there."
- "[We would meet] the least number of times necessary for the work environment and the most numbers of times appropriate in such an environment. There is a natural tendency in many cultures to 'over meet.' But my belief is that if you are working on a small team, you should meet very infrequently, in fact, only as often as you absolutely need to."
- "I'm an informal type of person. For project updates, just throw some papers on the table and that's just fine by me."

The phrases "Detailed Info" and "Ambiguous Info" in Fig. 1 capture the essence of a group of behaviors associated with the degree to which one needs certainty, either high Need for Certainty or low Need for Certainty, respectively, and the process of assessing a situation. When the team function is sharing information among team members on resources and constraints, tasks and goals, and priorities, individuals with a high Need for Certainty prefer to give and receive detailed information and tend to focus on transmitting and acquiring a great deal of information, whereas individuals with a low Need for Certainty are comfortable with general information and may actually experience frustration if they perceive too much time is being spent on details. Accuracy of information sent or received is of paramount importance to individuals with a high Need for Certainty, who will check, double-check, and triple-check a particular piece of information before using that information in decision making. Contrary to those with a high Need for Certainty, individuals with a low Need for Certainty find it easier to make decisions, when necessary when information is unclear, unverifiable, or incomplete. Specifically, individuals with a low Need for Certainty will be more comfortable than those with a high Need for Certainty utilizing ambiguous information. Further, when assessing a situation, individuals with a high Need for Certainty tend to be intolerant of ideas that deviate from the norm and are resistant to changing established ways of problem solving. They prefer a regulated process for information acquisition and information reporting. Individuals with a low Need for Certainty are more tolerant of novel and innovative ideas and, rather than being constrained by a regulated process of information exchange, appreciate free-flowing acquisition and reporting of information. A final comment on behavioral tendencies associated with Uncertainty Avoidance and situation assessment is that individuals with a high Need for Certainty tend to focus on planning what actions to take, whereas individuals with a low Need for Certainty tend to be more focused on the execution of plans that were developed during situation assessment.

The terms "Well-defined" and "Ad-hoc" in Fig. 1 are descriptive of behavioral manifestations of high and low Need for Certainty that are associated with team coordination activities. "Well-defined," the high Need for Certainty descriptor, refers to a preference for pre-determined coordination processes and structured interactions. The term connotes risk-aversion. The team function of coordination involves activity sequencing, response sequencing, and time and position coordination. During the coordination process, individuals with a low Need for Certainty are more willing to take risks than individuals with a high Need for Certainty. Another aspect of high Need for Certainty in coordination activity that reflects the degree to which individuals are comfortable with risk is the perception of time. When coordinating activities, individuals with a high Need for Certainty tend to focus on the time available to complete a task rather than the amount of time it would actually take to complete the task. For example, given 30 days to complete a task, team members with a high Need for Certainty will create a plan that takes 30 days to complete. Individuals with a low Need for Certainty take a different approach. Given 30 days to complete a task, team members with a low Need for Certainty will determine how much time it should take to complete the task (e.g., 10 days) and plan to complete the task within that time frame. In the case of low Need for Certainty, *ad hoc* coordination is the preferred working style. Further, individuals with a low Need for Certainty prefer unstructured interactions with others while individuals with a high Need for Certainty seek out a more structured format for interaction with others.

The cultural dimension of Uncertainty Avoidance also affects the assignment of roles and responsibilities on teams. Individuals with a high Need for Certainty are more comfortable when team member roles are clearly differentiated as indicated by the term "Highly Specialized" in the cell representing the intersection of high Need for Certainty and assigning roles and responsibilities (see Fig. 1). Individuals with a high Need for Certainty thrive on structure, rules, and regulations governing the interaction of team members in the completion of their individual tasks. The term "Multi-functional" is a descriptor for behavior of individuals with a low Need for Certainty in the assignment of roles and responsibilities. The term implies that individuals with a low Need for Certainty prefer overlapping roles with other team members and are comfortable with a lack of structure regarding responsibilities of each team member.

The terms "Formal" and "Informal" in Fig. 1 represent high and low Need for Certainty, respectively, as those culturally based biases relate to team support behavior. For example, when providing status updates of the team's progress toward the goal, individuals with a high Need for Certainty tend to require detailed progress reviews when in a leadership position, or deliver detailed progress reviews when in a subordinate position. The review process itself is more likely to use a formal format when initiated by individuals with a high Need for Certainty, whereas a general progress review presented in an informal format is preferred by individuals with a low Need for Certainty.

Activity Orientation is the third culturally based dimension found to significantly impact multicultural teamwork at HQ SFOR. The terms "Independent" and Interdependent" indicate endpoints on a theoretical continuum of behaviors associated with Activity Orientation and are intended to be similar in meaning to the terms "Individualism" and "Collectivism."

At the intersection of Activity Orientation and situation assessment in Fig. 1 are the phrases "Direct Comms," and "Indirect Comms," which indicate a direct or indirect communication style, respectively. When meeting with team members either formally or informally, individuals oriented toward Independence will tend to use a direct, low-context communication style, whereas individuals oriented to Interdependence will tend to use an indirect, high-context communication style. Those with a direct communication style believe that speaking one's mind indicates honesty and is, therefore, the best way to interact when assessing a situation with team members. Questioning the logic of others' thoughts is acceptable behavior for individuals with an Independent Activity Orientation but viewed as confrontational by individuals with an Interdependent Activity Orientation, but interdependency implies that harmony should be maintained and conflict avoided, even during situation assessment.

With regard to team assignment of roles and responsibilities, the terms "Doing" and "Being" in Fig. 1 reflect significant differences in Activity Orientation. A Doing orientation supports the idea that who someone *is* determines which role that person will play on the team. It is the belief that assignment of responsibilities should be based on specific skill sets or even a set of pre-determined rules for task assignment. A Being orientation supports the idea that who someone *knows* determines which role that person will play on the team. For individuals with a Being orientation, assignment of responsibilities reflect a person's relationship to the group and, possibly, a person's connections outside the group.

With regard to coordination activities, individuals with an Independent orientation believe that dependence should be on individuals. This idea is captured in the words "Skills and Abilities" which marks the intersection of Independent Activity Orientation and coordination in Fig. 1. From an Independent perspective, management of the team should involve management of each individual on the team separately, as each individual has a unique set of skills and abilities. Individuals with an Interdependent orientation are more likely to rely on the team as a unit to take responsibility for coordination activities. This perspective is captured with the word "Connections" at the intersection of Interdependent Activity Orientation and coordination. With an Independent orientation, management of coordination activity is, therefore, best achieved by managing the team as a whole unit and not managing team members on an individual basis.

"Task" and "Relationship" are terms shown in Fig. 1 to indicate an Independent and Interdependent Activity Orientation, respectively, to team support behavior. Support behavior can be defined as assisting team members in monitoring and correcting errors and providing backup to other members. Individuals with an Independent orientation are independent in thought and action and tend to emphasize task over relationship when working with others. On the contrary, individuals with an Interdependent orientation tend to restrain actions that might violate the norm for social behavior on the team and, therefore, upset others when monitoring team progress toward the goal. In other words, relationships prevails over task when performing the support function for individuals with an Interdependent orientation Table 5.

Table 5. Statements by HQ SFOR Staff that are Reflective of an Orientation Toward Activity Orientation.

Independent

- "Well, I hate to be a dictator, but the truth of the matter is that decisions by committee are generally not the best decisions. Of course, you can't ignore recommendations, especially by the so-called experts in their field, unless there would be some overriding factor that would make me veto the recommendation."
- "Competition is a good thing. My work stands by itself. I'm not really concerned about how other people are completing their tasks."

Interdependent

- "I want everyone to have their say in the meeting on how things are done, as long as it does not cause conflict."
- "I would look for consensus in a team as well, because it's a team effort and we're bringing it to everyone for consideration."
- "It's not a question of teaching. It is a way of thinking. We can't do our mission if we don't know each other."

DISCUSSION

As we begin to define what constitutes adaptable behavior on multicultural teams, we must look closely at barriers and enablers of cultural adaptability. As presented in this chapter, both can be attributed to differences in manifested behaviors rooted in culture. Bowman (2002) provided several examples: (1a) When considering the implications of Power Distance on multicultural teamwork, it is possible that team members will not be used to exploit their best skills, resulting in miscommunication, lack of coordination, and loss of situation awareness if a team leader has a Hierarchical relationship pattern rather than an Egalitarian relationship pattern. (1b) If team members have a Hierarchical relationship pattern, they might not share information that could alter a decision, believing that it is the leader's responsibility to discover the information and make the decisions. (2a) With regard to the dimension of Uncertainty Avoidance, if a team leader has a high Need for Certainty, the task may become so detailed and structured that it obviates the purpose of team action. (2b) If team members have a high Need for Certainty, they might ask for so much guidance and information that they no longer provide unique contributions to the task at hand. (3a) If a team leader has an Independent rather than Interdependent Activity Orientation, contributions of team members may be disregarded if those contributions do not obviously contribute to the task at hand. Information and opportunities for shared situation awareness may be lost. (3b) If team members have an Independent rather than Interdependent orientation, they may move from task to task without developing a team culture or team situation awareness. Given these possible scenarios, one hypothesis could be that it is more difficult for individuals with a Hierarchical relationship pattern, a high Need for Certainty, and an Independent Activity Orientation, to achieve the requisite cultural competencies needed for adaptable performance on multicultural teams (i.e., cultural adaptability).

It is conceivable that there is an interaction between two or among all three dimensions. Perhaps cultural adaptability varies by team function. For example, it might be that an Egalitarian relationship pattern and low Need for Certainty is the best profile for achieving comprehensive situation awareness where team members represent multiple cultures, yet a Hierarchical relationship pattern and a high Need for Certainty is the best profile for coordination activities. Further research is needed to expand the body of knowledge in the domain of cultural adaptability. Research questions might include: Is there a particular behavioral profile that is more adaptive regardless of the situation? Is there an interaction between culturally based dimensions that reflects cultural adaptability to a greater extent than others? Which relationship pattern, Hierarchical or Egalitarian, is most indicative of cultural competence?

Adaptable leaders and teams appreciate diverse beliefs, values, behaviors, and practices and are able to map their team strategies in light of this appreciation. The implications of culture for teamwork are profound. Multicultural teams must be able to rapidly form into cohesive, high performing units despite differences, and in light of behavioral similarities. Leadership approaches are also affected by cultural diversity, for example, centralized vs. decentralized decision making, safety vs. risk, individual vs. group rewards, short-term vs. long-term horizons, stability vs. innovation, cooperation vs. competition, high vs. low team loyalty, and informal vs. formal procedures. Collaboration on multicultural teams places a premium on cultural competence and adaptable teamwork.

There are many permutations to the cultural dimensions and team functions presented in this chapter that could provide rich fodder for research. We propose that the framework for understanding cultural diversity in teamwork (Fig. 1) be used as the basis for social and cognitive scientists to investigate the impact of culture on teamwork for the purpose of contributing empirical data sorely needed in the culture and team literature. We understand that framework design is an evolving process and encourage research that improves on the basic design. Changes to the model that are based on solid data can only help to expand the construct of cultural adaptability.

REFERENCES

Adler, N. J. (1986). *International dimensions of organizational behavior*. Belmont, CA: Wadsworth.

Bagby, J. W. (1970). Dominance in binocular rivalry in Mexico and the United States. In: I. Al-Issan & W. Dennis (Eds), *Cross cultural studies of behavior* (pp. 49–56). New York: Holt, Rinehart, & Winston.

Beamer, L. (2000). Finding a way to teach cultural dimensions. *Business Communication Quarterly*, *63*(3), 111.

Berube, M. S., et al. (1999). *Webster's II new college dictionary, 1995*. New York: Houghton Mifflin Company.

Bogan, J. E., De Zure, R., TenHouten, W. D., & Marsh, J. F. (1972). The other side of the brain, IV: The A/P ratio. *Bulletin of Neurological Science*, *37*, 49–61.

Bowman, E. K. (2002). *Cultural factors affecting MNT communications in the SFOR environment*. Unpublished manuscript.

Brown, F. J. (2002). Imperatives for tomorrow. *Military Review*, *82*(5), 81–91.

Choi, I., & Nisbett, R. E. (2000). Cultural psychology of surprise: Holistic theories and recognition of contradiction. *Journal of Personality and Social Psychology*, *79*(6), 890–905.

Fleishman, E. A., & Quaintance, M. K. (1984). *Taxonomies of human performance*. Orlando, FL: Academic Press.

Fleishman, E. A., & Zacarro, S. J. (1992). Toward a taxonomy of team performance functions. In: R. W. Swezey & E. Salas (Eds), *Teams: Their training and performance*. Orlando, FL: Academic Press.

Hall, E. T., & Hall, M. R. (1990). *Understanding cultural differences*. Garden City, NY: Intercultural Press.

Heuser, B. (2000). Beliefs, culture, proliferation and use of nuclear weapons. *Journal of Strategic Studies*, *23*(1), 74–100.

Hofstede, G. (1980). *Culture's consequences: International differences in work-related values*. Thousand Oaks, CA: Sage.

Javidan, M., & House, R. J. (2001). Cultural acumen for the global manager: Less from project GLOBE. *Organizational Dynamics*, *29*(4), 289–305.

Kaplan, M. F. (1989). Task, situational, and personal determinants of influence processes in group decision making. In: E. J. Lawler (Ed.), *Advances in group processes* (Vol. 6). Greenwich, CT: JAI Press.

Klein, G., & Pierce, L. G. (2001). Adaptive teams. *Proceedings of the sixth international command and control research and technology symposium*, http://www.dodccrp.org/6thICCRTS/Pres/track_4.htm

Kluckhohn, F., & Strodtbeck, F. L. (1961). *Variations in value orientation*. Evanston, IL: Row, Peterson.

Korzenny, B. A. G. (1984). Intercultural communication training for adult educators. *Lifelong Learning Adult Years*, *7*(4), 7–9, 27.

Krulak, C. C. (1997). The three block war: Fighting in urban areas. Presented at National Press Club, Washington, DC, 10 October 1997, *Vital speeches of the day*, 15 December, p. 139.

Manzevski, M., & Peterson, M. F. (1997). Societal values, social interpretation, and multinational teams. In: C. C. Granrose & S. Oskamp (Eds), *Cross-cultural work groups* (pp. 61–89). Thousand Oaks, CA: Sage.

Markus, H., & Kitayama, S. (1991). Culture and the self: Implications for cognition, emotion, and motivation. *Psychological Review*, *98*, 224–253.

Maruyama, M. (1994). *Mindscapes in management: Use of individual differences in multicultural management*. Aldershot, England: Dartmouth Publishing Company.

McGlynn, R. P., Sutton, J. L., Sprague, B. L., Demski, R. M., & Pierce, L. G. (1997). *Development of a team performance task battery to evaluate performance of the command and control vehicle (C2V) crew*. Aberdeen Proving Ground, MD: US Army Research Laboratory. (Contract No. DAAL01-96-P-0875).

McGrath, J. E. (1984). *Groups: Interactions and performance*. Englewood Cliffs, NJ: Prentice-Hall.

Morris, C. W. (1942). *Paths of life: Preface to a world religion*. New York: Harper and Brothers.

Morris, C. W. (1948). *The open self*. New York: Prentice-Hall.

Morris, C. W. (1956). *Varieties in human value*. Chicago: University of Chicago Press (Reprinted, 1973).

Nisbett, R. E., Peng, K., Choi, I., & Norenzayan, A. (2001). Culture and systems of thought: Holistic versus analytic cognition. *Psychological Review*, *108*(2), 291–310.

Norenzayan, A., & Nisbet, R. (2000). Culture and causal cognition. *Current Directions in Psychological Science*, *9*(4), 132–135.

Parsons, T., & Shils, E. (1951). *Toward a general theory of social action*. Cambridge, MA: Harvard University Press.

Pierce, L. G. (2002). Barriers to adaptability in a multinational team. *Proceedings of the human factors and ergonomics society 46th annual meeting* (pp. 225–229).

Pierce, L. G., & Pomranky, R. (2001). The Chameleon Project for adaptable commanders and teams. *Proceedings of the human factors and ergonomics society 45th annual meeting* (pp. 513–517).

Salas, E., Burke, C. S., Fowlkes, J. E., & Wilson, K. A. (2004). Challenges and approaches to understanding leadership efficacy in multi-cultural teams. In: M. Kaplan (Ed.), *Advances in human performance and cognitive engineering research* (Vol. 4, pp. 341–384). Oxford, UK: Elsevier.

Salas, E., Dickinson, T. L., Converse, S. A., & Tannenbaum, S. I. (1992). Toward an understanding of team performance and training. In: R. J. Swezey & E. Salas (Eds), *Teams: Their training and performance* (pp. 3–29). Norwood, NJ: Ablex.

Snodgrass, S. E. (1990). Sex role stereotypes are alive and well. Paper presented at the American Psychological Association annual meeting, Boston, MA.

Sutton, J. L., & Pierce, L. G. (2003). A framework for understanding cultural diversity in cognition and teamwork. *Proceedings of the 8th international command and control research and technology symposium*, www.dodccrp.org/8thICCRTS/Pres/track_1.htm.

Schwartz, S. J. (1999). A theory of cultural values and some implications for work. *Applied Psychology: An International Review*, *48*(1), 23–37.

Triandis, H. C. (1989). The self and social behavior in differing cultural contexts. *Psychological Review*, *96*, 506–520.

Trompanaars, F., & Hampdon-Turner, C. (1997). *Riding the wave of culture: Understanding diversity in global business* (2nd ed.). London: Nicholas Brealey.

Witkin, H. A., & Berry, J. W. (1975). Psychological differentiation in cross-cultural perspective. *Journal of Cross-Cultural Psychology*, *6*(1), 4–87.

BUILDING THE ADAPTIVE CAPACITY TO LEAD MULTI-CULTURAL TEAMS

C. Shawn Burke, Kathleen P. Hess and Eduardo Salas

A U.S. Lieutenant is assigned to be the leader of the embedded training team responsible for training Iraqi security forces. Within this role, the U.S. LT (Murphy) serves as an advisor to the Iraqi LT (Abdul) responsible for training the security forces. While observing training exercises, LT Murphy notices that the Iraqi troops have lost enthusiasm for the training and in some cases are not paying attention. This is especially true when the Iraqi non-commissioned officer in charge (SGT Karzi) is present. LT Murphy decides that the situation must be remedied before training can continue. LT Murphy uses his translator to advise LT Abdul to question the SGT and, if that does not work, to pose the question back to the training force all at once to save time. LT Abdul agrees to the advisement and proceeds to question SGT Karzi, from whom he learns nothing, and then moves on to question the training force. After this discussion, even more problems seem to arise. The resentment and resistance the Iraqi troops display seems to increase. Their opinion of SGT Karzi has decreased even further and they are beginning to resent LT Abdul. This situation is not acceptable as the training of an Iraqi security force is a key element of the U.S. exit strategy from Iraq. What happened in this situation; LT Murphy has used this strategy numerous times within U.S. forces with success?

Understanding Adaptability: A Prerequisite for Effective Performance within Complex Environments
Advances in Human Performance and Cognitive Engineering Research, Volume 6, 175–211

ISSN: 1479-3601/doi:10.1016/S1479-3601(05)06006-6

The example above illustrates that leadership within multi-cultural teams can be tricky. While it was but a short time ago that researchers and practitioners believed that teams and leadership were nearly mutually exclusive, progress is beginning to be made in this area with leaders being likened to the rudder which provides direction for a ship (Rawles, 1996; Zaccaro, Rittman, & Marks, 2001). Much has been learned about leadership within teams over the last decade, but what remains elusive is how to best prepare leaders for operating within multi-cultural contexts, specifically multi-cultural teams. While there are many questions that remain unanswered one thing is all too clear – leadership within multi-cultural teams is far more complex than that within culturally homogeneous teams. Team leaders of the 21st century and beyond, whether military or civilian, need to possess the adaptive capacity to lead along a continuum of cultural diversity. At present this capacity is not being effectively endowed upon team leaders prior to being placed 'in the fire.' This is evidenced by high expatriate return rates and observations and interviews with U.S. military forces returning from deployment overseas (Pierce, 2002; Pierce & Pomranky, 2001; Tomasovic, 2001).

Therefore, the purpose of this chapter is to examine components of adaptive capacity with respect to leading multi-cultural teams and one possible manner in which it can be fostered. In doing so, the literature on leadership and culture will first be reviewed to identify challenges. Second, the literature on creation of a 'third culture' will be briefly examined as one mechanism by which the team leader can create an enabling performance environment. Finally, a web-based training tool that was created to facilitate a leader's adaptive capacity with respect to multi-cultural team leadership will be reviewed.

ADAPTIVE CAPACITY

Adaptive capacity has commonly been defined as the "general ability of institutions, systems, and individuals to adjust to potential damage, to take advantage of opportunities, or to cope with the consequences" (http://www.greenfacts.org). Adaptive capacity is herein described as the ability to facilitate the process of adaptive team performance and the resulting outcome of team adaptation (see Stagl, Burke, Salas, & Pierce, this volume). More specifically, although often spoken of with regard to environmental and global changes, it is spoken of here with regard to the ability of individuals (and correspondingly teams) to recognize and understand contextual changes, dynamically revise and implement plans accordingly, and learn from each implementation so as to be better prepared in the future.

It should be of no surprise given the breadth, complexity, and dynamism of operating environments within public, private, and military organizations that the need for adaptive capacity within leaders as well as the teams they lead is on the rise. Here the focus is on promoting the adaptive capacity of the team leader such that they are able to properly develop, maintain, and recover team coherence (Kozlowski, Gully, McHugh, Salas, & Cannon–Bowers, 1996a) and the resulting common ground needed to collaboratively coordinate team member action within multi-cultural teams. However, prior to examining the leadership of multi-cultural teams, we must first examine what it is that leader's do in general to facilitate team effectiveness. This information will be used to determine the need for adaptive capacity and how things may change within multi-cultural teams.

WHAT FUNCTIONS DO TEAM LEADERS COMPLETE FOR TEAMS?

Within the last 10 years, many have begun to argue that team leaders play a key role in promoting, developing, and maintaining team effectiveness (Entin, Serfarty, & Deckert, 1994; Kozlowski, Gully, Salas, & Cannon-Bowers, 1996b). Yet most conceptualizations of leadership focus solely on individual-based leadership as opposed to team-based leadership. Kozlowski (2002) argues that team leadership dynamically varies with the situation and acknowledges the tight interdependencies and subsequent coordination requirements among team members. Within team leadership there is a focus on structuring and regulating team processes to meet shifting internal and external contingencies as opposed to fitting the leader to the situation, task or subordinates as within traditional individual-based leadership theories.

Researchers who are beginning to investigate team leadership and what it is that team leaders do primarily leverage against the functional approach to leadership. McGrath (1962) describes the key assertion within this approach to be, "that [the leader's] main job is to do, or get done, whatever is not being adequately handled for group needs" (p. 5, as cited in Hackman & Walton, 1986). Within this approach the leader is effective to the degree to which he/she ensures that all functions critical to task and team maintenance are completed, either through personal action or via the action of other team members. Five conditions have been argued to increase the likelihood that teams will be effective. Specifically, Hackman (2002) argued that teams must be a real team, have compelling direction, an enabling structure, a supportive organizational context, and expert coaching. The first three of these conditions (i.e., real team, compelling direction, enabling structure) have been argued to be core conditions while the later two (i.e., supportive context, expert coaching) are additional enablers.

A real team is one in which there is a team task, clear boundaries, specified authority to manage work processes, and some degree of membership stability (Hackman, 2002). The team leader may or may not have the ability to control this first condition as in some cases the form, design, and nature of the work is dictated by the organization with little input from the team leader; thereby it will not be a key focus here. In order for the second condition, compelling direction, to exist direction must be seen as challenging, clear, and consequential (Hackman, 2002). It should provide members with a sense of what is expected and why it is important in relation to the team's common goal. While specifying an end, the direction should not specify detailed means on how to achieve the end. Direction given according to the above guidance should serve to motivate team members, align strategy, and promote the full use of the team's capabilities. However, the exact nature of what each team member will consider compelling will depend, in part, on the member's personal interests, values, and aspirations.

Compelling direction may also assist in the promotion of the third core condition, an enabling structure, by promoting norms that allow teams to capitalize on potential synergy that exists within the team. Norms that promote real time adjustment of strategy, environmental scanning, and team self-correction can promote an enabling structure. Work design (e.g., autonomy, task significance) and team composition factors (e.g., size, heterogeneity) also determine the degree to which this core condition exists.

Finally, the leader can facilitate the final two enabling conditions for effective teams (i.e., a supportive organizational context, provision of expert coaching). While both are important here the provision of expert coaching is elaborated upon as it is felt that the team leader can have an impact on this condition no matter the level at which the leader resides. Hackman and Wageman (2005) argue that, dependent on the team's developmental stage, the leader can intervene with one of the three types of coaching (motivational, consultative, educational). Similarly, others have argued that across the course of team development, leaders progress from mentor to instructor, to coach, and finally to the facilitator. (Kozlowski et al., 1996a). So by what manner can the team leader ensure that the team needs specified above are met?

Leadership Functions

Fleishman et al. (1991) created a taxonomy of four super-ordinate leadership functions which can provide some insight to the question posed above. Specifically, Fleishman et al. (1991) argue for the existence of four leadership functions: search for and structuring of information, use of information in problem solving, management of personnel resources, and management of material resources. Information search and structuring refers to "the leader's systematic search, acquisition, evaluation, and organization of information regarding team goals and operations" (Zaccaro et al., 2001, p. 455). The second dimension, information use in problem solving, refers to the leader using information gained through boundary spanning activities toward solving the problem at hand. Fleishman et al. (1991) argue that it is within this leadership dimension that cognitive problem solving actually resides. The remaining two dimensions, managing personnel resources and managing material resources, revolve around the actual implementation of the developed plan (Zaccaro et al., 2001). Managing personnel resources refers to the leader obtaining, allocating, developing, and motivating his/her personnel resources as well as utilizing these resources to enact the developed plan and monitor progress. Managing material resources subsume similar dimensions, but do not include developing and motivating.

THE IMPACT OF CONTEXT: ADAPTIVE APPLICATION OF TEAM LEADERSHIP FUNCTIONS

While specifying a broad set of leader functions, researchers operating from a functional approach to leadership note that the same set of behaviors may not have the same instrumentality in all situations (Lord, 1977), but that a generic set of leadership functions exist that can be tailored to the specific situation. Therefore, this begs the following questions – how might the contextual factor of multi-cultural teams impact the enactment of these functions? What areas might pose challenges? What are the areas where the cultural diversity within the team might act as a facilitator? Before these questions can be answered, the context within which the leader is operating must be understood. In the present case the context that will be focused upon is that of mid-level officers in the United States military who are leading multi-cultural teams. Therefore, first a brief review of those cultural dimensions deemed most relevant will be discussed and later specific leadership skills will be identified. For a more detailed review regarding cultural dimensions the interested reader is referred to Sutton, Pierce, Burke, and Salas (this volume).

Culture

Culture has been defined as "a pattern of shared basic assumptions that was learned by a group as it solved problems of external adaptation and internal integration, that has worked well enough to be considered valid and, therefore, to be taught to new members as the correct way to perceive, think, and feel in relation to those problems" (Schein, 2004, p. 17). Although Schein's definition was offered with regard to organizational culture one finds similar definitions when examining national culture. For example, Hofstede (2001) defines culture as the "collective programming of the mind that distinguishes the members of one group or category of people from another" (p. 9). Similarly, GLOBE researchers have defined culture as, "shared motives, values, beliefs, identities, and interpretations or meanings of significant events that result from common experiences of members of collectives that are transmitted across generations" (House & Javidan, 2004, p.15).

It has long been acknowledged that national cultures differ with regard to the values, beliefs, and affect, which guide member behavior. As evidence of this, Salas, Burke, Wilson-Donnelly, and Fowlkes (2004) identified over 64 conceptualizations of cultural dimensions. An examination of the definitions of the identified cultural dimensions revealed that several themes could be delineated with regard to differences in preferences, attitudes, and beliefs. Specifically, it appears that there are individual and national differences with regard to human relations, power distribution, rules for status ascription, rules of behavior, orientation to time, affective expressions, context, and cognitive style.

The human relations theme contains cultural dimensions that address how members of cultures react, interact, and develop relationships with others. Specifically, this theme includes dimensions that describe the identification of in- versus out-groups and corresponding expectations (Hofstede, 1980), preferences for individualistic tendencies versus group consensus and corresponding behavioral consequences (Trompenaars & Hampden-Turner, 1998), and the maintenance of the status quo (Schwartz, 1999). Similar in focus to the human relations theme are those themes that deal with preferences for communication and degree of involvement in others lives. Specifically, cultures differ with regard to the degree to which the meaning contained within a communicated message is explicit or implicit (Hall & Hall, 1990) and degree to which instant gratification is acceptable (Parsons & Shils, 1951). One way in which this is operationalized is by whether it is deemed acceptable to express emotions and affect or whether emotions should be delayed or suppressed.

The power relations theme contains cultural dimensions that revolve around peoples' beliefs, values, and subsequent behaviors resulting from perceptions of power. Cultural dimensions within this theme guide rules and regulations regarding people's reaction to power as well as the perception, acceptance, and adherence of power being distributed unequally (Hofstede, 1980). While originally categorized as a separate theme cultural dimensions that describe how status is allocated may be considered a sub-theme within power relations. Allocation of status refers to how members assign status (i.e., based on relationships or achievement, Trompenaars & Hampden-Turner, 1998). This is closely related to power, as status is one manner in which power is manifested.

While the first four themes deal primarily with direct social interactions, the next several themes pertain to differences in cultures' orientation to more inanimate objects (i.e., rules, times, nature). Dimensions, which pertain to a culture's orientation to rules include those that describe the adherence to, application of, and comfort with rules for members of a certain culture. Specifically, this theme refers to attitudes and preferences for ambiguity, rules guiding actions, and the amount of rules that govern behavior for a particular society (Hofstede, 1980). National cultures also have different preferences with regard to perception of time and how those perceptions guide behavior. The time orientation theme refers to dimensions that explain how time perceptions of members relate to rewards, how time is viewed, and whether or not members pay attention to time (Hofstede, 2001; Hall & Hall, 1990).

The final theme deals with cognitive style. Cultural diversity exists with regard to the degree to which members employ a specific-diffuse continuum such that members with an analytic style tend to use formal logic and partition the problem space into parts similar to the manner in which specific cultures partition objects. In contrast, diffuse cultures tend to view objects and the environment in a holistic manner, tending to the entire field (Triandis, 2000). While we do not argue that the themes presented above are all inclusive we argue that they represent a major sampling of the most prominent cultural dimensions. The reader is referred to Table 1 to see what cultural dimensions are subsumed within each broader category.

Table 1. Sampling of Cross-Cultural Dimensions Discussed Within Chapter.

Cross-Cultural Dimension	Category	Definition
Individualism–collectivism	Human relations	"A loosely knit social framework in which people are supposed to take care of themselves and of their immediate families only" (Hofstede, 1980, p. 45). A tight social framework "in which people distinguish between in-groups and out-groups, they expect their in-group to look out after them, and in exchange for that they feel they owe absolute loyalty to the in-group" (Hofstede, 1980, p. 45).
Conservatism–autonomy	Human relations	Conservatism is "a cultural emphasis on maintenance of the status quo, propriety, and restraint of actions or inclinations that might disrupt the solidarity group or the traditional order (social order, respect for tradition, family security, wisdom" (Schwartz, 1999, p. 27). Autonomy describes "cultures in which the person is viewed as an autonomous, bounded entity who finds meaning in his or her own uniqueness, who seeks to express his or her own internal attributes (preferences, traits, feelings, motives) and is encouraged to do so." (Schwartz, 1999, p. 27). Intellectual autonomy is the extent to which individuals independently pursue their own ideas, while affective autonomy is the extent to which individuals independently pursue affectively positive experiences (Schwartz, 1999).
Power distance	Power relations	"The extent to which a society accepts the fact that power in institutions is distributed unequally" (Hofstede, 1980, p. 45). High power distance cultures accept this and social exchanges are based on this fact. Low power distance cultures do not see a strict hierarchy among social exchanges.
Achievement–ascription	Power relations: allocation of status	Relationship with power. The degree to which status is given based on one's achievements (doing) or based on personal characteristics (e.g., age, class, gender, education; being) (Trompenaars, 2002).
Ascription–achievement	Power relations: allocation of status	Refers to how an individual is judged in society; Individuals in ascriptive cultures are judged by their attributes, those in achievement cultures are judged by their actions and performance (Parson & Shils, 1951).

Uncertainty avoidance	Rules orientation	"The extent to which a society feels threatened by uncertain and ambiguous situations and tries to avoid these situations by providing greater career stability, establishing more formal rules, not tolerating deviant ideas and behaviors, and believing in absolute truths and the attainment of expertise" (Hofstede, 1980, p. 45). Ranges from high to low.
Tightness	Rules orientation	Tight cultures have many rules, norms, and ideas about what is correct behavior in each situation and conformity is high; Loose cultures have fewer rules and norms and people are tolerant of many deviations from normal behavior (Triandis, 2000).
Long/short-term orientation	Time orientation	"LTO stands for the fostering of virtues orientated towards future rewards, in particular perseverance and thrift"; "STO the fostering of virtues related to the past and present, in particular respect for tradition, preservation of 'face' and fulfilling social orientations" (Hofstede, 2001, p. 359).
Past-future orientated	Time orientation	Refers to the segments of time frame that are emphasized (Hall & Hall, 1990).
Monochronic-polychronice	Time orientation	Refers to the degree to which members of a culture pay attention to and do things one at a time (monochromic) versus being involved in many things at once (polychronic). Within monochromic cultures time is experienced and used in a linear way; segmented; compartmentalized (Hall & Hall, 1990).
Neutral-emotional	Affect	Degree to which people express affect (Trompenaars, 2002).
Affective-affective neutrality	Affect	"Extent to which it is acceptable for individuals to experience instant gratification" (Erez & Earley, 1993, p. 46).
Emotional expression-suppression	Affect	Refers to the degree to which people freely express their emotions no matter what the consequences (i.e., emotional expression). Suppression refers to controlling the expression of emotion (Triandis, 2000).
Analytic-holistic	Cognitive styles	Analytic cultures pay attention primarily to the object and the categories to which it belongs, use rules and formal logic to understand its behavior. Holistic cultures attend to the entire field and assign causality to interactions between the object and the field, making relatively little use of categories and formal logic; rely on dialectical reasoning (Choi & Nisbett, 2000).

Table 1. *(Continued)*

Cross-Cultural Dimension	Category	Definition
Field dependence-independence	Cognitive styles	Field independence is a cognitive style or "the ability to highly differentiate between stimuli and to think analytically, whereas field dependence refers to lower levels of differentiation and global thinking." (Erez & Earley, 1993, p. 127); field dependent rely more on external social referent, field independent less likely to be engaged in information seeking behavior. Field dependent people more likely to have an interpersonal orientation.
Specific-diffuse	Context; how far we get involved	How far we get involved. "Degree to which we engage people in specific areas of life and single levels of personality or diffusely in multiple areas of our lives and at several levels of personality at once" (Trompenaars & Hampden-Turner, 1998, p. 83).
Specific-diffuse	Context; how far we get involved	"… the degree to which relations among actors and objects are limited"; diffuse culture this relationship can be quite indirect; specific culture the relationship is narrow and limited (Parson & Shils, 1951).
Specific-diffuse	Context; how far we get involved	Diffuse cultures respond to the environment in a holistic manner; Specific cultures discriminate different aspects of the stimulus complex (Triandis, 2000).
High-low context	Context; how far we get involved	In high context cultures communication involves messages "in which most of the information is already in the person, while very little is in the coded, explicit, transmitted part of the message" While low context the mass of the information is vested in explicit code (Hall & Hall, 1990, p. 6).
Masculinity-feminity	Miscellaneous	"The extent to which the dominant values of society are 'masculine' – that is, assertiveness, the acquisition of money and things, and not caring for others, the quality of life, or people" (Hofstede, 1980, p. 45).

Source: Adapted from Salas et al. (2004).

Cultural Diversity

While the cultural dimensions themselves do not present challenges to team performance when team composition is homogeneous a different picture unfolds when examining multi-cultural teams (i.e., within team cultural diversity). Cox (1994) defines cultural diversity as, "the representation in one social system, of people with distinctly different group affiliations of cultural significance" (p. 6). While members often report that multi-cultural teams are frustrating and challenging (Helmreich & Merritt, 1998), the broader diversity literature would suggest the potential for great synergy exists within multi-cultural teams due to the differences in perspectives and resources each member brings to the table (e.g., Thomas, 1999; Watson, Kumar, & Michaelsen, 1993). Others have also reported conflicting results with regard to the impact of cultural diversity on team and organizational outcomes (see Jackson, Joshi, & Erhardt, 2003). This begs the question – what is the distinguishing factor between those teams in which multi-culturalism is an advantage as compared to those where it serves as a barrier to effectiveness?

Some have argued that the team leader can make the difference between cultural diversity as a maximizer and a minimizer (Adler, 1997; Graen, Hui, & Gu, 2004a; Bass, 1997). Specifically, it has been argued that in order to be effective within multi-cultural teams, leaders must be aware that they are dealing with different 'fabrics' of meaning, which at first glance may look similar (i.e., words are same, but metaphorical and literal meaning is not, Geertz, 1973). It has been suggested that through the creation of a 'third culture' the leader can mitigate the difficulties that surround interdependent action within a culturally diverse team. Graen et al (2004a) define a third culture as, "a culture in which the different cultural backgrounds of the organization or group members are synthesized into a new culture that is acceptable to members" (p. 226). The creation of a third culture has been argued to foster a flexible structure in which the requirements of multiple cultures can be integrated in such a way to enhance coordination and co-operation (Graen, Hui, & Taylor, 2004b); in turn, leading to improved team performance.

Researchers have argued that the first step in this process is the identification of the volatile areas that may cause conflict or ambiguity with regard to the cultural composition of the team (Graen et al., 2004a). Once these areas are mapped (i.e., leverage points), recommendations can be made for changes that will serve to create something acceptable to all. In an effort to create awareness of how leadership functions, broadly defined, may translate to different 'fabrics' of meaning (which, in turn, create volatile areas when leader's are not aware) within multi-cultural teams, a conceptual framework of how culture may impact the aforementioned leadership functions and enabling conditions for team effectiveness has been created (see Fig. 1). Corresponding propositions are put forth below:

Proposition 1. Culture will impact the leader's search and structuring of information.

As depicted in Fig. 1, the first functional requirement is that the leader enacts his/her role as a boundary spanner to scan the environment for cues that indicate whether or not an adaptation in strategy or design is needed. Here it is argued that the leader's cultural tendencies will not only influence the cues that elicit attention, but the characteristics of the search, and the manner in which meaning is assigned (i.e., structuring of information). Cultural dimensions such as uncertainty avoidance, high-low context, field dependence-independence, and analytic-holistic reasoning are all cultural dimensions that may impact the leader's search (see Salas et al., 2004). For example, as uncertainty avoidance deals with preferences for certainty this dimension may impact the breadth and timeliness of the search. Similarly, cognitive style (i.e., analytic-holistic) may impact the type of cues which call elicit the leader's attention. Although this leadership function is usually used to refer to the leader's search for information external to the team, in theory it might also include the leader's search and structuring of information within the team (i.e., external versus internal focus).

Once information is gathered, meaning is assigned through the structuring of this information within one's mental model. The values and beliefs, which are the foundation of culture, serve to form the basis of an individual's cognitive framework (i.e., mental model). In assigning meaning to events, individuals compare new information to existing mental models and attempt to integrate the new information into existing frameworks. When there is a mismatch, information may be disregarded or existing mental models may be updated. Therefore, the values, beliefs, and perceptions contained within mental models serve to influence meaning assignment. Others have similarly argued that the encoding and decoding of information is culturally dependent (Klopf & Park, 1982).

Proposition 2. Cultural heterogeneity will impact information use in problem solving.

Once information has been gathered from the environment and incorporated into one's mental models this information is then used in the actual

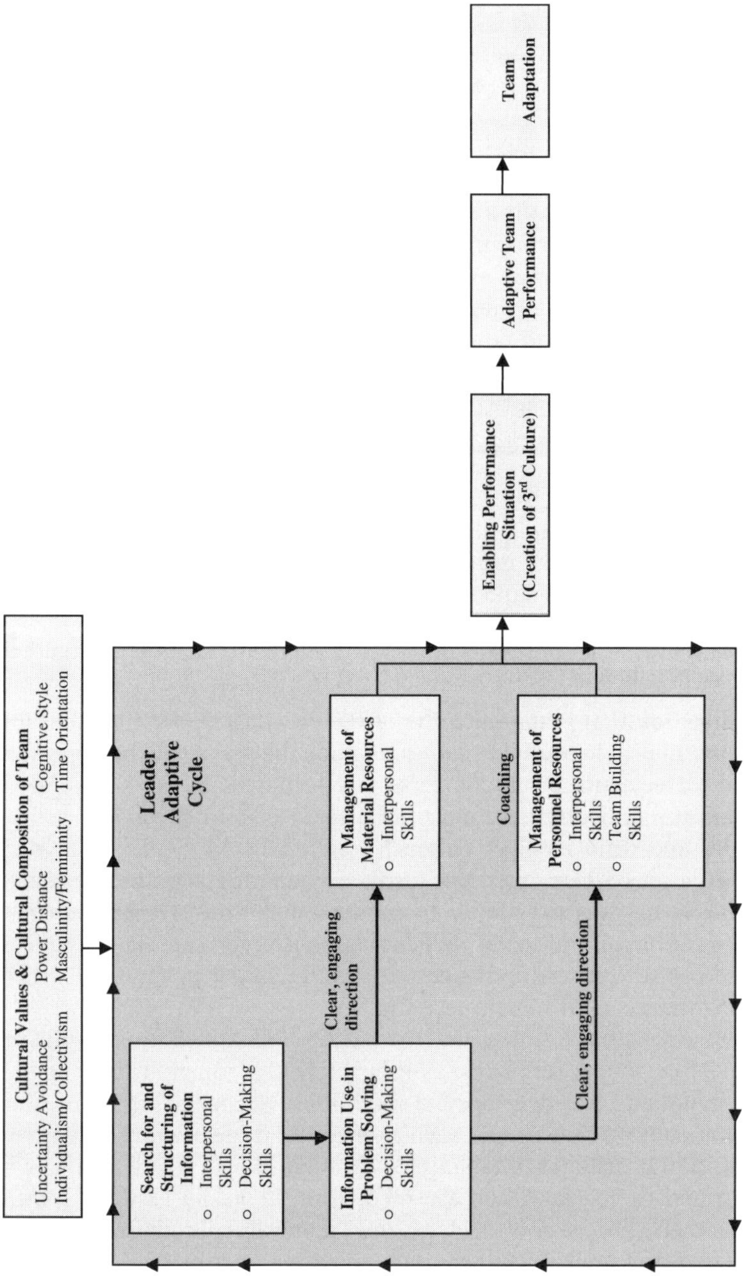

Fig. 1. A Conceptual Model of Effective Multi-Cultural Team Leadership.

problem solving process. It is during this process when a plan is crafted that depicts how the newly acquired information will be put to use in order to keep the team adaptive to its environment and viable. This, second function may be enacted by the leader or team members; either way cultural preferences play a large role in this process. Cultural dimensions such as, but not limited to: time orientation, cognitive style, affective expression, uncertainty avoidance, and individualism/collectivism will impact the enactment of this leadership function. For example, time orientation may impact horizon at which the plan is set as well as the linearity of the plan. Uncertainty avoidance and similar cultural dimensions, on the other hand, will impact the amount of detail and autonomy given within the plan. Those cultures that are not comfortable with uncertainty will expect a more detailed plan than those who are. Furthermore, where members fall on individualism/collectivism may impact plan development with regard to how interconnected various segments are.

This second function is an important enabler to effective team performance as it is from the output of this stage that compelling direction is created and transmitted to team members to guide subsequent action and align members' mental models and form common ground.

Proposition 3. Cultural heterogeneity will impact how the leader needs to manage personnel resources.

The direction that is the outcome of the previous leader function, information use in problem solving serves to guide the management of personnel resources. The management of personnel resources might be the area in which cultural difficulties are most often seen, as there is the interaction of the leader and team member cultural preferences. Moreover, this is often within situations where interdependent, coordinated action is needed and where the leader has the ability to perhaps make the largest impact with regard to multi-cultural teams. When personnel and material resources are managed properly it sets up the conditions that allow an enabling structure and performance environment (see Fig. 1).

Almost any cultural dimension that has been identified impacts the management of personnel resources, as it is within this function that the leader creates, maintains, and develops the conditions for coordinated team action. Therefore, cultural dimensions such as masculinity/femininity, affective expression, power distance, and status ascription impact the degree to which direction and feedback will be accepted from the leader as well as various team members. Dimensions such as, individualism/collectivism will impact the tendency and preferences for communication and interaction that either reflect independence or interdependence. These and other cultural dimensions are elaborated upon more later with regard to management of personnel resources.

> **Proposition 4.** Cultural heterogeneity will impact the leader's management of material resources.

Similar to Proposition 3, the direction that is the outcome of information use in problem solving serves to guide the management of material resources, which in turn, provide an enabling structure and supportive context for team members. In terms of how cultural may impact the management of these resources many of the cultural dimensions that deal with preferences regarding cognition and time orientation have an impact here. For example, preferences with regard to past or future time orientation will impact how and what materials are used, while other aspects of time orientation may impact the sequencing of materials. Preferences for certainty, cognitive style, and individualism/collectivism may impact how often resource availability is checked as well as who is likely to be given preferences with regard to valued material resources.

The above propositions begin to highlight how culture may interact with the implementation of the broadly defined leadership functions; thereby highlighting the fact that the 'cultural lens' of team members and correspondingly their leader may be different. These are broad propositions that provide an initial view to some potential barriers or considerations; however, to create the adaptive capacity needed to truly be able to create a 'third culture,' another layer needs to be peeled.

IDENTIFICATION OF LEVERAGE POINTS: CREATING ADAPTIVE CAPACITY

When placed within the context of leading a multi-national team it is the interaction between the leadership skills required to manage personnel resources and the leader's cultural awareness that leads to effective leadership behavior and the creation of an enabling performance environment for team members. With the above in mind, a set of leadership skills and corresponding behaviors that provide the bare foundation for effective leadership within multi-cultural teams were identified. This effort sought to identify those leadership skills that we felt would: (a) be the most important within the current context (guided by Army leadership source documents) and

(b) would be most affected by cultural differences (guided by theory, subject matter experts, source documents). This resulted in the identification of 3 team leadership skills (i.e., decision-making, interpersonal skills, and team building) along with a set of behaviors that underlie each of the respective skills (see Table 2). We are in no way arguing that these are the only leadership skills that are important within multi-cultural environments, but based on common difficulties reported and a focus on the areas in which we feel that team leaders can have the most opportunities for leverage (management of personnel resources, information use in problem solving) these three leadership skills have been identified.

Leader Interpersonal Skills

Since leadership is about people, it is not surprising to find interpersonal skills, at the top of the list of what an Army leader must possess. As defined here, interpersonal skill refers to skills, which impact how the leader interacts with team members and contribute to a leader's ability to manage personnel resources. Interpersonal skills were deemed as an important leverage point for when adaptively applied within a multi-cultural environment, these skills and corresponding behaviors can mitigate some of the conditions which cause multi-cultural teams to be frustrating (i.e., miscommunication, loss of communication, lack of trust, inappropriate use of stereotypes, Helmreich & Merritt, 1998). Additionally, the diversity present in multi-cultural teams often means that there is little common ground existing among team members. This, in turn, drives the importance of interpersonal skills such as, active listening, negotiation, empathy, and conflict resolution. However, in order for leaders to effectively enact the behavioral manifestations of such skills, they must understand how the cultural diversity present within the team may impact how interpersonal skills and corresponding behaviors are enacted.

Active Listening

Active listening is an important form of two-way communication that involves observing the sender's words and mannerisms and communicating that the exchanged information has been received (Department of the Army, 1999). The acknowledgement can involve either verbal or non-verbal communication. Active listening is a behavior that is essential within multi-cultural teams for it can assist in mitigating some of the miscommunication that often occurs. For example, Geertz (1973) argues that even when the

Table 2. U.S. Army Field Grade Competency Map.

Competency	Skill	Example Behaviors	Supporting Performance
Interpersonal	• Communicating • Understanding soldiers	• Coach, teach, counsel, motivate, empower and encourage initiative • In subordinates by employing • Transformational leadership • Convince others to follow • Ideas, make a commitment, and • Take action by using the style of • Communication appropriate to the • Situation	• Active listening • Negotiating • Gaining consensus • Conflict resolution • Leading change • Effective oral/written communication
Conceptual	• Understanding systems • Creative thinking • Adaptation • Establish intent • Critical reasoning • Reflective thinking • Predicting order effects	• Encourage subordinates to take action on their own to transform intent into reality even when unanticipated events arise • Visualize the sequence of activities that will move the organization • Use a systems perspective to assess feedback on their performance from multiple perspectives—seniors, peers, and subordinates	• Ethical Reasoning • Multi-dimensional problem solving • Cultural awareness • Historical nature of war - Attrition - Asymmetrical - Decisive
Technical	• Doctrine • Predicting effects • Leveraging technology • Information dominance	• Demonstrate proficiency in required professional knowledge, judgment, and warfighting, apply warfighting doctrine within the commander's intent • Resource, allocate, exploit and apply systems under their control to gain a decisive military advantage	• Digital systems • Analog and digital processing procedures • Understanding how the army runs • Training management
Tactical	• Warfighting • Synchronization orchestration	• Demonstrate proficiency in employing (within the commander's intent) units and combat organizations (up to corps/JTF levels, to include coalition partners) in a warfighting environment	• Army operational doctrine requirements joint operational doctrine capabilities • Elements of combat power (maneuver, firepower, leadership, protection and information)

Table 2. *(Continued)*

Competency	Skill	Example Behaviors	Supporting Performance
		• Arrange activities in space, time, and purpose to focus complementary and reinforcing effects of all military and nonmilitary assets; in order to achieve maximum relative military power at one or more decisive points	• Full spectrum operations (dominant maneuver, precision engagement, focused logistics, full dimensional protection)
Influencing	• Decision making • Communication	• Assess environment (people, events, and systems), tailor message to target audience, clearly communicate by persuading and conveying intent, standards, goals and priorities • Live the 'Warrior Ethos' and embody	• Envisioning • Media support • Motivating and building teams • Enduring army values (Loyalty, Duty, Respect, Self-less service, Honor, Integrity, Personal courage)
Operating	• Executing • Assessing • Planning/preparing	• Vigorously implement the seven steps of systems planning; in order to integrate planning of all assets • Successfully integrate (horizontally and vertically) and synchronize all elements and Systems	• Simultaneous planning and execution • Coalition planning • Decentralized decision making • Joint vision strategy • Army transformation strategy • Creative staff process (build, train, sustain) • Coalition building and assessment
Improving	• Developing /life-long learning • Self-awareness • Building	• Maintain organizational focus; ensure conditions are set for developing subordinates for positions of increased responsibility • Promote desirable mental, physical, and emotional attributes for self and subordinates	• Combined arms teams/operations • Leadership Assessment • Assessing cognitive and creative capacity • People assessment • Developing people and leaders • Mentoring • Use military Theory and history

Source: Adapted from Department of the Army (1999).

words are the same within multi-cultural teams the meaning is often different; active listening could assist in this area. The following are several propositions that depict potential volatile areas with regard to active listening:

Proposition 5. Cultural diversity with respect to context and individualism/collectivism will impact the manner in which active listening must be carried out.

Carrying out active listening via the typical manner within collectivist societies, who tend to be high context, might cause team members to take offense as they feel that the leader is not truly listening. Within cultural situations such as these, team leaders should attempt to determine meaning from the words and only ask clarification as a last resort. Do not ask questions or 'close the loop' as a matter of course as would happen within individualistic cultures or those low in context.

Proposition 6. Team members' beliefs concerning the appropriateness of power-distance will impact the effectiveness of active listening.

Active listening will be best used with team members who are low in power distance for when a message is not received clearly, members will ask questions and expect that leaders will do the same. When the leader is asked questions, they should be answered directly realizing that members are trying to obtain additional clarification. Conversely, when attempting to implement active listening within high power distance cultures, leaders must monitor non-verbal communications and ask direct questions to ensure understanding as members of high power distance cultures will not question or interrupt a higher status individual.

Empathy

Empathy has been defined as entailing a capacity to share other's experiences, feelings, and ideas (http://www.dictionary.com). It is a way of identifying with others by sharing in their circumstances and can focus leaders' attention on the right objects, enabling them to make better decisions about how to listen, care, and lead. As such, empathy forms the foundation for many of the team leadership functions reviewed earlier. For those who have low levels of empathy, it will be difficult to have an accurate awareness of what is happening with team members.

Proposition 7. Masculinity/femininity will impact the manner in which team members expect empathy to be shown by the leader.

When dealing with cultures where the dominant values are feminine the display of empathy will be associated with caring for others and being able to put oneself in members' shoes. Conversely, in dealing with members from masculine cultures where the dominant values are assertiveness, independence, and the acquisition of material things, empathy displayed in the same manner will be viewed as weak. It is expected that while empathy is still appreciated it must be shown in an indirect, more task related manner.

Proposition 8. The cues for determining when empathy needs to be shown will vary depending on cultural diversity with respect to individualism/collectivism.

Within cultures characterized by collectivist values, leaders are expected to intuitively understand members' needs and offense will be taken if leaders do not comply with this expectation. Within these cultural situations, leaders must watch subtle cues or find out member needs indirectly as they will likely not ask directly for help. While empathy is also valued within individualistic cultures leaders can expect members to ask if they have needs. Team members are less likely than those in collectivist cultures to expect leaders to determine what their needs are intuitively.

Negotiation/Conflict Resolution

Negotiation is a problem-solving process, where people voluntarily discuss their differences and attempt to reach a joint decision on common concerns (Department of the Army, 1999). Negotiation differs from conflict resolution in that high emotions are not normally involved in the former, while they are common in the later. It requires participants to identify issues about which they differ, educate each other about their needs and interests, generate possible settlement options, and bargain over the terms of the final agreement. While normally not involving high emotions, it does assume some blocking of goal attainment has already occurred (i.e., goal incompatibility exists).

Proposition 9. The manner in which conflict is viewed will differ dependent on cultural composition with regard to uncertainty avoidance.

Within cultures that are not threatened by uncertainty, conflicts that occur during negotiations or conflict resolution are viewed as stimulating progress (a natural progression). Therefore, leaders should be prepared to openly discuss issues and accept input and contradictory views on issues. Conversely, when there is a preference for certainty and stability, members will be uncomfortable with conflict that often occurs during negotiation and conflict resolution. In these situations, leaders must find a middle ground, attempting to negotiate in a non-combative manner and minimizing open disagreements, while still resolving the problem. Negotiation needs more subtly.

Proposition 10. Cultural diversity with respect to masculinity/femininity will impact negotiation and conflict resolution.

When negotiating with members who prefer feminine values, the process will be characterized by members valuing compromise where the solution benefits all members. Leaders in this situation should openly discuss the situation and try to reach a middle ground solution that incorporates the inputs of all members. Conversely, negotiations that take place with members valuing masculine tendencies will be more combative, more openly difficult, and compromise will be less likely. Within these cultures team members will value assertive behavior on the part of the leader or negotiator.

Communication

Effective communication requires that leaders commit to a few common, powerful, and consistent messages and repeat them over and over in different forms and settings. Finding some apparent success with the medium, frequency, and words of the message, leaders must determine the best way to measure the message's effectiveness and continually scan and assess the environment to make sure the message is going to all the right groups in the right format.

Proposition 11. The degree of uncertainty avoidance within the team will impact the manner in which communication must be structured.

Within cultures where there is a preference for certainty, members prefer that there be rules and norms for communication. These rules will likely dictate the form, structure, and method by which communication takes place. Team members will expect structured communication norms to be in place and will be uncomfortable with ad-hoc, emergent communication structures. Additionally, communication typically is more verbose, operating on the assumption that complex ideas take complex communication to explain. Communication tends to be explicit with meaning embedded within the actual words. Conversely, within cultures that are not threatened by uncertainty or ambiguity, communication is more free flowing and structures are often adhoc. Communication that communicates complex ideas in simple language is appreciated.

Proposition 12. Perceived power relationships within the team will impact communication.

When communicating with members who readily accept status differences and base social interactions on those differences, team members will typically not initiate communication with higher status members (i.e., the leader). In these cases, the burden of keeping communication lines open typically falls on the higher status member. Team leaders should engage subordinates in conversation and be proactive in seeking information paying particular attention to non-verbal cues. Members will typically not explicitly disagree with leaders, but may come to resent them internally. Conversely, within cultures characterized by low levels of power distance subordinates will freely communicate with superiors and freely challenge ideas. Leaders should expect that communication channels will be very open. Here it is common to receive a mix of positive and negative comments and communication exchanges.

Team Building

Within the current context, team building may be defined as developing subordinates and forming a cohesive team. The goal within team building is to build a solid and effective team through team member development and training. This involves such behaviors as providing feedback, mentoring, motivating, assigning roles appropriately, and enacting the appropriate leadership style. The behavioral manifestation of team building skills are essential within complex, dynamic environments where teams must continually learn from their actions and adapt accordingly. These skills contribute to the leader's ability to ensure that personnel resources are managed and an enabling performance environment created. Therefore, such behaviors as: feedback, motivating and developing, and building teams are important.

While team building is important within any team, it becomes even more important within multi-cultural teams where mistrust is often common. In addition, as multi-cultural teams are often challenging and frustrating due to the process loss, which often occurs initially, the ability to keep team members motivated is essential. Team leaders, which operate within multicultural teams, must be able to see the world through the 'cultural lens' of fellow team members in order to make sense of ambiguous team actions. Seeing the other's perspective can also assist in the team leader's determination of how and when feedback should be delivered to continue developing a learning and adaptive team. In order for leaders to effectively enact the behavioral manifestations of such skills, they must understand how the cultural diversity present within the team may impact how team-building skills and corresponding behaviors are enacted.

Feedback

It has been argued that within effective teams where adaptation is required feedback is essential (Burke, Stagl, Salas, Pierce, & Kendall, in press; Edmondson, 1999; Kozlowski et al., 1996a, b). In order to learn as a team and self-regulate as individuals, process and outcome feedback must be provided. This includes the provision of positive and negative feedback; yet to be effective it must be constructive (i.e., focused on the task) and diagnostic (i.e., providing constructive suggestions for improvement). This feedback may or may not involve the active participation of the team members, but the guiding of the team members through self-correction of ineffective behavior should be initially facilitated by the leader.

Proposition 13. Diversity with regard to power distance will impact the delivery and form of feedback.

Members coming from cultures with a norm of low power distance will expect to have a voice in evaluating team behavior and may actively question the leader's analysis of a situation. When dealing with low power distance members, the leader should actively involve subordinates in feedback delivery by providing tools for self-evaluation and correction (see team self-correction, Smith-Jentsch, Zeisig, Acton, & McPherson, 1998). Conversely, when delivering feedback to members with a high power distance orientation, the leader will be expected to be well versed in the domain and members will accept the feedback that is given. Saying I do not know is not acceptable when dealing with high power distance members.

Proposition 14. Individualism/Collectivism will impact the structure of feedback that will result in internalization.

Members of collectivist cultures do not value standing apart or being singled out from the rest of the team (Hofstede, 1980). Therefore, direct confrontation is considered rude and members will be embarrassed by blunt feedback. The leader must provide feedback in a more indirect manner when dealing with collectivist cultures. One approach which may facilitate the acceptance and effectiveness of feedback delivery is to provide feedback with regard to the team as a whole as opposed to singling an individual out. This is especially true if the feedback is negative. Conversely, those members who hold values of an individualistic culture will value and expect direct and pointed feedback. The leader should state clearly and concisely what the areas in need of improvement are in a constructive, diagnostic manner.

Developing People

Many leadership researchers would argue that a key function of team leaders is to ensure expert coaching and developmental opportunities are available for team members. Development may take a number of forms including mentoring, stretch assignments, and coaching. Developmental behaviors may also include the leader sharing the benefit of perspective and experience; thereby serving to broaden the depth and breadth of members' mental models. This can incorporate developmental guidance on what to study, where to focus, whom to watch, and how to proceed.

> **Proposition 15.** Cultural diversity with respect to context will determine the acceptability of sharing personal experiences as a way to develop subordinates.

In high context cultures communication tends to involve messages in which most of the meaning is implicit (i.e., already in the person), while in low context cultures the meaning of communication is explicitly contained in the words of the message (Hofstede, 1980). The notion underlying this difference is that cultures differ with regard to preferences for the degree to which relations among people are limited or broad. While the sharing of personal experiences is a common practice through which to develop people within some cultures, other cultures may view this method as being intrusive and out of line.

> **Proposition 16.** Cultural diversity with respect to uncertainty avoidance will determine the acceptance and potential effectiveness of stretch assignments as a developmental method.

Recent work within leadership development has begun to indicate that operational assignments that are challenging and serve to stretch the leader beyond his/her current comfort zone can be used to efficiently develop new competencies. These stretch assignments must be challenging, yet not impossible, in order to be developmental. Specifically, recent evidence suggests that the tacit knowledge derived from these experiences is essential to leader learning and subsequent development (Banks, Bader, Fleming, Zaccaro, & Barber, 2001; McCall, Lombardo, & Morrison, 1988; Tesluk, Dragoni, & Russell, 2002).

While typically spoken of in regard to leader development, stretch assignments can be used to develop team members as well. However, the degree to which stretch assignments are valued may be differentially related to cultural preferences. For example, in cultures where is it perceived as threatening to be placed within uncertain and ambiguous situations, stretch assignments may not be as highly valued as a developmental mechanism. Members within these cultures tend to prefer development techniques that pose a little less ambiguity. If stretch assignments are to be applied within cultures with a low tolerance for ambiguity, the leader needs to carefully structure the situation and provide sub-goals to assist in reducing the ambiguity. Conversely, within cultures where ambiguity is not perceived as threatening, stretch assignments may work very well.

Motivating

Motivating is the ability to inspire great efforts in team members, it also requires leaders to cultivate a challenging, supportive, and respectful environment for members to operate in. The types of goals that are set and the degree of empowerment or involvement in decisions are aspects that have been found to be related to motivation in U.S. culture (see Hackman & Oldham, 1980).

> **Proposition 17.** Cultural diversity with respect to uncertainty avoidance will determine the manner in which goals should be structured to be motivating.

Hackman (2002) argues that the direction provided to the team by the leader needs to be clear and engaging. It is argued that what is considered engaging will be determined, in part, by members' personal interests, values, and aspirations. Given this state of affairs the leader must be careful to align direction with cultural expectations. Research has shown that goals that are quantifiable, specific, and challenging are motivating (Locke & Latham, 1994); yet most of this work has been done in the United States. The degree of uncertainty avoidance that guides member actions may require that goals be differentially set to be viewed as motivating. For example, cultures high in uncertainty avoidance are not comfortable with risk, therefore challenging goals may be perceived as threatening. The opposite is true of low uncertainty avoidance cultures; here challenging goals motivate.

> **Proposition 18.** Cultural diversity with respect to masculinity/femininity will determine the manner in which goals should be structured to be seen as valued.

Cultures within which the dominant values are indicative of masculine characteristics are likely to value different goals than those where the dominant values are feminine. For example, masculine cultures value assertiveness, independence, and the acquisition of money. Team members from these cultures are likely to more easily value goals in which these things are emphasized. Conversely, feminine cultures prefer collaboration, helping others out, and doing things for the good of the group. Goals that are structured in such a way as to emphasize these values are likely to be internalized and valued.

Building Teams

This behavior refers to leaders working to effectively create a viable team. In particular, there is an emphasis here on the assignment of members roles and functions to specific tasking.

Proposition 19. Cultural diversity with respect to masculinity/femininity will partially determine how members are assigned to task.

This proposition flows directly from the fact that within masculine cultures there is an emphasis on being assertive and independent, while in feminine cultures the emphasis is on collaboration. In building teams and matching members to task roles the leader should take these tendencies into account. For example, given that two team members have similar levels of expertise and skill yet there are two tasks which differ in the amount of self-initiative required the leader may assign the person with the more masculine tendencies to the task requiring the most due to the valued independence. Similarly, time critical tasks where assertiveness is required might fall to the person with the masculine orientation whereas tasks that are highly collaborative might be assigned to the culture which has a more feminine orientation; assuming all other things are equal.

Proposition 20. Cultural diversity with respect to time orientation will impact how member roles are structured and to whom they are assigned.

Time orientation may also impact how team roles are assigned. While there are several cultural dimensions that fall under the time orientation theme, the one that will be focused on within this proposition is mono-chronic versus polychromic. Within mono-chronic cultures individuals tend to view time as segmented and attend to things one at a time. Polychromic cultures view time as more continous in nature and as such tend to be involved in many things at once (Hall & Hall, 1990). Therefore, one might expect that members with a polychronic orientation might be better assigned to tasks or situations in which multi-tasking or boundary spanning between different entities is required. Conversely, members with a mono-chronic orientation might be best assigned to tasks where things can be accomplished sequentially and deadlines are clear and concise.

Decision-Making

Within the current context, decision-making can be defined as the ability to gather and integrate information, use sound judgment, identify alternatives, select a solution, and evaluate the consequences (Cannon-Bowers, Tannenbaum, Salas, & Volpe, 1995). Displaying this leadership skill involves such behaviors as knowing how to envision the problem, shape the environment, and determining what and who needs to be influenced.

Functional leadership argues that within complex environments leadership is comprised of a form of social problem-solving where the team leader must ensure that the task and developmental needs of the team are met. Given the focus on social problem-solving, decision-making skills are foundational to team leader effectiveness. The complexity that is brought about by the dynamic environments and multi-cultural teams that face military officers, drives the requirement that in order to be effective the leader must adaptively apply his/her knowledge and skill based on the contextual contingencies. Within this process the team leader must gather the necessary information, assign meaning to this information, decide on the necessary action or inaction, engage in plan development (determining whom he needs to influence and potential methods), communicate the plan to team members, and follow through adaptively redirecting action as needed. Almost all of the above processes entail elements of decision-making.

Envisioning

Envisioning means engaging in a process of designing a vision for your organization and inspiring collaborative efforts to articulate the vision in detail. Envisioning involves communicating your vision clearly, creating a plan, gaining support, and focusing members' effort.

Proposition 21. Cultural diversity will impact what is seen as clear direction.

Hackman (2002) argued that in order for direction to be compelling it must be clear. The cultural composition of the team may impact what is seen as clear; leader's need to take this into account. For example, uncertainty avoidance and high-low context may affect the degree to which directions are perceived as clear. It has been argued that cultures high in uncertainty avoidance prefer very clear instructions for they provide a sense of control and order (Harper & Rifkind, 1995). Cultural preferences with regard to context (Hall & Hall, 1990) may also impact what is deemed clear. For example, in low context cultures there is the expectation that provided direction will be very literal. Within high context cultures the expectation is not one of literal translation of direction, but one where much of the meaning is implicit. When these expectations are not met, it is likely that the direction will be viewed as confusing and unclear. In addition, in the case of high context cultures the leader may actually lose credibility in that the message may be seen as being overly complex.

Proposition 22. Cultural diversity will impact what is seen as motivating.

This proposition does not relate to any one cultural dimension or theme, but involves them all. The basic argument is that to the extent that the direction provided by the leader does not meet cultural expectations with regard to form, style, and content it is less likely to be seen as consequential or motivating. For example, within masculine cultures, direction that emphasizes collaboration without integrating something about personal gain will not be viewed as motivating as direction that does. Similarly, direction that is viewed as being unclear is also less likely to be seen as motivating (see Proposition 21). Finally, direction that is not aligned with members time orientations (long- versus short-term, Hofstede, 2001) will likely be seen as less motivating.

Shape Environment

Shaping the environment involves situations in which the leader takes action to ensure that each component of a unit is properly resourced, structured, and assigned missions to support the military's strategy (Department of the Army, 1999).

Proposition 23. Cultural diversity will impact the manner in which the environment is shaped and the success of that effort.

It is evident that cultures differ on a variety of dimensions, some of which relate to the manner in which credibility or power is gained; these dimensions have a large impact on the leader's ability to shape the environment. Shaping the environment is largely about influencing people. If the leader is not seen as credible with those parties who he/she is trying to influence, the attempt to shape events, people, and situations will not be successful. Mismatches in cultural dimensions such as the allocation of status, masculinity-femininity, and emotional expression-suppression will impact the leader's ability to influence. For example, cultures differ in the manner in which status is allocated. In some cultures status is allocated by achievement (i.e., what has been accomplished, resume, medals), while in others it is based on social relationships and has nothing to do with actual ability. When a leader has gained status through social relationships, yet is dealing with a culture where achievement dictates status, credibility will be lost. This can also work the other way.

Another case in point is that if a leader enacts primarily feminine values, but is working with a culture where masculine values are valued, he/she will be seen as weak; thereby not having much influence. Similar arguments can be made with regard to whether it is acceptable to express emotion in an influence attempt or whether that emotion should be suppressed. When this mismatch occurs leaders may be viewed as being irrational or conversely having no feelings.

Decision-Making Steps

The behaviors contained within this section are referred to by a number of different names, but represent steps for leaders to identify their preferred course of action so that leaders and their staff can work on detailing the improvement, specification, and execution of the specified course of action. The stages include situational information gathering, mission identification, operationalizing the course of action, rehearsal/war game, development of orders, and execution.

> **Proposition 25.** Cultural diversity with respect to cognitive style will impact the decision-making process; specifically the information gathering stage.

Cultural tendencies will influence the cues that elicit attention. Specifically, members who tend to be field independent or analytic in their cognitive style are able to highly differentiate between various stimuli, whereas field dependent styles are less likely to be so explicit in their differentiation (Erez & Earley, 1993; Choi & Nisbett, 2000). Therefore, the cues that elicit attention for individuals with a field dependent style are likely to be more global in orientation than those cues that elicit attention for the field independent style. Erez and Earley (1993) have argued that field dependent people rely more on social referents in gathering information, whereas field dependent people are less likely to be engaged in information seeking behavior as they have a more interpersonal orientation.

Proposition 26. Cultural diversity with respect to time orientation will impact the emphasis within plan development.

Cultures differ in their perceptions of time along several lines, but the one that will be considered within this proposition is long-short term orientation (Hofstede, 2001). Cultures with a long-term orientation tend to emphasize values orientated toward the future, including an emphasis on perseverance, thrift, and development. Conversely, those with a short-term orientation emphasize a respect for tradition, preservation of face, immediate gratification, and fulfilling of social obligations. These differences across cultures are likely to be represented in the plans and strategies that are chosen once information is gained. These differences not only appear with respect to the team leader, but must be taken into account when soliciting input from the team.

FuLL TiLT: A WAY FORWARD

Development of cultural awareness begins with an awareness of culturally learned assumptions (Connerley & Pedersen, 2005). Yet it goes beyond knowledge; the leader must understand how cultural awareness is translated into appropriate cultural behavior. The propositions offered in the previous sections begin to provide not only an awareness of culturally learned assumptions, but also begin to highlight possible volatile areas where leaders can adaptively leverage their cultural skills to begin to create a third culture. The propositions offered above are but a small part of a broader set of propositions which are all being used to design an intervention that will assist in developing adaptive capacity with regard to the leadership of multicultural teams. The tool, Functional Learning Levers – The Team Leader Toolkit (FuLL TiLT) is designed to leverage the natural points for a leader to intervene (i.e., the volatile areas or black holes, as described by Graen and collegues).

In order to best structure this tool we relied on the science of learning and recent best practice reviews. For example, Day and Halpin (2001) conducted a review of best practices of leadership development currently in use by industry to identify the basic tenets of successful leadership development programs and to identify evaluation issues. Results indicated that effective leadership development appears to be a function of the interdependence of the various practices rather than a collection of independent programs. In other words, programs that rely on what is known about human learning and combine multiple approaches based on targeted learning objectives tend to be effective when consistently applied (see Salas & Cannon-Bowers, 2000).

Based on this, it was felt that an effective training tool for leaders of multinational teams should combine elements of self-learning (e.g., community links), skill training, role-play, guided facilitation, and scenario-based training (Hess, Salas, Burke, Paley, Gamty, & Bradley, 2003). Following this structure, multimedia, diagnostic feedback, and practice could guide participants through a series of vignettes designed to target specific skills and behaviors (some of which are depicted in the propositions above). Instruction would be accomplished through a series of video-based vignettes, which were written to target the intersection between culture and the behaviors underlying the broader skill dimensions. The foundation for the content underlying each scripted vignette should be the real-life experiences, extracted during focus groups and interviews.

Bottom Line Up Front

FuLL TiLT is a web-based application, which meets SCORM compliance standards and is designed such that a user can complete the entire training in $2\frac{1}{4}$ h. It is comprised of 9 separate modules that provide cultural awareness and skill development with regard to the intersection between culture and the following leadership skills: interpersonal, decision-making, and team building. A complete training sequence for each skill requires that the user progress through three modules. Each module targets the relationship between 2 behaviors, which represent different manifestations of the targeted skill, and a subset of the cultural dimensions deemed to be important within a team context. Furthermore, FuLL TiLT represents a blended approach to learning by combining aspects of a scenario-based approach to learning with web-based, collaborative, and self-paced learning. In addition, the tool has aspects which facilitate 'just-in-time'/refresher training and its use as a job aide.

Structure of Individual Modules

Each module is structured such that it contains three scripted scenarios, which follow one overarching storyline. Once the participant logs into the training and completes the assessment phase (which establishes a baseline for where the participant should begin training), he/she is directed to the modules of one of the three skills targeted. Each module is structured such that the first scenario the user views illustrates a situation in which current leadership training is applied and results in effective performance outcomes. This "good" example illustrates a leader within a homogeneous team (i.e., an American military team) dealing with a situation and having to direct team members. The purpose of the first scenario is twofold: (a) capture user's attention and (b) illustrate the effectiveness of existing training in certain situations. At the conclusion of the first scenario, users hear a narrator provide a contextual-based explanation that describes the behavior the leader used to accomplish the goal and a rationale for its effect on team member behavior (i.e., tying the leadership behavior to cultural factors).

Participants then view a second scripted vignette that illustrates when their current training on interpersonal, decision-making, or team building skills may not work. This "bad" example illustrates a leader within a nationally heterogeneous team (e.g., a team with both American and Spanish team members) faced with the same situation shown in the "good" example, applying the same strategies, and targeting the same behaviors. However, in this case, the outcomes of the behavior are not desirable. The purpose is to illustrate how the application of the same strategies within multi-cultural teams may backfire. Following this example, participants receive "lessons learned" that are contextually grounded within the vignette just viewed.

Following the lessons learned, participants view a final vignette, completing the storyline. This final vignette is built to also illustrate the intersection between the behavioral manifestation of the targeted skill and culture. However, this final vignette is different from the first two in that it illustrates a different situation and participants "choose their own ending," rather than a solution playing out automatically. Answers to the "choose your own ending" vignette are based on interviews with subject matter experts and researcher knowledge of the impact of culture on the targeted skill behavior. Furthermore, to increase transfer, answers begin to mimic the complex cognitive choices that have to be made within multi-cultural teams in that no one answer is completely correct or incorrect, but differ by sophistication of understanding of multi-cultural effects. Diagnostic feedback is provided for each response chosen, followed by more "lessons learned," and recommendations for further training needs. In addition to the training content, the tool contains "community" links, including message boards, chat rooms, fact sheets, quick tips, frequently asked questions, and other reference material. We see FuLL TiLT not only as a training interface, but also as a reference that can help the leader better understand multi-cultural team issues and therefore be better prepared to lead such a team.

CONCLUSION

Operational environments within business, as well as the military, are becoming increasingly multi-cultural in nature. It is important for those operating in these contexts to know that the specific manner in which leadership functions are enacted may differ across cultures. Therefore, leaders of multi-cultural teams need the adaptive capacity to not only understand cultural differences (i.e., cultural awareness), but adaptively apply the behaviors underlying broad leadership functions. The knowledge and skill which underlies such adaptive capacity is the first step to creating a third culture which is able to take advantage of the potential synergy that is often present within multi-cultural teams.

Few would argue against the assertion that team leaders are in a role where they have great potential to influence and develop team members; therefore providing leaders with the adaptive capacity to capitalize on the synergy is a natural step. However, Graen and Wakabayashi (1994) acknowledge that capturing this synergy is not an easy task as many potential barriers often exist within multi-cultural teams. Barriers these authors mention include: (1) low partner commitment to personally invest, (2) 'them versus us' stigma, (3) lack of openness, (4) multiple leaks of knowledge, (5) static network for knowledge acquisition and testing, (6) losing influence with a partner, (7) confused reward systems, and (8) few regular venues for information input. It is our hope that the conceptual framework put forth within this chapter, the propositions that flow from it, and the leader's toolkit that has been briefly described (i.e., FuLL TiLT) are the first step toward facilitating such synergy. Finally, as we continue to learn more about the interaction between cultural dimensions and leadership functions, competencies, and KSAs it is expected that the framework and propositions within will be expanded upon.

ACKNOWLEDGMENT

The views expressed in this work are those of the authors and do not necessarily reflect official Army policy. This work was supported by funding from the Army Research Institute, Contract # DASW01-04-C-0005. The view, opinions, and/or findings contained in this report are those of the author(s) and should not be construed as an official Department of the Army position, policy, or decision.

REFERENCES

Adler, N. J. (1997). *International dimensions of organizational behavior* (3rd ed.). Cincinnati, OH: International Thomson Publishing.

Banks, D., Bader, P., Fleming, P., Zaccaro, S., & Barber, H. (2001). Leader adaptability: The role of work experiences and leader attributes. In: S. J. Zaccaro (Chair), *Leadership and team adaptation: Examining the attributes and training strategies that promote effective performance in dynamic environments*. Symposium presented at the 16th Annual Conference of the Society for Industrial and Organizational Psychology San Diego, CA.

Bass, B. M. (1997). Does the transactional-transformational leadership paradigm transcend organizational and national boundaries? *American Psychologist*, *52*(2), 130–139.

Burke, C. S., Stagl, K. C., Salas, E., Pierce, L., & Kendall, D. L. (in press). Understanding team adaptation: A conceptual analysis and model. *Journal of Applied Psychology*.

Cannon-Bowers, J. A., Tannenbaum, S. I., Salas, E., & Volpe, C. E. (1995). Defining competencies and establishing team training requirements. In: R. A. Guzzo & E. Salas (Eds), *Team effectiveness and decision making in organizations* (pp. 333–381). San Francisco, CA: Jossey-Bass.

Choi, I., & Nisbett, R. E. (2000). Cultural psychology of surprise: Holistic theories and recognition of contradiction. *Journal of Personality and Social Psychology*, *79*(6), 890–905.

Connerley, M. L., & Pedersen, P. B. (2005). *Leadership in a diverse and multicultural environment: Developing awareness, knowledge, and skills*. Thousand Oaks, CA: Sage.

Cox, T. H., Jr. (1994). *Cultural diversity in organizations: Theory, research, and practice*. San Francisco, CA: Bernett–Koehler.

Day, D. V., & Halpin, S. M. (2001). *Leadership development: A review of industry best practices*. Technical Report no. 1111. US Army Research Institute for the Behavioral and Social Sciences, Alexandria, VA.

Department of the Army. (1999). *Field manual 22–100, Army leadership: Be, know, do*. Washington, DC: U.S. Government Printing Office.

Edmondson, A. (1999). Psychological safety and learning behavior in work teams. *Administrative Science Quarterly*, *44*, 350–383.

Entin, E. E., Sefarty, D., & Deckert, J. C. (1994). *Team adaptation and coordination training*. Technical Report. no. 648-1. ALPHATECH, Inc., Burlington, MA.

Erez, M., & Earley, P. C. (1993). *Culture, self-identity, and work*. New York: Oxford University Press.

Fleishman, E. A., Mumford, M. D., Zaccaro, S. J., Kevin, K. Y., Korotkin, A. L., & Hein, M. B. (1991). Taxonomic efforts in the description of leader behavior: A synthesis and functional interpretation. *Leadership Quarterly*, *2*(4), 245–287.

Geertz, C. (1973). *The interpretation of cultures: Selected essays*. New York: Basic Books.

Graen, G. B., Hui, C., & Gu, Q. L. (2004a). A new approach to intercultural cooperation. In: G. B. Graen (Ed.), *New Frontiers of Leadership* (pp. 225–246). Greenwich, CT: Information Age Publishing.

Graen, G. B., Hui, C., & Taylor, E. T. (2004b). A new approach to team leadership: Upward, downward and horizontal differentiation. In: G. B. Graen (Ed.), *New frontiers of leadership*. Greenwich, CT: Information Age Publishing.

Graen, G. B., & Wakabayashi, M. (1994). Cross-cultural leadership-making: Bridging American & Japanese diversity for team advantage. In: H. C. Triandis, M. D. Dunnette & L. M. Hough (Eds), *Handbook of Industrial and Organizational Psychology* (Vol. 4, pp. 415–446). New York: Consulting Psychologist Press.

Hackman, J. R. (2002). *Leading teams: Setting the stage for great performances*. Boston, MA: Harvard.

Hackman, J. R., & Oldham, G. R. (1980). *Work redesign*. Reading, MA: Addison-Wesley.

Hackman, J. R., & Wageman, R. (2005). A theory of team coaching. *Academy of Management Review*, *30*(2), 269–287 Business School Press.

Hackman, J. R., & Walton, R. E. (1986). Leading groups in organizations. In: P. S. Goodman & Associates (Eds), *Designing effective work groups* (pp. 72–119). San Francisco, CA: Jossey-Bass.

Hall, E. T., & Hall, M. R. (1990). *Understanding cultural differences: The Germans, French and Americans*. Yarmouth, Maine: Intercultural Press.

Harper, L. F., & Rifkind, L. J. (1995). Intercultural communication in the diversified quality workplace. In: L. F. Harper & L. R. Rifkind (Eds), *Cultural collision: Quality teamwork in the diverse workplace* (pp. 41–61). Dubuque, IA: Kendall/Hunt Publishing Company.

Helmreich, R. L., & Merritt, A. C. (1998). *Culture at work in aviation and medicine: National, organizational, and professional influences*. Aldershot: Ashgate.

Hess, K. P., Salas, E., Burke, C. S., Paley, M., Gamty, M., & Bradley, J. (2003). *Going FuLL TiLT toward warrior readiness for coalition and collaborative teams*. SBIR Phase I Final Technical Report (Contract DASW01-03-P-0182). Unpublished Manuscript, Aptima, Inc., Woburn, MA.

Hofstede, G. (1980). *Culture's consequences: International differences in work related values*. Beverly Hills, CA: Sage.

Hofstede, G. (2001). *Culture's consequences: Comparing values, behaviors, institutions, and organizations across nations* (2nd ed.). Thousand Oaks, CA: Sage.

House, R. J., & Javidan, M. (2004). Overview of GLOBE. In: R. J. House, P. J. Hanges, M. Javidan, P. W. Dorfman & V. Gupta (Eds), *Culture, leadership, and organizations: The GLOBE study of 62 societies* (pp. 9–28). Thousand Oaks, CA: Sage.

Jackson, S., Joshi, A., & Erhardt, N. L. (2003). Recent research on team and organizational diversity: SWOT analysis and implications. *Journal of Management*, *29*(6), 801–830.

Klopf, D. W., & Park, M. (1982). *Cross-cultural communication: An introduction to the fundamentals*. Seoul: Han Shin Publishers.

Kozlowski, S. W. J. (2002). Discussant. In: J. C. Ziegert & K. J. Klein (Chairs), *Team leadership: Current theoretical and research perspectives*. Symposium presented at the 17th annual conference of the Society for Industrial and Organizational Psychology, Toronto, Canada.

Kozlowski, S. W. J., Gully, S. M., McHugh, P. P., Salas, E., & Cannon-Bowers, J. A. (1996a). A dynamic theory of leadership and team effectiveness: Developmental and task contingent leader roles. In: G. R. Ferris (Ed.), *Research in personnel and human resources management* (Vol. 14, pp. 253–305). Greenwich, CT: JAI.

Kozlowski, S. W. J., Gully, S. M., Salas, E., & Cannon-Bowers, J. A. (1996b). Team leadership and development: Theory, principles, and guidelines for training leaders and teams.

In: M. Beyerlein, S. Beyerlein & D. Johnson (Eds), *Advances in interdisciplinary studies of work teams: Team leadership* (Vol. 3, pp. 253–292). Greenwich, CT: JAI.

Locke, E. A., & Latham, G. P. (1994). Goal setting theory. In: H. F. O'Neil, Jr. & M. Drillings (Eds), *Motivation: Theory and research* (pp. 13–29). Hillsdale, NJ: Lawrence Erlbaum Associates.

Lord, R. G. (1977). Functional leadership behavior: Measurement and relation to social power and leadership perceptions. *Administrative Science Quarterly*, *22*, 114–133.

McCall, M. W., Lombardo, M. M., & Morrison, A. M. (1988). *The lessons of experience: How successful executives develop on the job*. Lexington, MA: Lexington Books.

Parsons, T., & Shils, E. (1951). *Toward a general theory of social action*. Cambridge, MA: Harvard University Press.

Pierce, L. G. (2002). Barriers to adaptability in a multinational team. *Proceedings of the Human Factors and Ergonomics society 46th Annual Meeting*, (pp. 225–229).

Pierce, L., & Pomranky, R. (2001). The Chameleon Project for adaptable commanders and teams. *Proceedings of the Human Factors and Ergonomics Society 45th annual meeting*, (pp. 513–517).

Rawles, D. (1996). Foreword. In: M. M. Beyerlein, D. A. Johnson & S. Beyerlein (Eds), *Advances in interdisciplinary studies of work teams: Team leadership* (Vol. 3, pp. xvii–xviii). Greenwich, CT: Jai Press, Inc.

Salas, E., Burke, C. S., Wilson-Donnelly, K. A., & Fowlkes, J. E. (2004). Promoting effective leadership within multicultural teams: An event-based approach. In: D. Day, S. J. Zaccaro & S. M. Halpin (Eds), *Leader development for transforming organizations* (pp. 293–323). Mahwah, NJ: Lawrence Erlbaum Associates, Inc.

Salas, E., & Cannon-Bowers, J. A. (2000). The anatomy of team training. In: S. Tobias & J. D. Fletcher (Eds), *Training & retraining: A handbook for business, industry, government, and the military* (pp. 312–335). New York: Macmillan Reference.

Schein, E. H. (2004). *Organizational culture and leadership* (3rd ed.). San Francisco, CA: Jossey-Bass Publishers.

Schwartz, S. H. (1999). A theory of cultural values and some implications for work. *Applied Psychology: An International Review*, *48*(1), 23–37.

Smith-Jentsch, K. A., Zeisig, R. L., Acton, B., & McPherson, J. A. (1998). Team dimensional training: A strategy for guided team self-correction. In: J. A. Cannon-Bowes & E. Salas (Eds), *Making decisions under stress: Implications for individual and team training*, (pp. 271–297). Washington, DC: American Psychological Association.

Stagl, K. C., Burke, C. S., Salas, E., & Pierce, L. (this volume). Team adaptation: The realization of team synergy. In: C. S. Burke, L. Pierce & E. Salas (Eds), *Advances in human performance and cognitive engineering research* (Edited volume in preparation). Oxford, UK: Elsevier Science.

Tesluk, P. E., Dragoni, L., & Russell, J. A. (2002). Growing management talent: Role of developmental work experiences, learning orientation, and access to opportunities in shaping managerial competencies and advancement potential. Paper presented at 17th annual conference of the Society for Industrial and Organizational Psychology, Toronto, Canada.

Thomas, D. C. (1999). Cultural diversity and work group effectiveness. *Journal of Cross-cultural Psychology*, *30*(2), 242–263.

Tomasovic, R. (2001). *Leader development and education for sustained peace*. Executive Summary Presentation. Center for Civil Military Relations, Naval Postgraduate School, Monterey, CA.

Triandis, H. C. (2000). Culture and conflict. *International Journal of Psychology*, *35*(2), 145–152.
Trompenaars, F. (2002). In: V. Gupta & R. House (Chairs), *Building effective networks: Reconciling cultural dimensions of five international programs*. Symposium conducted at the annual meeting of the Academy of Management Conference, Denver, CO.
Trompenaars, F., & Hampden-Turner, C. (1998). *Riding the waves of culture: Understanding cultural diversity in global business*. New York, NY: McGraw-Hill.
Watson, W. E., Kumar, K., & Michaelsen, L. K. (1993). Cultural diversity's impact on interaction process and performance: Comparing homogeneous and diverse task groups. *Academy of Management Journal*, *36*(3), 590–602.
Zaccaro, S. J., Rittman, A., & Marks, M. A. (2001). Team leadership. *Leadership Quarterly*, *12*, 451–483.

ADAPTIVE AUTOMATION: BUILDING FLEXIBILITY INTO HUMAN-MACHINE SYSTEMS ☆

Mary T. Dzindolet, Hall P. Beck and Linda G. Pierce

ABSTRACT

In complex environments, the use of technology to enhance the capability of people is commonplace. In rapidly changing and often unpredictable environments, it is not enough that these human-automated "teams" perform well when events go as expected. Instead, the human operators and automated aids must be flexible, capable of responding to rare or unanticipated events. The purpose of this chapter is to discuss the Framework of Automation Use (Dzindolet, Beck, Pierce, & Dawe, 2001) as it relates to adaptive automation. Specifically, our objectives are to: (1) examine a number of factors that determine how people can effectively integrate their activities with their machine partners in fluid environments and (2) consider the implications of these findings for future research.

☆Portions of this paper were presented in a previous technical report: Dzindolet, M. T., Beck, H. P., Pierce, L. G., & Dawe, L. A. (2001). A framework of automation use (Rep. No. ARL-TR-2412). Aberdeen Proving Ground, MD: Army Research Laboratory and at a conference: Dzindolet, M. T., Pierce, L. G., & Beck, H. (2003, May). Understanding the Human-Computer Team. Paper presented at the North Atlantic Treaty Organization's Critical Design Issues for the Human-Machine Interface, Prague, Czech Republic.

Understanding Adaptability: A Prerequisite for Effective Performance within Complex Environments
Advances in Human Performance and Cognitive Engineering Research, Volume 6, 213–245

ISSN: 1479-3601/doi:10.1016/S1479-3601(05)06007-8

On a snowy evening in 1996, a Washington Metropolitan Area Transit Authority (WMATA) subway train overran the Shady Grove station and crashed into an unoccupied train. At the time of the wreck, the driver, abiding by WMATA procedures, had set the train to automatic mode. The subsequent study by the National Transportation Safety Board (1996) revealed that administrative decisions by the WMATA did not take into account the limitations of automation during inclemency. Had the driver been authorized to change to manual control, he could have allowed for the icy tracks, slowed the subway train, and prevented the accident.

In most circumstances, using the automatic rather than the manual mode to control the train was appropriate. Automation was generally safer and produced less equipment wear than manual operation. What the WMATA system designers failed to consider was that the normally safe and efficient automatic mode became deadly when conditions changed. Administrative decisions by the WMATA set the level of automation (LOA) at the system design stage. Only under the direst circumstances was an operator intended to assume manual control of the train.

Accidents such as the crash of the subway at Shady Grove provide some of the most graphic demonstrations of the need for system designers and operators to exhibit adaptability when developing and working with human-machine systems. In rapidly changing and often unpredictable environments, it is not enough that people and machines perform well when events go as expected. Instead, systems must be flexible, capable of responding to rare or unanticipated events.

In static human-automation teams, such as the one used at Shady Grove, system designers make the LOA decisions. However, in adaptive environments, the final authority of the LOA decisions is shared by the automated aid and the human operator. In contrast to static automation, adaptive automation (e.g., Parasuraman, Bahri, Deaton, Morrison, & Barnes, 1992; Rouse, 1988; Scallen, Hancock, & Duley, 1995) is context dependent. The goal of adaptive automation (AA) is not to identify the best overall LOA, but to determine the best LOA under a given set of circumstances. AA has been proposed as a means of attenuating some of the problems arising from static automation such as degradation of skills and decrease in situational awareness.

The purpose of this chapter is to introduce a framework that we have found useful in organizing much of the automation usage literature. Specifically, our objectives are to: (1) examine a number of factors that determine how people can effectively integrate their activities with their machine partners in fluid environments and (2) consider the implications of these findings for future research.

A BRIEF OVERVIEW OF AUTOMATION USAGE

Automation is "any sensing, detection, information-processing, decision-making, or control action that could be performed by humans but is actually performed by a machine" (Moray, Inagaki, & Itoh, 2000, p. 44). Although automation is often regarded as a radical technological development, it is a natural extension of the trend toward mechanization that produced the Industrial Revolution (Coleman, 1992). Most of the early uses of automation emulated or expanded upon human muscles and senses. Recent scientific achievements, especially within the field of computer science, have greatly expanded the realm of automation making it possible to simulate many of the mental processes that were once the sole domain of people.

Because a task can be automated does not necessarily mean that the task should be automated. While there are many examples of successful application, the introduction of automation onto the battlefield and into the workplace has frequently failed to produce expected gains (e.g., Bainbridge, 1983; Parasuraman & Riley, 1997; Wiener & Curry, 1980; Woods, 1996). Too often military and civilian organizations have funded the development of expensive devices only to discover that operators were unwilling to use them or that the task could be better performed by a manual or less technologically advanced alternative.

Not all of the disappointments associated with automation are hardware and software failures. Some decision aids that meet designer specifications have no functional utility. The prevalence of electronically sophisticated but useless automation clearly highlights the main weakness in the state-of-the-art. We are better at creating electronic marvels than we are at building useful automated aids.

Though automation can serve many purposes, the most common goal is to improve task performance. In choosing between automated and manual alternatives, the optimal decision is typically the one that has the highest probability of accomplishing the task. Viewing automation usage from a decision-making perspective allows us to specify two types of choices that would result in suboptimal LOAs. Misuse is over utilization, relying on automation when the manual option is more likely to achieve the goal (Parasuraman & Riley, 1997). Disuse is under utilization, manually performing a task that could best be done by automation (Parasuraman & Riley, 1997).

While it is often convenient to speak of automated versus manual modes as a dichotomy, in actuality the move from manual to automated control is seldom all-or-none. A number of different classification systems (e.g.,

McDaniel, 1988; Riley, 1989; Sheridan & Verplank, 1978; Wickens, 1997) incorporate the idea that automation is more accurately seen as a continuum. The vertical axis in Table 1 shows the ten LOAs originally proposed by Sheridan and Verplank (1978). Manual operation, in which a person carries out an activity without intervention from a machine, is at one end of the continuum. At the higher levels of the scale, the machine becomes increasingly autonomous of human control. The tenth level is full automation; the machine performs all aspects of the task independent of human input.

Parasuraman, Sheridan, and Wickens (2000) extended Sheridan and Verplank's original scheme to include four information-processing functions or stages. The first stage, "information acquisition," refers to the sensing and registration of input data. Telescopes, which can be programmed to locate a particular star or planet, are examples of information acquisition. The second stage called, "information analysis," involves cognitive functions such as working memory and inference. Actuarial equations used to predict college grades (e.g., Beck & Davidson, 2001) are conducting information analysis. "Decision and action selection" is the third stage and involves a comparison of alternatives. Computer programs, which select the fastest driving route between cities, are performing decision and action selection. "Action implementation" is the final stage and refers to the execution of the response following the decision. Usually, a sensor or triggering mechanism initiates this function. Electronic doors, which activate when a person or other object breaks a photo beam, and photocopiers that may be programmed to print, collate and staple are examples of action implementation. Parasuraman et al.'s (2000) model forms a 10×4 matrix in which LOAs and stages of information processing serve as factors.

Good taxonomies are extremely useful devices. They present a set of possible systems, identify key variables, and often suggest approaches to automation that the designer may not have considered. However, taxonomies per se do not indicate which functions to automate and to what levels. For example, Parasuraman et al.'s taxonomy suggests that an artillery battery could, within engineering limits, be fully automated. Their taxonomy also implies many alternatives to full automation, all of which would give more control to the human operator and less to the machine. What the taxonomy does not do is predict the LOA that will produce the most effective gun battery. Taxonomies present the potential routes without selecting the best path.

Until recently, many task allocation decisions were based solely on engineering limitations. Machines were assigned tasks whenever feasible and human input was restricted to those activities that could not be efficiently

Table 1. Automation Usage Decisions as a Function of Information Processing and Automation Levels.

		Information Acquisition	Information Analysis	Action Selection	Action Implementation
10.	The computer decides everything, acts autonomously, ignoring the human.				
9.	Informs the human only if it, the computer, decides to				
8.	Informs the human only if asked, or				
7.	Executes automatically, then necessarily informs the human, and				
6.	Allows the human a restricted time to veto before automatic execution, or				
5.	Executes that suggestion if human approves, or				
4.	Suggests one alternative				
3.	Narrows the selections down to a few, or				
2.	The computer offers a complete set of decision/action alternatives, or				
1.	The computer offers no assistance: human must make all decisions and actions.				

Note: This table was adopted from Parasuraman, Sheridan, and Wickens (2000). Shaded areas represent functions and automation levels requiring automation usage decisions.

automated. Full automation provided an ideal, a goal that system designers hoped to increasingly approximate. An alternative perspective holds that full automation is not always an attainable or even desirable objective. Full automation can lead to skill degradation (Wickens, 1992) and limit the situational awareness of human operators (Endsley & Kiris, 1995). Others argue that human operators should always be given final authority over automated aids (e.g., Billings & Woods, 1994). AA allows automation and human operators to share in determining appropriate LOAs. If the human operator were bored or noticed the automated aid were making errors, the human operator could move from a more automated LOA to a more manual one. Similarly, automation, noticing a change in the human operator's heart rate variability (Byrne & Parasuraman, 1996) or a decrement in performance on a secondary task (Kaber & Riley, 1999), could move from a more manual LOA to a more automated one.

Instead of creating ever more automated systems, the goal is to develop a synergy based upon a harmonious blend of human and machine attributes, human strengths to offset machine weaknesses, and machine strengths to offset human weaknesses. In order to achieve this "harmonious blend," we must understand the processes human operators use when making LOAs. Armed with this understanding, system designers and those who train human operators can predict the conditions in which human operators are likely to make suboptimal allocation decisions (Fig. 1).

THE FRAMEWORK OF AUTOMATION USE

The Framework of Automation Use (see Fig. 1; Dzindolet, Beck, Pierce, & Dawe, 2001) provides a conceptual framework to help in understanding the processes that human operators use when deciding on an appropriate LOA. The original framework viewed automation as a dichotomous variable. In this chapter, we have adapted the framework to include various LOAs. The Framework of Automation relies heavily on the work of Mosier and Skitka (1996), who outlined three possible reasons why people inappropriately use automation or choose suboptimal LOA decisions: (1) cognitive miser hypothesis, (2) authority hypothesis, and (3) diffusion of responsibility. Paralleling this work is the group dynamics literature, which identified cognitive, social, and motivational processes as causes of productivity loss in groups (e.g., Mullen, Johnson, & Salas, 1991). Since many researchers have considered a human-computer "team" to be a group in which one member happens not to be human (e.g., Bowers, Oser, Salas, & Cannon-Bowers,

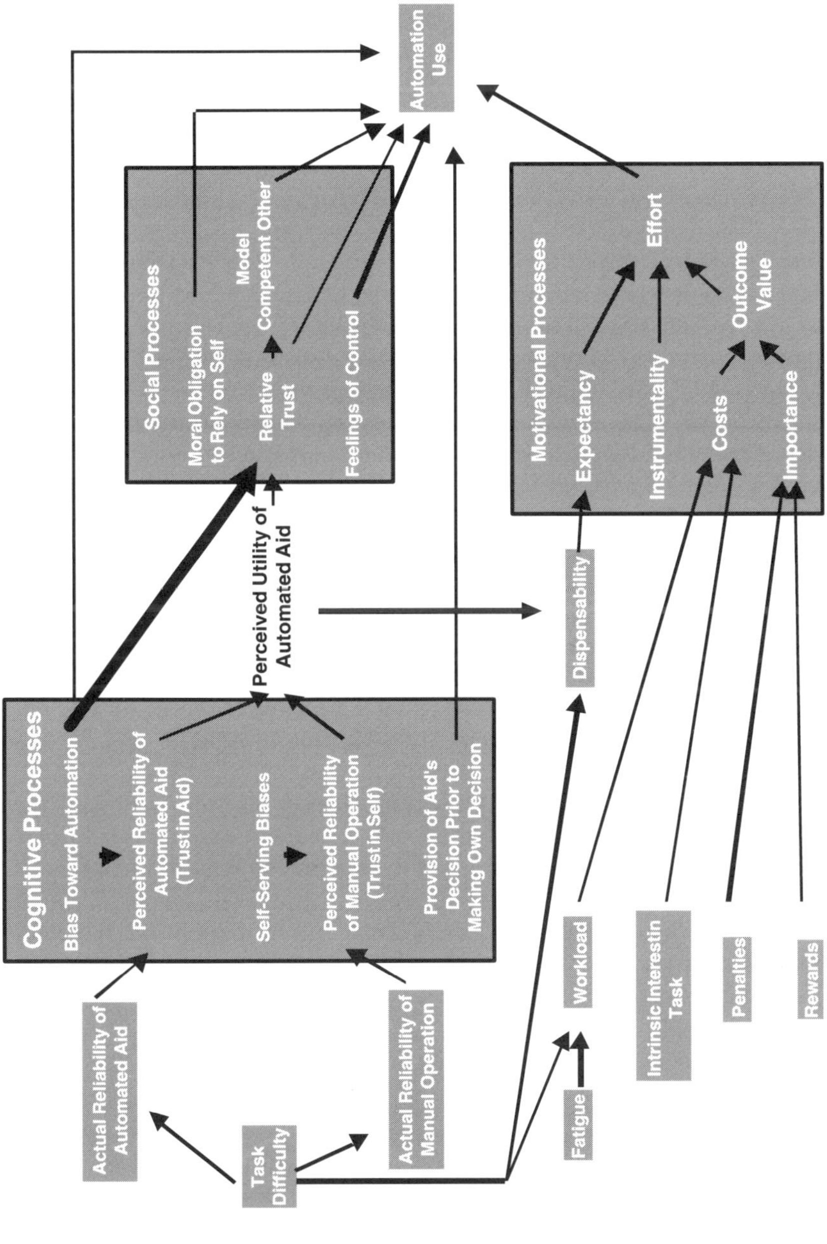

Fig. 1. Dzindolet et al. (2001) Framework of Automation.

1996; Christoffersen & Woods, 2002; Sarter, 2001; Sarter & Woods, 2000; Scerbo, 1996), Dzindolet et al. hypothesized that these group dynamic processes could lead to suboptimal LOA decisions and performance in human-computer teams. A discussion of the three processes follows.

Cognitive Processes: Cognitive Miser Hypothesis/Automation Bias

Mosier and Skitka (1996) hypothesized that people may overly rely on automated systems when making decisions due to faulty cognitive processing. The cognitive literature contains an examination of a myriad of errors due to flawed cognitive processing in *individual* decision-making (Tversky & Kahneman, 1973). In addition, the social cognition literature is replete with examples of less-than-ideal cognitive processing while working in teams or groups. Errors and biases have been identified in various domains of social psychology (e.g., illusory correlation and in-group differentiation/out-group homogeneity in stereotype formation (Hamilton & Sherman, 1989; Mullen & Hu, 1989), the halo effect and the negativity bias in impression formation (Skowronski & Carlston, 1989), the confirmation bias and self-handicapping in attribution (Arkin & Baumgardner, 1985; Leyens & Yzerbyt, 1992)). Rather than logically processing relevant pieces of information, people often adopt effort-saving strategies called heuristics. Mosier and Skitka (1996) coined the term "automation bias" to refer to, "the tendency to use automated cues as a heuristic replacement for vigilant information seeking and processing" (p. 205).

The fact that the automated system provides a decision may lead the decision-maker to rely on this information in a heuristic manner (see Fig. 2). Relying on the aid's decisions heuristically, the human operator chooses an LOA that is skewed toward automation reliance. Rather than going through the cognitive effort of gathering and processing information, the information supplied by the automated system is used (Mosier & Skitka, 1996). The

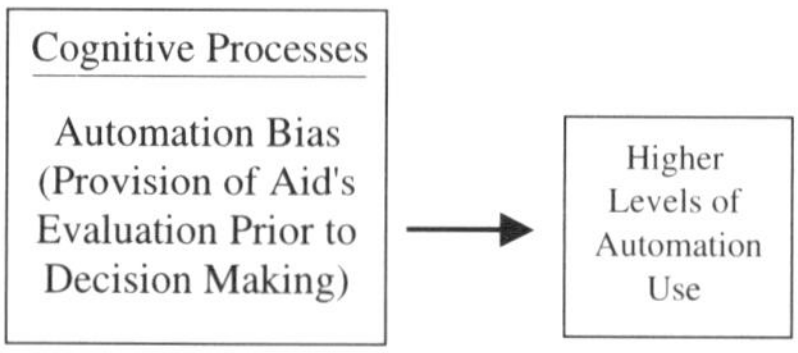

Fig. 2. Automation Bias.

amount of skewing may occur in various degrees. In its most extreme form, the decision reached by the automated aid is immediately adopted. In a less extreme form, the decision reached by the aid may be given an inappropriately large role in the human's decision-making process. For example, Layton, Smith, and McCoy (1994) found many pilots provided with an automated aid's poor en-route flight plan did not explore other solutions (e.g., they did not generate actual flight plans on screen) as much as pilots not provided with the automated aid's decision.

Indirect evidence to support the existence of automation bias has been found by examining task allocation decisions across two experimental paradigms. In one paradigm, the automation bias was allowed to flourish; in the other, it was prevented from occurring. In both paradigms, the LOA decision was simple and dichotomous. Participants either relied on the automated aid's decision or on their own decision. In addition, an adaptive environment did not exist in either paradigm. The human had complete authority for determining the LOA. In one paradigm, the LOA could vary from trial to trial; in the other paradigm, the LOA was measured only once and could not vary. A description of each paradigm follows.

Automation Bias Present

In one of the paradigms, participants viewed about 200 slides displaying pictures of Fort Sill terrain on a computer screen (see Fig. 3 for a sample slide). About half of the slides contained one soldier ("target") in various levels of camouflage; the remaining slides were of terrain only. Sometimes the target was easy to detect (as in Fig. 3); other times it was more difficult to find.

Each slide was presented on the computer screen for about $\frac{3}{4}$ of a second. Participants did not need to make their absent–present decision alone; they were provided with the decision of an automated decision aid. Specifically, participants were told that a computer routine had been written to assist them in performing their task. They were told that the routine performed a rapid scan of the photograph looking for contrasts that suggested the presence of a human being. If the contrast detector routine determined the soldier was probably present, the word "PRESENT" and a red circle appeared. If the contrast detector routine determined the soldier was probably absent, the word "ABSENT" and a green circle appeared.

The next screen asked the participants to indicate whether or not they believed the soldier was in the slide. They were given as much time as they needed to make their decision. Participants were informed that there were two possible errors that they could make. One error was made when they

Fig. 3. Sample Slide Containing Soldier.

indicated that the soldier was present when, in fact, he was not. The other error was made when they indicated that the soldier was not present when, in fact, he was. Participants were told that both errors were equally serious and that they should attempt to avoid them.

Finally, the participants indicated the extent to which they were certain their decision was correct. A five-point Likert scale ranging from "highly confident" to "not at all confident" was provided. Because participants viewed the automated decision aid's decision before making their own decision, the automation bias was allowed to flourish.

To analyze reliance in this paradigm, participants' overall error rate was determined [p(error)]. To examine error type, the participants' error rate was determined for the trials in which the aid gave the correct decision [p(error|aid correct)] and for the trials in which the aid gave an incorrect decision [p(error|aid error)]. Misuse, or overreliance on the contrast detector, existed when p(error|aid error) > p(error|aid correct). Disuse, or underutilization of the contrast detector, existed when p(error|aid error) = p(error|aid correct).

Repeatedly, misuse was found. For example, Dzindolet et al. (2001) found that regardless of the reliability of the automated aid, participants were more likely to err by relying on their decision aids than by ignoring them, p(error|aid error) = 0.27; p(error|aid correct) = 0.13. In some studies, participants not provided with the automated decision aid outperformed those provided with the aid due to the inappropriate LOA used by the participants (Beck, Dzindolet, Pierce, & McKinney, 2003; Dzindolet et al., 2001).

Therefore, when provided with the aid's decisions first, thereby allowing the automation bias to operate, participants were more likely to misuse than disuse their automated aids.

Automation Bias Absent

Changing this paradigm slightly, we were able to create a paradigm in which the automation bias was eliminated. Participants were not provided with the decisions reached by the contrast detector until after they had indicated their decision and their level of confidence in their decision. Without the automation bias, were participants still more likely to misuse than disuse their automated aids?

Participants in these studies viewed the slide of Fort Sill terrain for about $\frac{3}{4}$ of a second, indicated their decision, rated their confidence, and, only then, were provided with the contrast detector's decision. After completing 200 slides, students were told they could earn $5 in coupons to be used at the university cafeteria (or in some studies, extra credit in a course) for every correct decision made on ten randomly chosen trials. Participants had to choose whether the performance would be based on their decisions or on the decisions of their aid. After making their choice, students were asked to justify their choice in writing.

Rather than misusing the contrast detector, participants in these studies disused the automated aid (Dzindolet, Peterson, Pomranky, Pierce, & Beck, 2003; Dzindolet, Pierce, Beck, & Dawe, 2002). Even among participants provided with feedback that their aid's performance was far superior to their own, the majority chose to rely on their own decisions rather than on the decisions of the automated aid. For example, Beck, Dzindolet, Pierce, Poole, and McDowell (2000) found that 83% of participants in their study chose self-reliance rather than relying on the decisions of a superior automated decision aid.

Therefore, when the automation bias could play a role in the LOA decision, misuse occurred more than disuse. However, when the automation bias was eliminated by providing the automated aid's decisions only after participants recorded their decision, disuse, not misuse, was found on a subsequent task allocation decision.

The automation bias may not only play a role in a human operator's decision when choosing an appropriate LOA, it may also play a role in the human operator's performance in ascertaining when conditions warrant that the current LOA should be reassessed. For example, if an automated aid is designed to monitor its own performance and notify the human operator when a more manual mode of operation should be employed, the human operator, under the automation bias, may be likely to rely too heavily on the automated decision aid's assessment.

Although the automation bias may play a role in assessing and predicting LOA decisions, it cannot account for human operators' choice of an LOA that is skewed toward reliance on the human operator. Automation bias cannot account for disuse. The information received from the automated aid is predicted to influence the human's response. Ignoring an automated aid's decision would not be expected. Other factors must also play a role in determining LOAs. Analyses of the justifications of the task allocation decisions provided by participants indicated some of these variables (Dzindolet et al., 2002). For example, nearly one-quarter (23%) of the participants in Dzindolet et al. (2003) study justified their disuse by stating that they did not trust the automated aid as much as they trusted themselves. Similarly, many of the participants who chose self-reliance in the Dzindolet et al. (2003) Study 2 justified their decision by stating that they did not trust the automated decision aid. Trust, a social process, clearly influences LOA determination and maintenance.

Social Processes: Authority Hypothesis/Trust in Automation

A second explanation of the inappropriate LOA decisions has to do with the role of the computer as the expert. According to Mosier and Skitka's (1996) authority hypothesis, people rely on the automated system's decision because they believe it to be more reliable, and thus place greater trust in it. Many other researchers have expanded on trust influences in automation use (Beck, Dzindolet, & Pierce, 2002; Cohen, Parasuraman, & Freeman, 1998; Jian, Bisantz, & Drury, 2000; Lee & Moray, 1992, 1994; Lee & See, 2004; Lewandowsky, Mundy, & Tan, 2000; Liu & Hwang, 2000; Moray, 2001; Moray et al., 2000; Muir, 1987, 1994; Singh, Molloy, & Parasuraman, 1993; Tan & Lewandowsky, 1996; Wiegmann, Rich, & Zhang, 2001). Inappropriate levels of trust will lead to inappropriate LOA decisions. Overly trusting an automated aid will lead human operators to misuse; lack of trust in a superior aid will lead to disuse. In addition, trust may affect the human operator's performance in assessing a previously determined LOA. Overly trusting an automated aid, a human operator may not vigilantly monitor the situation to be sure that the LOA is appropriate as time and conditions change. Not trusting a superior aid may lead a human operator to ignore decrements in manual performance as time and conditions change.

Parasuraman and Riley (1997) described many real-world incidences in which disastrous results occurred due to people ignoring automated warning signals they saw as untrustworthy. Ignoring automated alarm systems that have previously signaled in error has been dubbed the "cry wolf effect" (Bliss, 1997; Bliss, Dunn, & Fuller, 1995). Publicizing the alarm's trustworthiness was one strategy that proved effective in reducing the cry wolf phenomenon (Bliss et al., 1995).

Muir (1987, 1994), one of the first researchers to focus on automation trust, relied on the literature on human trust to understand human operator's trust of automation. She hypothesized that automation that is predictable, dependable, and inspires faith that it will behave as expected in unknown situations, will be seen as more trustworthy.

To test some of Muir's hypotheses, Lee and Moray (1992, 1994) examined the effect of trust in automation on task allocation decisions in an adaptable environment. Participants in Lee and Moray's studies always had the final LOA decision as they controlled a simulated orange juice pasteurization plant for two hours each day for three days. The simulation included three subsystems, each of which could be operated manually or automatically. Participants could allocate tasks any way they wished and could change their allocations easily. As part of the experiment, whether controlled automatically or manually, one of the subsystems failed periodically. Lee and Moray (1992, 1994) were especially interested in task allocation changes after these failure events, since Muir predicted that after failure events, trust would decline rapidly and slowly increase as the system performed without making errors. Thus, based on Muir's work LOA decisions should be adjusted to more manual levels after failure events. With exposure to repeated trials in which the automated aid did not err, the human operator may again change the LOA to a more automated level.

Results indicated strong individual differences in automation use. Some participants were prone to use manual control; others were prone to use automation.

Status Quo Bias

Inconsistent with Muir's hypotheses, the Lee and Moray (1992, 1994) participants rarely changed their allocation task decisions. The extent to which the resistance to change in LOA decisions is due to trust in automation, trust in manual performance, lack of vigilance in monitoring human-automation team performance, or some other cause is unknown. For example, personality may influence trust in automation. Singh et al. (1993) created a scale to determine individual differences in the propensity to misuse automated aids that may have been able to predict which individuals would be prone to rely on automation and which would be prone to rely on manual operation. Once the human operator assigned a subsystem to automated or manual control, he or she was unlikely to change the decision during that session – even after failure events. In the decision-making literature, such a decision has been termed the status quo bias (Anderson, 2003). Human operators operating under the status quo bias have an "inflated preference for the current state of affairs" (p. 145).

Perceived Utility of Aid

In Lee and Moray's (1992, 1994) and Tan and Lewandowsky's (1996) earlier work, LOA decisions could be determined through a comparison process of trust in the automated aid and trust in manual operation. Thus, the Framework of Automation hypothesized that LOA decisions, under some conditions, are determined from the outcome of a comparison process between the perceived reliability of the automated aid (trust in aid) and the perceived reliability of manual control (trust in self). Dzindolet et al. (2001) called the outcome of the decision process the perceived utility of the automated aid (see Fig. 4). If one perceives the ability of the aid to be greater than one's own, perceived utility of the aid will be high. If one perceives the ability of the aid to be inferior to one's own, perceived utility of the aid will be low.

Perceived utility is one variable that affects LOA decisions. When perceived utility is high, greater LOAs are favored over more manual alternatives. However, when perceived utility is low, manual alternatives are favored over more automated levels.

Since accurately perceiving the utility of the aid might lead to appropriate LOA decisions, it is very important that we gain an understanding of how

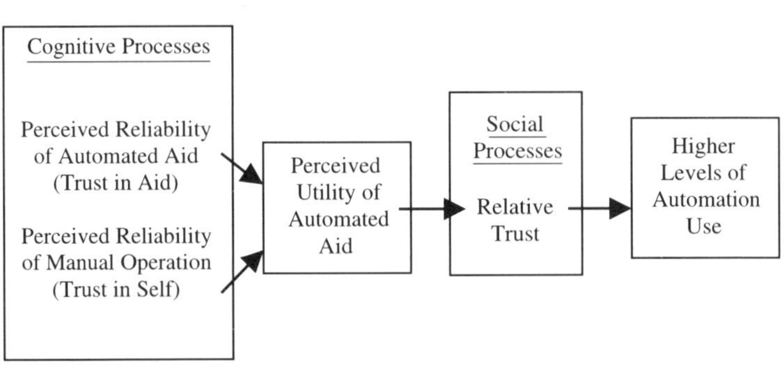

Fig. 4. Relative Trust.

this perception is formed. The perceived utility of the aid will be most accurate when the actual ability of the aid and actual ability of the manual operator are compared. However, the "actual" ability is never known. Perceived ability is determined through a function of actual ability and error. The larger the error, the more likely misuse and disuse is to occur. We suspect that at least two types of errors occur.

Self-Serving Bias

One type of error occurs when human operators estimate their own performance. Human operators tend to overestimate their own ability. Social psychological literature is fraught with examples of self-serving biases. Humans exaggerate their contribution to a group product (appropriation of ideas, Wicklund, 1989), overestimate the number of tasks they can complete in a given period of time (planning fallacy, Buehler, Griffin, & Ross, 1994), are overconfident in negotiations (Neale & Bazerman, 1985), and inflate their role in positive outcomes (Whitley & Frieze, 1985). Thus, we hypothesize that human operators will be likely to overestimate their manual ability.

The extent of the self-serving bias may be, in part, determined by the LOA being examined for use. It might be that LOAs closer to full manual operation are influenced more (or less) by self-serving biases than LOAs that are closer to full automation. The strength of self-serving biases may consistently decline (or increase) as one moves from full-manual operation to full automation, or the strength may vary in a less linear fashion. These hypotheses have not been explored in the AA literature.

At any given moment, a human operator may evaluate his or her manual performance inappropriately due to self-serving biases. In addition, actual manual ability may change over time and vary from situation to situation. The extent to which self-serving biases remain constant (or change) with actual manual ability is unknown. Automation research has virtually ignored how the reliability of one's estimation of manual performance varies over time and situation. Clearly, this area of research is needed to understand adaptable automation decisions.

Bias Toward Automation

Human operators' estimates of manual ability represent one type of error. The other type of error occurs when human operators estimate the performance of their automated aid. Prior to working with the aid, the human must rely on stereotypes formed concerning the performance of automated aids. Although individual differences exist, a bias toward automation leads many people to predict near-perfect performances from automated aids. Dzindolet et al. (2002) told half the participants they would be provided with the decisions reached by the contrast detector before they made their soldier absent/present decision for each of the 200 slides. Other participants were told they would be provided with the decisions reached by the prior participant before making their soldier absent/present decision for each of the 200 trials. The instructions informed the participants that their aid (human or automated) was not perfect. When asked to estimate the number of errors the automated aid would make in the upcoming 200 trials, participants predicted, on average, the aid would make only 14.19 errors (i.e., correct nearly 93% of the time). When asked to estimate the number of errors the human aid would make, participants predicted, on average, 46.17 errors (i.e., correct only 77% of the time – only 27% better than chance). Other researchers have also found a bias toward automation. For example, Dijkstra, Liebrand, and Timminga (1998) found students judged advice from an expert system to be more rational and objective than the same advice from a human advisor. However, Lerch, Prietula, and Kulik (1997) found greater trust in automated systems than human advisors only when the automation was an expert system and the human advisor was a novice. They did not find participants were more likely to trust an automated expert system than a human expert advisor.

As with self-serving biases, the bias toward automation may vary with LOA either linearly or in some other fashion. In addition, the bias toward automation may vary as the actual reliability of automation changes. Parasuraman, Molloy, and Singh (1993) and Singh, Molloy, and Parasuraman (1997) varied the actual reliability of the automation over time. Some participants worked with an automated system that was consistently correct 87.5% of the time; others worked with a system that was consistently correct 56.25% of the time. Others worked with machines that varied in reliability. Some participants started with automated systems that were accurate 87.5% of the time for the first ten minutes of the session of the experiment, but then alternated in reliability between 56.25% and 87.5% during 10-min intervals for the rest of the experimental session. Other participants started working with a less reliable automated system that alternated to a more reliable one every 10 min during the experimental session. In addition to monitoring the automated task, participants were required to simultaneously perform two manual tasks.

Overreliance on automation was found by participants in both of the constant conditions (Parasuraman et al., 1993) and the salience of the automation failure signals did not affect the results (Singh et al., 1997). Thus, when the reliability of the automation varied, participants appropriately relied on the automated monitoring system. However, when the system was consistent in its reliability (either high or low), participants tended to overly rely on the system's monitoring capabilities. Singh et al. (1997) hypothesize that complacency was due to the participants being too trusting of the automation. "Participants may have begun the automated sessions with an equal amount of trust in the automation. However, as the reliability of the automation fluctuated for the variable group their trust may have declined. Therefore, the variability group may have been more skeptical of the automation, and, thus, been more vigilant for automation failures" (p. 28). However, participants' trust was not measured in the study, so the relationship between trust and the status quo bias has yet to be empirically tested.

In summary, the perceived reliability of the automated aid is determined by the actual reliability of the automated aid and by the bias toward automation. The perceived reliability of manual operation is determined by the actual reliability of the human operator and by self-serving biases. Perceived utility is the comparison of the perceived reliability of the automated aid and manual operation. Perceived utility is one factor that affects LOA decisions. In addition, we hypothesize that perceived utility may play a role in the diligence the human operator chooses to take in assessing whether changes in LOA decisions need to be made. The status quo bias may keep LOA decisions constant over time and situations may be affected by perceived utility.

Increasing the actual reliability of the aid will not necessarily affect LOA decisions. Only if the aid's perceived reliability surpasses that of perceived manual operations will human operators choose a more automated LOA. This can explain the inconsistent findings concerning automation reliability and human-computer performance. For example, Riley (1994) and Moray et al. (2000) found people were more likely to overly rely on a more reliable than a less reliable automated system. Yet, Dzindolet et al. (2001), Parasuraman et al. (1993) and Singh et al. (1997) did not find participants to rely on more reliable decision aids than less reliable ones.

Therefore, we hypothesize that people may misuse an automated aid when the perceived utility of the aid is overestimated and disuse an aid when the perceived utility of the aid is underestimated. The perceived utility of the system results from a comparison between the perceived ability of the automated system and one's own perceived ability. Perceived ability is hypothesized to be affected by actual ability and various biases (self-serving and bias toward automation). In addition, the constancy of the reliability may affect trust and the status quo bias.

Improving LOA Decisions

Reducing the biases should decrease inappropriate automation use. Providing accurate feedback will assuage the self-serving biases. Dzindolet et al. (2002) found that providing feedback of the contrast detector's superior performance after each trial and/or at the end of the 200 trials reduced disuse. Beck and Davidson (2001) found that disuse could be reduced by providing participants multiple forms of feedback of their own and of the superior aid's performance. However, in both of these studies, some disuse was found – even when participants were continually reminded of the number of errors both they and their aid had made (and the aid had made half as many errors).

Understanding the reliability of the automated aid may be difficult for human operators, especially if they begin with a bias toward automation. Dzindolet et al. (2003) hypothesize that when a participant views an easy slide, quickly spots a target, and makes his or her decision with a high degree of confidence, he or she assumes that the automated aid will be in concurrence. When the automated aid indicates that the target is absent, the participant is likely to notice the obvious error just committed by the aid. Without an understanding of why this error was made, this obvious error violates the trust the operator has in the aid's decisions. Trust may diminish slowly or may immediately drop to a low level. As long as participants are able to view the decisions made by their automated aids, obvious errors can be detected setting in motion the violation of trust. In some of the conditions in Study 2 of Dzindolet et al. (2003), participants could not view the aid's decisions. Results indicated appropriate automation reliance only among participants who received continuous feedback of their aid's superiority and were unable to view errors made by the decision aid.

In Study 3 of Dzindolet et al. (2003), participants were provided with an explanation as to why their automated aid might err. This manipulation was successful in increasing the participants' level of trust in the automated decision aid and reliance on the aid. Unfortunately, participants provided with inferior aids were just as likely to rely on them as those provided with superior aids. Thus, although providing participants with a rationale as to their aid's errors was successful in reducing disuse, in certain conditions, it led to misuse.

How do these variables affect trust in an adaptive environment? Moray et al. (2000) examined trust among human operators using AA. In a microworld, human operators were to control the temperature of apartments using a central heating system and determine what to do if leaks or breaks occurred in pipes. The automated aid provided diagnoses of potential problems. If the situation was not time-critical, then the human operator could either solve the problem indicated by the diagnosis (low LOA) or indicate that the automated aid should solve the problem (moderate LOA). But, if the situation was time-critical, then the automation would automatically take over (high LOA). The automation's diagnosis was correct either, 70, 90, or 100 percent of the time. After each trial, participants completed a short automated questionnaire to measure the level of trust in the aid and trust in manual operation. In addition, participants were provided with performance feedback at the end of each trial.

Using time-series modeling, they determined that trust in the automated aid was determined by the automated aid's reliability, the occurrence of false diagnoses, and the number of times that the human operator disagreed with the automated aid's diagnosis. Trust in manual operation was determined by prior trust in manual operation and the number of accidents. They conclude that different processes are used to determine trust in aid and trust in manual operation. "Trust [in aid] seems to be reduced by properties of the system (real or apparent false diagnoses), whereas self confidence [i.e., trust in manual operation] is reduced by experiences of the operator (experience of accidents)" (Moray et al., 2000, p. 54). One fascinating finding was that no differences in trust in aid and trust in manual operation were found among the three LOAs examined. "The transfer of authority in the face of fast dynamic faults appears to be well tolerated. Some operators indicated informally that when the severe Break L1 was controlled automatically by SVL 7 automation, their feeling of self-confidence [trust in manual operation] increased, whereas others stated the contrary" (Moray et al., 2000, p. 55).

Need for Control

In addition to perceived utility affecting LOA decisions, we conjecture that two other social processes may affect automation use: feelings of control and moral obligation to rely on self. Fig. 5 illustrates the social processes.

Analyses of the justifications of the task allocation decisions provided by participants in one of the Dzindolet et al. (2002) experiments revealed that 71% of the students, who were provided with cumulative feedback that indicated that the aid made about an equal number of errors as the participant, justified self-reliance with statements indicating they would not earn more rewards if they relied on the aid. Since the task allocation decision would not affect the size of their reward, why did participants opt for self-reliance? We hypothesize that lower LOAs provide participants with an illusion of control. Langer (1983) has found that people often behave illogically in order to have an illusion of control.

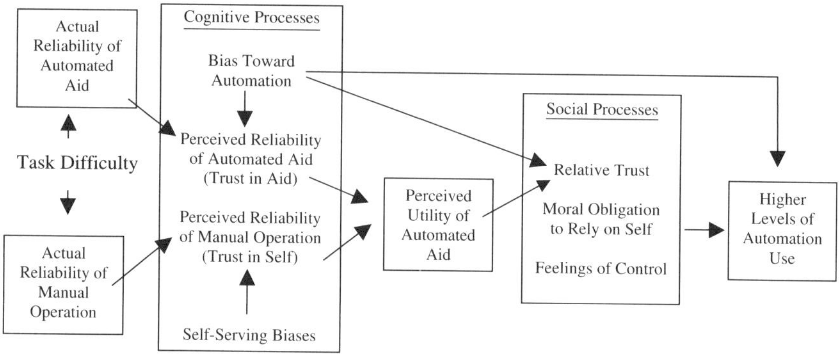

Fig. 5. Social Processes.

Moral Obligation

In addition, many participants (though more working with human aids ($n = 24$, 43.64%) than automated aids ($n = 9$, 16.67%; $X^2 = 8.58$, $p < 0.01$) justified self-reliance with statements concerning a moral obligation to rely on oneself. One student wrote, "I would rather the amount of coupons I receive be based on my performance – it seems more 'fair' to myself." Another wrote, "I feel anything earned should be based on how well I did or didn't do."

Much research remains to be performed to explore the social processes and their effect on automation use. Beck, Dzindolet, Pierce, and McKinney (2003) recently found that students taking a multiple choice test who could request help from an automated aid known to be correct about 70 percent of the time performed better than those who could not request to view the automated aid's responses. What is surprising about this result was that the performance difference existed even for the trials in which the students did not view the aid's help. Just knowing that one could be aided by automation led to better performance. Whether this was due to social facilitation, motivation, or other factors has yet to be explored. Only with a more clear understanding of these processes will we be able to suggest ways in which misuse and disuse can be reduced. The variables which affect perceived utility are of special interest to us because perceived utility is not only predicted to affect trust, but also to affect the last of the processes, motivational processes.

Motivational Processes: Diffusion of Responsibility

A third explanation of the overreliance on automation discussed by Mosier and Skitka (1996) involves the idea that when working in a group, the responsibility for the group's product is diffused among the group members. In this case, the group is the human-computer system (Bowers et al., 1996; Scerbo, 1996; Woods, 1996). Thus, the human may feel less responsible for the outcome when working with an automated system than when working without one. The person may not be as motivated to extend as much effort when paired with an automated system as when working alone. In addition, the human operator may not be as motivated to diligently monitor the performance of the human-computer team to determine when shifts in LOA are appropriate in an AA environment as in an adaptable environment. In the social–psychological literature, this phenomenon has been dubbed social loafing (cf. Latane, Williams, & Harkins, 1979) or free riding (Kerr & Bruun, 1983).

One theory which has been successful in accounting for much of the findings in the social loafing literature is Shepperd's (1993, 1998) Expectancy-Value Theory. According to this theory, motivation is predicted by a function of three factors: expectancy, instrumentality, and outcome value.

Expectancy

The first factor, expectancy, is the extent to which members feel that their efforts are necessary for the group to succeed (see Fig. 6). When members feel their contributions are dispensable, or when one's individual contribution is unidentifiable or not evaluated, one is likely to free ride, or work less hard (Kerr & Bruun, 1983; Williams & Karau, 1991).

With a human–computer system, individual contributions tend to be identifiable and evaluated, thus these variables are not thought to affect motivational processes. However, when the perceived utility of a system is high, one is likely to feel his or her efforts are more dispensable than when working with a system low in perceived utility. Thus, we would expect human operators to be likely to misuse an automated system deemed more reliable than themselves in the same way people free ride on group members

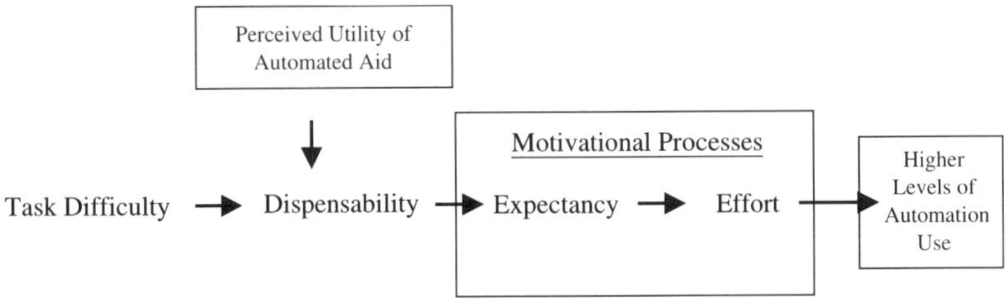

Fig. 6. Expectancy.

deemed more reliable than themselves. Thus, as perceived utility of the automated aid increases, LOA decisions should become more and more skewed toward full automation. Most of the time, this decision may be optimal. However, if changes in the situation occur, or if the automated aid's or human operator's reliability changes, then the LOA decision may need to be revised.

Task difficulty, which is predicted to affect perceived utility (see Fig. 5), has also been found to directly affect dispensability. In fact, one of the methods researchers have used to make group members feel their efforts are indispensable has been to imply that the difficulty of the task makes the demands on each group member particularly high (Shepperd, 1993). For example, Harkins and Petty (1982) asked participants to generate as many uses as they could for either a knife (easy task) or for a detached door knob (difficult task) either alone or in nine-member groups. Although they found social loafing with the easy task (group members did not generate as many ideas as those working alone), they did not find social loafing with the difficult task.

In summary, the more dispensable the human operator is made to feel, the lower expectancy will be; effort will probably be low and the likelihood that the automated aid will be relied upon will be high. In some instances, this will lead to suboptimal LOA decisions. In addition, dispensability may affect the diligence human operators use as they monitor the current LOA for possible modification.

Instrumentality

Instrumentality, the extent to which members feel that the group's successful performance will lead to a positive overall outcome, is also predicted to affect effort. Members who feel the outcome is not contingent on the group's performance are less likely to work hard. Thus, human operators who feel their human-automated team's performance is irrelevant are likely to rely on higher LOAs and to allow the automated aid to determine when changes in LOA are necessary. In one study, Shepperd (1998) varied instrumentality. Half the participants were told that the seven groups with the highest number of ideas generated (out of ten groups) would earn a reward. Other participants were told that the members of the four groups with the highest number of ideas generated (out of 40 groups) would have their names entered into a lottery. One name would be drawn and that person would earn a reward. Thus, in the former condition, members had a 7 in 10 chance of attaining the reward; in the latter condition, there was only a 1 in 200 chance of attaining the reward. In addition to the optimistic bias (participants estimated their chance of winning to be about 1 in 4), he found that performance suffered when instrumentality was lowered.

In many situations, there will be more than one human-automated team. For example, on the battlefield, there will be many soldier-computer teams. If the human determines that the overall outcome is not contingent on his or her human-computer team (either because he estimates other teams are more able to do the task or that his human-computer team is dispensable), then the human will put little effort into the task. High LOAs will be used and changes in LOA decisions as conditions and time changes will be unlikely.

Outcome Value

Finally, the value of the outcome is predicted to affect motivation. Outcome value is the difference between the importance of the outcome and the costs associated with working hard. Increasing the costs or minimizing the importance of the reward will lead members to put forth less effort. More effort may lead to better awareness of variables that should indicate changes in LOA decisions. People who are highly motivated may be more likely to make optimal LOA decisions in a dynamic context.

More effort will be extended toward tasks that lead to valuable outcomes without requiring much cost. Costs vary with the number of other tasks one must perform, fatigue, intrinsic interest of the task, and cognitive overhead (see Fig. 7).

Workload. As workload increases, the cost of performing a specific task increases, thereby leading to more automated LOA decisions (and the

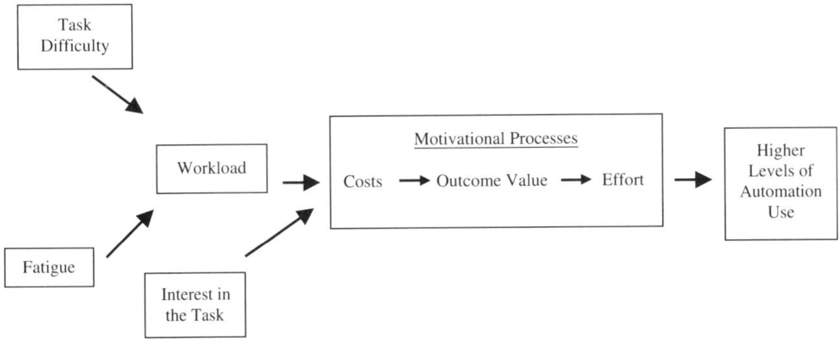

Fig. 7. Costs.

potential for misuse). In Study 2 of Parasuraman et al. (1993), misuse did not occur among participants who were required only to perform the automated task. Overreliance on automation was found only among participants who had to manually perform two additional tasks. Similarly, Thackray and Touchstone (1989) did not find differences in detection of failures between aided and unaided participants performing a single task. With AA, human operators may move from more manual LOAs to more automated LOAs when they perceive increases in workload may occur. Unfortunately, in high workload situations, human operators may be the least able to make appropriate LOA shifts. Parasuraman and Riley (1997) found that human operators may overestimate the stresses of increased workload and prematurely switch to more automated LOAs.

Measures of human operator workload have been explored as the basis for automation controlling LOA decisions and taking the human temporarily out of the loop. Using physiological measures of arousal, automation could monitor the human operator's arousal state. Measures such as heart rate variability, EEG signals, eye fixation, and scanning have been suggested as ways of assessing the human operator's arousal level (Byrne & Parasuraman, 1996; Parasuraman & Byrne, 2003). If arousal level was deemed as high (or low) enough to impede performance, then automation would modify the LOA to a more automated and less manual solution.

Just having to make an LOA shift may affect workload in an AA environment. For example, when human operators feel responsible for assessing and monitoring the performance of the human-computer team to determine when changes in LOA are warranted, workload may be increased. Support for this idea was found in a study performed by Kaber and Riley (1999). Participants simultaneously performed two tasks. In the primary task, participants were to monitor moving shapes on a "radar scope" and destroy shapes before they moved to the center of the screen or collided with another shape. Participants were told that the primary task was the most important one and to work on the second task only with what attention resources remained. In the secondary task, participants were to monitor a moving pointer and respond when the pointer moved out of range. Half the participants were told that if their performance on the secondary task became satisfactory, then an automated system would take over the primary task (i.e., the automated system would make the LOA change). The other half of the participants were told that if their performance on the secondary task became unsatisfactory, then an automated system would suggest that it should take over the primary task (i.e., the human operator would determine whether or not to make an LOA change). When comparing the performances in the manual mode on the primary task, participants who did not have to decide whether or not to change the LOA decisions performed better. Kaber and Riley suggest that having to monitor and assess the human-computer team's performance to determine if changes in LOA are necessary increased the human operator's workload.

Workload may affect optimal LOA decisions in unintended ways. For example, if high LOAs are used under low workload conditions then the human operator is likely to become bored and uninterested. This may make it more difficult for the human operator to respond to a sudden threat or system failure. Clearly, optimal LOAs change as conditions change. AA allows the human and the automation to respond to such changes.

Fatigue. The more fatigued the human operator is, the higher the cost of performing a task. Therefore, we would expect human operators to choose higher LOAs and to change the LOA decisions less often when fatigued than when well rested. Of course, when fatigued, human operators may be less likely to alter the LOA, especially if changing the LOA demands an exertion of effort. Physiological and/or performance assessments of the human operator would allow the automated aid to "know" that the human has reached a level of fatigue that is detrimental to performance and change the LOA to a more automated level. Kaber and Riley (1999) used performance on a secondary task to determine human operator's fatigue level. Parasuraman and Byrne (2003) outline various physiological measures that could be used, for example, heart rate variability, EEG, eye–scanning, and fixations to determine fatigue and workload.

Interest in the Task. The cost of performing a task that is intrinsically interesting is less than the cost of performing a less interesting task. For example, the cost of performing boring, redundant tasks is higher than the cost of performing interesting tasks. If the task is boring enough, the cost might outweigh the importance; outcome value will be decreased, effort will be lower, and higher LOAs will be continually used. The potential for misuse will rise.

In summary, if costs of manual operation are larger than importance due to large workload, fatigue of the human operator, and/or boredom of the task, then outcome value will be low. The amount of effort expended on the task is predicted to be low. Thus, high LOAs will be used; monitoring of the performance of the human-computer team to assess the need for changes in the LOA decision will be unlikely.

Costs will only affect automation use, however, if they are deemed greater than the importance of the outcome. If the importance of the outcome is deemed greater than the cost, outcome value will be high, thereby increasing effort. With increased performance, more manual LOAs may be selected initially. Diligent monitoring of the performance of the human-computer team to determine when the LOA decision should be modified will probably lead to changes in LOA decisions as time and situations change. Importance is predicted to be affected by the rewards of successful task completion and the penalties of task failure (see Fig. 8).

Rewards. When successful completion of the task leads to highly valued resources (e.g., money, prestige), and if the rewards are not outweighed by the costs of succeeding, then outcome value will be high and participants are predicted to work hard.

Penalties. Similarly, when grave penalties are a consequence of successful completion of the task not occurring, specifically, when the penalties of failure outweigh the costs of succeeding, then outcome value will be high and participants are predicted to work hard.

On the battlefield, suboptimal human-computer performance can be lethal; outcome value is extremely high. In combat, disuse may be more of a problem than misuse. Among such highly motivated people, misuse may not exist at all. Human operators who show such high levels of motivation may prematurely change LOA decisions toward manual operation. This is consistent with findings from some interviews with Gulf War soldiers, who indicated they turned off their automated systems.

For this reason, it is imperative that some of the research testing the model be performed in more combat-like environments. Virtual reality simulators may be useful to meet this end. At the very least, researchers should

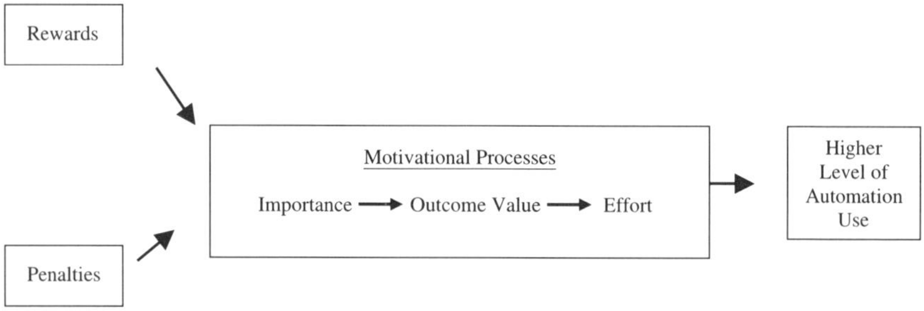

Fig. 8. Importance of Outcome.

examine automation reliance while varying the consequences for successful task performance. Although it is intuitively appealing, albeit, somewhat obvious, to predict that instituting positive consequences for successful performance would lead to improved automation reliance, this may not necessarily occur. In the Dzindolet et al. (2002) and Moes, Knox, Pierce, and Beck (1999) experiments using static automation, participants earned coupons or extra-credit for correct decisions. Yet, in all three studies, disuse prevailed. Of course, in these studies, the consequences were not varied. Future research needs to manipulate rewards and penalties in an AA environment to determine the effects on performance.

In summary, penalties and rewards will affect the importance of successful completion of the task. If importance is greater than costs associated with performing the task, outcome value will be high, leading effort to be expended, and LOA decisions to be skewed toward manual operation and less stable than when less effort is expended. In some situations, this will lead to optimal task allocation decisions; sometimes it will lead to inappropriate LOA decisions.

CONCLUSIONS

The Framework of Automation Use predicts that human operators use cognitive, social, and motivational processes to make and maintain LOA decisions. Research has found several errors that are commonly made by human operators that may lead to suboptimal LOA decisions. With a deeper understanding of these tendencies, system designers and human operator trainers can determine the conditions under which the automated aid should make the LOA decisions and the conditions under which the human operator should be given control of the LOA decisions. Fig. 9 summarizes some of the biases and errors human operators may have.

Many factors affect each of the processes, and may therefore, affect LOA decisions. The reliability of the automated aid, the reliability of manual operation and several cognitive biases (including self-serving and the bias toward automation) combine to affect the perceived utility of the aid. When the perceived utility of the aid is high, the operator is likely to trust the aid and feel dispensable; his or her efforts are not necessary for the task to be completed. LOA is predicted to be stable and high through both social and motivational processes. Fatigue, workload, intrinsic interest in the task, penalties for task failure, and rewards for task completion combine to affect

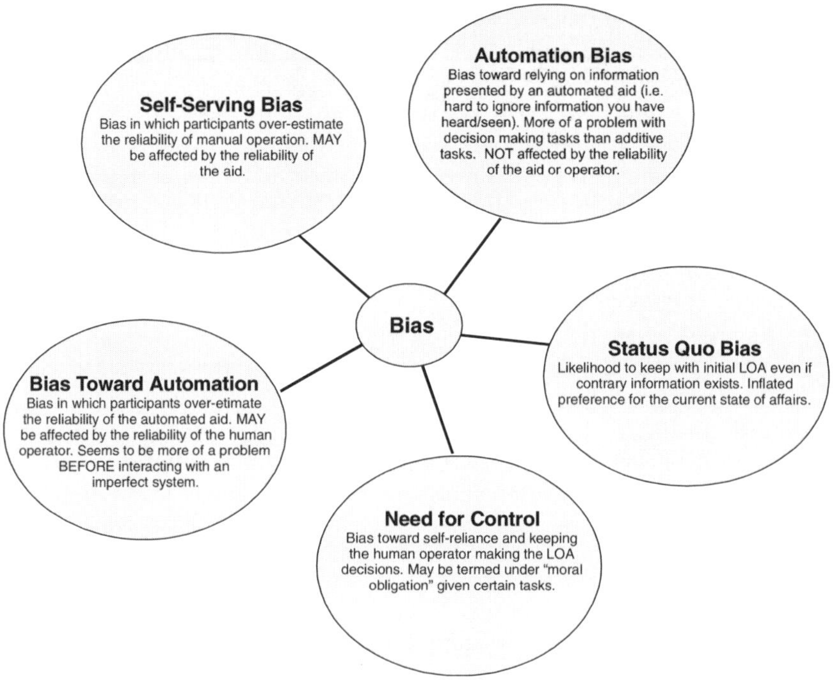

Fig. 9. Biases.

the outcome value, which also will affect the effort the human will expend on the task. Effort also affects the variability and LOA likely to be used.

Future researchers need to further examine this framework, determine the effect of each of the cognitive, social, and motivational processes on automation use, and examine the interaction of the three processes. We believe the framework will prove useful to researchers interested in reducing automation misuse and disuse.

In addition to this theoretical perspective, a strong look at the empirical evidence gained from the studies performed with the paradigms discussed at the beginning of the paper and from other researchers may help to guide system designers and trainers. System designers and trainers can use the empirical findings and the Framework of Automation Use to help create situations, which encourage human operators to appropriately rely on automated decision aids. One can view adaptive automation within a 2 (decision: change LOA vs. status quo) $\times$ 2 (decision-maker: human operator vs. automation) matrix. We have focused on the human decision-maker's processes and biases in changing and maintaining LOAs; system designers should explore the automated system's processes and determine the potential errors it is likely to make. Future researchers could aid system designers in this feat.

Our level of analysis has focused on the human-automated team. However, each team is often working with other human-automated teams to accomplish tasks and goals. Often the human-computer teams work with other lateral teams and teams both higher and lower within an organizational structure. At each of these levels, adaptability is needed to ensure optimal performance. Future research should explore variables that affect the entire system's performance.

Armed with knowledge of the biases human operators are likely to use when making LOA decisions, system designers, human operators, and their trainers can help to make human-automated teams operate synergistically compensating for each other's weaknesses, adapting to complex, ambiguous, ever changing environments in order to perform optimally.

ACKNOWLEDGMENT

We would like to thank Scott Peterson for reviewing earlier drafts of the paper. In addition, we are indebted to many students who spend countless hours collecting data reported in this paper: Jennifer Batka, Emily Beadles, Regina Pomranky, Lori (Purcell) Sawyer, Tamara Young.

REFERENCES

Anderson, C. J. (2003). The psychology of doing nothing: Forms of decision avoidance result from reason and emotion. *Psychological Bulletin, 129*, 139–167.

Arkin, R., & Baumgardner, A. H. (1985). Self-handicapping. In: J. H. Harvey & G. Weary (Eds), *Basic issues in attribution theory and research*. New York: Academic Press.

Bainbridge, L. (1983). Ironies of automation. *Automatica, 19*, 775–779.

Beck, H. P., & Davidson, W. B. (2001). Establishing an early warning system: Predicting low grades in college students from Survey of Academic Orientations Scores. *Research in Higher Education, 42*, 709–723.

Beck, H. P., Dzindolet, M. T., & Pierce, L. G. (2002). Applying a decision-making model to understand misuse, disuse, and appropriate automation use. In: E. Salas, C. A. Bower, N. Cooke, J. Driskell & D. Stone (Eds), *Advances in human factors and cognitive engineering* (Vol. 2). Boston: JAI Press.

Beck, H. P., Dzindolet, M. T., Pierce, L. G., & McKinney, J. B. (2003). Looking to the future: A simulation of decision aids in tomorrow's classroom. Paper presented at the Human Factors and Ergonomics Society Meeting, Denver, CO.

Beck, H. P., Dzindolet, M. T., Pierce, L. G., Poole, A. H., & McDowell, L R. (2000). Feedback mitigates bias against machines with decision-making capabilities. Poster session presented at the annual meeting of the Southeastern Psychological Association, New Orleans, LA.

Billings, C. E., & Woods, D. D. (1994). Concerns about adaptive automation in aviation systems. In: R. Parasuraman & M. Mouloua (Eds), *Human performance in automated systems: Current research and trends* (pp. 264–269). Hillsdale, NJ: Lawrence Erlbaum Associates.

Bliss, J. P. (1997). Alarm reaction patterns by pilots as a function of reaction modality. *International Journal of Aviation Psychology*, *7*, 1–14.

Bliss, J. P., Dunn, M., & Fuller, B. S. (1995). Reversal of the cry-wolf effect: An investigation of two methods to increase alarm response rates. *Perceptual and Motor Skills*, *80*, 1231–1242.

Bowers, C. A., Oser, R. L., Salas, E., & Cannon-Bowers, J. A. (1996). Team performance in automated systems. In: R. Parasuraman & M. Mouloua (Eds), *Automation and human performance: Theory and applications. Human factors in transportation*. Mahwah, NJ: Lawrence Erlbaum Associates.

Buehler, R., Griffin, D., & Ross, M. (1994). Exploring the "planning fallacy": Why people underestimate their task completion times. *Journal of Personality and Social Psychology*, *67*, 366–381.

Byrne, E. A., & Parasuraman, R. (1996). Psychophysiology and adaptive automation. *Biological Psychology*, *42*, 249–268.

Christoffersen, K., & Woods, D. D. (2002). How to make automated systems team players. In: E. Salas (Ed.), *Advances in human performance and cognitive engineering research: Automation* (Vol. 2, pp. 1–12). Kidlington, Oxford: Elsevier Science/JAI Press.

Cohen, M. S., Parasuraman, R., & Freeman, J. T. (1998). Trust in decision aids: A model and its training implications. *Proceedings of the 1998 command and control research and technology symposium*. CCRP, Washington, DC.

Coleman, D. C. (1992). *Myth, history, and the Industrial Revolution*. Rio Grande, OH: Hambledon Press.

Dijkstra, J. J., Liebrand, W. B. C., & Timminga, E. (1998). Persuasiveness of expert systems. *Behaviour and Information Technology*, *17*, 155–163.

Dzindolet, M. T., Beck, H. P., Pierce, L. G., & Dawe, L. A. (2001). *A framework of automation use*. Rep. No. ARL-TR-2412. Army Research Laboratory, Aberdeen Proving Ground, MD.

Dzindolet, M. T., Peterson, S. A., Pomranky, R. A., Pierce, L. G., & Beck, H. P. (2003). The role of trust in automation reliance. *International Journal of Human Computer Studies: Special Issue on Trust and Technology*, *58*, 697–718.

Dzindolet, M. T., Pierce, L. G., Beck, H. P., & Dawe, L. A. (2002). The perceived utility of human and automated aids in a visual detection task. *Human Factors*, *44*, 79–94.

Endsley, M., & Kiris, E. O. (1995). The out-of-the-loop performance problem and level of control in automation. *Human Factors*, *37*, 381–394.

Hamilton, D. L., & Sherman, S. J. (1989). Illusory correlations: Implications for stereotype theory and research. In: D. Bar-Tal, C. F. Graumann, A. W. Kruglanski & W. Stroebe (Eds), *Stereotyping and prejudice: Changing conceptions*. New York: Springer.

Harkins, C. G., & Petty, R. E. (1982). Effects of task difficulty and task uniqueness on social loafing. *Journal of Personality and Social Psychology*, *43*, 1214–1229.

Jian, J., Bisantz, A. M., & Drury, C. G. (2000). Foundations for an empirically determined scale of trust in automated systems. *International Journal of Cognitive Ergonomics*, *4*, 53–71.

Kaber, D. B., & Riley, J. M. (1999). Adaptive automation of a dynamic control task based on secondary task workload measurement. *International Journal of Cognitive Ergonomics*, *3*, 169–188.

Kerr, N. L., & Bruun, S. E. (1983). Dispensability of member effort and group motivation losses: Free-rider effects. *Journal of Personality and Social Psychology*, *44*, 78–94.

Langer, E. J. (1983). *The psychology of control*. Beverly Hills, CA: Sage.

Latane, B., Williams, K. D., & Harkins, S. (1979). Many hands make light the work: The causes and consequences of social loafing. *Journal of Personality and Social Psychology*, *37*, 822–832.

Layton, C., Smith, P. J., & McCoy, C. E. (1994). Design of a cooperative problem-solving system for enroute flight planning: An empirical evaluation. *Human Factors*, *36*, 94–119.

Lee, J. D., & Moray, N. (1992). Trust, control strategies and allocation of function in human-machine systems. *Ergonomics*, *35*, 1243–1270.

Lee, J. D., & Moray, N. (1994). Trust, self-confidence, and operators' adaptation to automation. *International Journal of Human-Computer Studies*, *40*, 153–184.

Lee, J. D., & See, K. A. (2004). Trust in automation: Designing for appropriate reliance. *Human Factors*, *46*, 50–80.

Lerch, F. J., Prietula, M. J., & Kulik, C. T. (1997). The turing effect: the nature of trust in expert system advice. In: P. J. Feltovich, K. M. Ford & R. R. Hoffman (Eds), *Expertise in context: Human and machine* (pp. 417–448). Menlo Park, CA: AAAI Press.

Lewandowsky, S., Mundy, M., & Tan, G. P. A. (2000). The dynamics of trust: Comparing humans to automation. *Journal of Experimental Psychology: Applied*, *6*, 104–123.

Leyens, J., & Yzerbyt, V. Y. (1992). The in-group overexclusion effect: Impact of valence and confirmation on stereotypical information search. *European Journal of Social Psychology*, *22*, 549–569.

Liu, C., & Hwang, S. L. (2000). Evaluating the effects of situation awareness and trust with robust design in automation. *International Journal of Cognitive Ergonomics*, *4*, 125–144.

McDaniel, J. W. (1988). Rules for fighter cockpit automation. In: *Proceedings of the IEEE national aerospace and electronics conference*, IEEE, New York (pp. 831–838).

Moes, M., Knox, K., Pierce, L. G., & Beck, H. P. (1999). Should I decide or let the machine decide for me? Poster presented at the meeting of the Southeastern Psychological Association, Savannah, GA.

Moray, N. (2001). Humans and machines: Allocation of function. In: J. Noyes, & M. Bransby (Eds), *People in control: Human factors in control room design*. Edison, NJ: Institution of Electrical Engineers (IEE control engineering series, 60).

Moray, N., Inagaki, T., & Itoh, M. (2000). Adaptive automation, trust, and self-confidence in fault management of time-critical tasks. *Journal of Experimental Psychology: Applied*, *6*, 44–58.

Mosier, K. L., & Skitka, L. J. (1996). Human decision-makers and automated decision aids: Made for each other? In: R. Parasuraman & M. Mouloua (Eds), *Automation and human performance: Theory and applications. Human factors in transportation*. Mahwah, NJ: Lawrence Erlbaum Associates.

Muir, B. M. (1987). Trust between humans and machines, and the design of decision aids. *International Journal of Man–Machine Studies*, *27*, 527–539.

Muir, B. M. (1994). Trust in automation: Part I. Theoretical issues in the study of trust and human intervention in automated systems. *Ergonomics*, *37*, 1905–1922.

Mullen, B., & Hu, L. (1989). Perceptions of ingroup and outgroup variability: A meta-analysis integration. *Basic and Applied Social Psychology*, *10*, 233–252.

Mullen, B., Johnson, C., & Salas, E. (1991). Productivity loss in brainstorming groups: A meta-analytic integration. *Basic & Applied Social Psychology*, *12*, 3–23.

National Transportation Safety Board. (1996). *Collision of Washington metropolitan transit authority train T111 with standing train at Shady Grove Station, Near Gaithersburg, MD*, (January 6), (Rep. PB 96-916304). Washington, DC.

Neale, M. A., & Bazerman, M. H. (1985). The effects of framing and negotiator overconfidence on bargaining behaviors and outcomes. *Academy of Management Journal*, *28*, 34–49.

Parasuraman, R., Bahri, T., Deaton, J., Morrison, J., & Barnes, M. (1992). *Theory and design of adaptive automation in aviation systems*. Progress Report No. NAWCADWAR-92033-60. US Naval Air Warfare Center, Warminster, PA.

Parasuraman, R., & Byrne, E. A. (2003). Automation and human performance in aviation. In: P. S. Tsang & M. A. Vidulich (Eds), *Principles and practice of aviation psychology: Human factors in transportation* (pp. 311–356). Mahwah, NJ: Lawrence Erlbaum Associates.

Parasuraman, R., Molloy, R., & Singh, I. L. (1993). Performance consequences of automation-induced "complacency". *International Journal of Aviation Psychology*, *3*, 1–23.

Parasuraman, R., & Riley, V. (1997). Humans and automation: Use, misuse, disuse, abuse. *Human Factors*, *39*, 230–253.

Parasuraman, R., Sheridan, T. B., & Wickens, C. D. (2000). A model for types and levels of human interaction with automation. *IEEE Transactions on Systems, Man, and Cybernetics*, *30*, 286–297.

Riley, V. (1989). A general model of mixed-initiative human–machine systems. In: *Proceedings of the human factors society 33rd annual meeting*, Human Factors Society, Santa Monica, CA (pp. 124–128).

Riley, V. (1994). Human use of automation. *Dissertation Abstracts International: Section B: The Sciences & Engineering*, *55*, 2425.

Rouse, W. B. (1988). Adaptive aiding for human/computer control. *Human Factors*, *30*, 431–443.

Sarter, N. (2001). Human technology interface: Multimodal communication and support of coordinated functions of human–machine teams. *Journal of Human Performance in Extreme Environments*, *5*, 50–54.

Sarter, N., & Woods, D. D. (2000). Team play with a powerful and independent agent: A full-mission simulation study. *Human Factors*, *4*, 390–402.

Scallen, S. F., Hancock, P. A., & Duley, J. A. (1995). Pilot performance and preference for short cycles of automation in adaptive function allocation. *Applied Ergonomics*, *26*, 397–403.

Scerbo, M. W. (1996). Theoretical perspectives on adaptive automation. In: R. Parasuraman & M. Mouloua (Eds), *Automation and human performance: Theory and applications. Human factors in transportation*. Mahwah, NJ: Lawrence Erlbaum Associates.

Shepperd, J. A. (1993). Productivity loss in performance groups: A motivation analysis. *Psychological Bulletin*, *113*, 67–81.

Shepperd, J. A. (1998). Expectancy Value Theory. Presentation presented at the Midwestern Psychological Association, Chicago, IL.

Sheridan, T. B., & Verplank, W. L. (1978). *Human and computer control of undersea teleoperators*. Technical Report. MIR Man–Machine Systems Laboratory, Cambridge, MA.

Singh, I. L., Molloy, R., & Parasuraman, R. (1993). Automation-induced "complacency": Development of the complacency-potential rating scale. *International Journal of Aviation Psychology*, *3*, 111–122.

Singh, I. L., Molloy, R., & Parasuraman, R. (1997). Automation-induced monitoring inefficiency: Role of display location. *International Journal of Human–Computer Studies*, *46*, 17–30.

Skowronski, J. J., & Carlston, D. E. (1989). Negativity and extremity biases in impression formation: A review of explanations. *Psychological Bulletin*, *105*, 131–142.

Tan, G., & Lewandowsky, S. (1996). *A comparison of operator trust in humans versus machines.* Presentation of the First International Cyberspace Conference on Ergonomics: http://www.curtin.edu.au/conference/cyberg/centre/paper/tan/paper.html.

Thackray, R. I., & Touchstone, R. M. (1989). Detection efficiency on an air traffic control monitoring task with and without computer aiding. *Aviation, Space & Environmental Medicine*, *60*, 744–748.

Tversky, A., & Kahneman, D. (1973). Availability: A heuristic for judging frequency and probability. *Cognitive Psychology*, *5*, 207–232.

Whitley, B. E., Jr., & Frieze, I. H. (1985). Children's causal attributions for success and failure in achievement settings: A meta-analysis. *Journal of Educational Psychology*, *77*, 608–616.

Wickens, C. D. (1992). *Engineering psychology and human performance* (2nd ed.). New York: Harper Collins.

Wickens, C. D. (1997). Automation. In: C. D. Wickens, A. S. Mavor & J. P. McGee (Eds), *Flight to the future: Human factors in air traffic control.* Washington, DC: National Academy Press.

Wicklund, R. A. (1989). The appropriation of ideas. In: P. B. Paulus, et al. (Eds), *Psychology of group influence.* Hillsdale, NJ: Lawrence Erlbaum Associates.

Wiener, E. L., & Curry, R. E. (1980). Flight-deck automation: Promises and problems. *Ergonomics*, *23*, 995–1011.

Wiegmann, D., Rich, A., & Zhang, H. (2001). Automated diagnostic aids: The effects of aid reliability on users' trust and reliance. *Theoretical Issues in Ergonomics Science*, *2*, 352–367.

Williams, K. D., & Karau, S. J. (1991). Social loafing and social compensation: The effects of expectations of coworker performance. *Journal of Personality and Social Psychology*, *61*, 570–581.

Woods, D. D. (1996). Decomposing automation: Apparent simplicity, real complexity. In: R. Parasuraman & M. Mouloua (Eds), *Automation and human performance: Theory and applications.* Mahwah, NJ: Lawrence Erlbaum Associates.

SECTION III: ORGANIZATIONAL LEVEL ADAPTABILITY

NORMATIVE DESIGN OF PROJECT-BASED ADAPTIVE ORGANIZATIONS

Georgiy Levchuk, Daniel Serfaty and Krishna R. Pattipati

In mid-2001 a carrier battle group was underway to its new assignment in the Persian Gulf. Its mission was to perform a presence patrol and to provide naval aviation to conduct Operation Southern Watch. The battle group arrived on location just after the September 11th attack on the World Trade Center and the Pentagon. Thus, its mission was changed significantly – from peacetime presence and Southern Watch to playing a major role in Operation Enduring Freedom. Many aspects of the mission were different: the *tempo* of operations changed from a moderate-tempo (where there was time allocated for maintenance and training in addition to flying) to high-tempo sustained operations in support of the troops (Special Operations Force, Marines, Afghani Freedom Fighters, etc.) on the ground. The *mission* had also changed radically: the country of interest was different and the mission tasks were different. That is, the previous tasks that involved countering anti-aircraft systems and an integrated air defence system changed to a totally different set of tasks, i.e., all in support of ground forces.

This actual scenario is but one example of how military forces need to be *adaptable* to accommodate changes in mission that will occur as part of the

Understanding Adaptability: A Prerequisite for Effective Performance within Complex Environments
Advances in Human Performance and Cognitive Engineering Research, Volume 6, 249–287

ISSN: 1479-3601/doi:10.1016/S1479-3601(05)06008-X

nature of warfare. The purpose of this chapter is to present the normative methodology developed under the Adaptive Architectures for Command and Control (A2C2) research program to address such needs for adaptation of military and other mission-based organizations. Our approach integrates optimization, modeling, and simulation-based research efforts with psychology-based and experimental activities to address key issues in command and control. Our research has followed a model-experiment-model paradigm wherein designs produced by the modeling/simulation support the formulation of hypotheses, the determination of key variables and parameter values, and the prediction of organizational performance and processes of adaptation. The experimental data, in turn, are collected and produced in such a way that allows for both examination of the hypotheses and ease of use by the modelers for post-experimental model-data comparison and model refinement.

One of the major thrusts of the A2C2 research has been the development of models and constructs to design organizations that are *matched* to a given mission that they plan to perform (Levchuk, Levchuk, Luo, Pattipati, & Kleinman, 2002). A salient factor that has emerged from this work and motivated our research of mission-based organizations is the concept of organizational "congruence". These congruence theories loosely state that the better an organization is matched to the overall mission (as measured using a multi-variant set of workload/congruence metrics), the better will that organization perform – and that mismatches are potential drivers for organizational adaptation. In this chapter, we first review the research in the area of organizational strategy and structure design. Next, problem settings and the model-based *congruent design* concept development, which formed the basis of our modeling paradigm, are described. Finally, we present the alternative *robust design* approach and discuss its benefits and disadvantages. Our research efforts have culminated in the development of an *adaptive design* process, which incorporates the notions of congruence and robustness, and allows developing cost-efficient adaptation strategies to achieve higher performance in the presence of uncertainty and/or changing environment.

RELATED RESEARCH

Over the past few years, mathematical and computational models of organizations have attracted a great deal of interest in various fields of scientific research (see Lin & Carley, 1993 for review). The mathematical models have focused on the problem of quantifying the structural (mis)match between organizations and their tasks. The notion of structural congruence has been generalized from the problem of optimizing distributed decision-making in structured decision networks (Pete, Pattipati, Levchuk, & Kleinman, 1998) to the multi-objective optimization problem of designing optimal organizational structures to complete a mission, while minimizing a set of criteria (Levchuk, Pattipati, Curry, & Shakeri, 1996, 1997, 1998). As computational models of decision-making in organizations began to emerge (see Carley & Svoboda, 1996; Carley, 1998; Vincke, 1992), the study of social networks (SSN) continued to focus on examining a network structure and its impact on individual, group, and organizational behavior (Wellman & Berkowitz, 1988). Most models, developed under the SSN, combined formal and informal structures when representing organizations as architectures (e.g., see Levitt et al., 1994; Carley & Svoboda, 1996). In addition, a large number of measures of structure and of the individual positions within the structure have been developed (Roberts, 1979; Scott, 1981; Wasserman & Faust, 1994; Wellman, 1991).

One of the keys in designing teams is to specify the performance criteria that differentiate one organization from another. Research in team performance has spanned industrial and organizational psychology, operations research, business management, and decision-making in command-and-control. Many researchers have studied the interplay among the task environment, the team organization, and team performance. In an effort to understand the complexity of contemporary team missions, researchers have examined a variety of teams (e.g., joint task force organizations, flight crew of a commercial airline, collaborative software development teams, medical teams, research and development teams, etc.) that represent different types of task environments and the concomitant distributed organizations. This in turn, has led to defining a variety of task and team variables relevant to team performance (Cameron, 1986; FAA, 1993; Hankins & Wilson, 1998; Kleinman & Serfaty, 1989; Kleinman, Pattipati, Luh, & Serfaty, 1992; Mackenzie et al., 1996; Mayk & Rubin, 1988; Sage, 1981; Salas, Dickinson, Converse, & Tannenbaum, 1992; Xiao & Mackenzie, 1997).

Over the years, research in team decision-making has demonstrated that an organization operates best when its structure and processes match the corresponding mission environment (Lin & Carley, 1993; Papastavrou & Athans, 1992; Pete, Kleinman, & Pattipati, 1994; Pete et al., 1998). Consequently, it has been concluded that the *optimality* of an organizational *design* ultimately depends on the actual mission structure and on key attributes of the environment in which the organization operates (Burton & Obel, 1998).

This premise has led to the application of systems engineering techniques to the process of designing human organizations (Levchuk et al., 1997; Levchuk, Pattipati, & Kleinman, 1998; Pete et al., 1994). The systems engineering approach to organizational design is as follows. First, a quantitative model describing the mission and the organizational constraints is built. Next, different criteria used to judge the optimality of an organization are combined into an (possibly non-scalar) objective function. Finally, an organizational design is generated to optimize the objective function.

When designing organizations to operate in an uncertain military environment, the specifics about many mission parameters may be inaccessible a priori, with only estimates available to the designer. Once the mission scenario unfolds, the *actual* values of the parameters may require the implementation of a particular strategy to achieve desirable performance. Furthermore, throughout the course of the mission, various causes (e.g., an erroneous initial mission parameter estimation, resource failures, malfunctioning of a decision node, etc.) may trigger unexpected changes in either the mission environment or in organizational constraints. Various strategies may be utilized to build an organization that accounts for dynamic and uncertain mission environments. At one extreme, one may construct an organization capable of processing a range of expected missions. At the other extreme, one may build a "finely tuned" organization for a specific mission, and allow online structural reconfiguration and/or strategy adaptation to cope with unforeseen changes in the mission and/or in the organization. The former (multi-mission) organizations, herein termed *robust*, are able to sustain high levels of performance in dynamic environments without having to alter their structures. The latter organizations, herein termed *adaptive*, are able to generate new strategies and/or reconfigure their structures to potentially achieve even higher performance.

Robustness in an organization introduces redundancies in task-resource allocation resulting in a stable organization with respect to environmental perturbations and/or decision/processing errors. Evidently, this insensitivity results in a slightly degraded performance on each specific sub-mission, but minimizes the organization's fragility. Organizational adaptation process is significantly simplified if specific causes of adaptation, or *adaptation triggers*, are anticipated a priori (e.g., the unexpected changes in the mission environment, resource failures, decision-maker (DM) failures, etc.). After a suitable adaptation option (e.g., strategy shift, resource reallocation, hierarchy reconfiguration) is selected, the organization needs to coordinate among its members to realize the selected change. For a sample of current research in robust and adaptive project-based organizational designs see

Booth (1996), Lee and Carley (1997), Levchuk, Levchuk, Meirina, Pattipati, and Kleinman (2004), and Song, Mathur, and Pattipati (1995).

Previous A2C2 experiments, and the concomitant models that supported the empirical efforts, focused extensively on the design of organizations that were congruent with a predefined mission. Over the course of these experiments, that have spanned over nine years, the analytical models and the experimentation tools – most notably the Distributed Dynamic Decision-making (DDD) simulator (Kleinman, Young, & Higgins, 1996) – have undergone considerable refinement, improvement, and extension in order to deal with the increasing complexity of relevant command and control (C2) issues (e.g., self-synchronization, network-centric operations, time-critical targeting, etc.). The newest experiment – number 8 on the list of A2C2 empirical milestones – was conducted at Naval Post-Graduate School (NPS) in August and November 2002. The objectives of this experiment were to compare theoretically predicted and experimentally observed measures of congruence between the missions and the organizations and to establish the experimental conditions in which the relationship between congruence and performance could be tested.

THE SETTINGS

The organizational design research described in this chapter is based on the notions of mission, task, resource, and DM. A *mission* is an overarching plan of objectives to be achieved by the organization. A *task* is an individual activity of sub-elements of the organization to accomplish the overall plan. A *resource* is a variable that quantifies the capabilities and defines requirements to execute tasks. Finally, a *DM* is a member of the team who controls resources, executes tasks, and coordinates its activities with other DMs. Resources and DMs together with concomitant supporting structures comprise the *organization*.

Mission

A mission analysis that details required courses of action by specifying a sequence of tasks, defining resource-to-task allocation, and a time-line for all task activities constitutes a *mission plan*. This implies that the mission must be *decomposable* into a set of entities generally referred to as tasks. A *task* is an activity that entails the use of relevant resources (provided by organization's assets) and is carried out by an individual DM or a group of DMs to accomplish the mission objectives. Every task in itself represents a "small mission", and can oftentimes be further decomposed into more elementary tasks. A *mission decomposition diagram* can be built to represent a hierarchical structure among the mission tasks. Different decomposition techniques (e.g., goal decomposition, functional decomposition, domain decomposition) represent different starting points of defining tasks and provide different task types required to complete the mission. The designer's choice of a particular decomposition technique and model granularity (number of tasks in the mission decomposition) must be contingent on the computational efficiency of the design process and its supporting algorithms.

Task attributes quantify various properties of the mission tasks that detail the specifics of task execution. They provide quantitative characteristics for the mission structure and specify the implications of commitment to task processing on both machine and human resources of an organization. In our model, we characterize every mission task T_i ($i = 1, \ldots, N$, where N is the total number of tasks) by specifying the following basic attributes. First, task temporal constraints are defined by specifying task release time and task processing window. Task *release time* is the time at which the task appears in the mission scenario. Task *processing time window* is the maximal time available from the start of task execution to its finish. This time window is a constraint on synchronizing assets assigned to the task. It indicates the time window during which these assets must be "applied" to execute the task with 100% accuracy. We also define two time variables that are obtained during mission execution: *task start time*, corresponding to the time that a task execution is started, and *task processing time*, which is a true interval between the time the first asset starts executing the task and the time at which the last asset finishes the task. The task processing time must not exceed the task processing time window. The success of accomplishing an individual task is quantified with the *task accuracy* variable, and the distribution of the tasks in the environment is quantified by specifying tasks' geographical *locations* in a state space. The location parameters can be used to compute the "distance" between tasks. A *task value* reflects the importance of individual tasks – either on a relative or absolute basis – and is taken as an indicator of the commander's intent or priority (all tasks are not equally important). A *resource requirement vector*, where each entry is equal to the number of units of corresponding resource type required for successful processing of the task, specifies how the tasks can be performed.

A variety of modeling techniques can be applied to capture the internal structure of a mission. One of the most popular modeling methodologies employs a graph formalism to describe the mission structure. In our research, we used graph formalism to construct a *mission task graph* – a dependency diagram that specifies task precedence, task input–output relationships, and inter-task information flow.

Organization

In large-scale organizations that involve humans, decision-making and operational functions are distributed among team members who coordinate their actions in order to achieve their common goal. Since the processing capabilities of a human are limited, the distribution of *information*, *resources*, and *activities* among DMs in an organization must be set up to guarantee that decision-making and operational load of each DM remains below the DM's capacity thresholds. In a highly competitive and distributed environment, a proper balance among information acquisition, decision hierarchy, and resource allocation, in short, *a proper organizational structure and its processes*, is critical to superior organizational performance.

In defining an organization, we differentiate between two classes of *entities*: (i) *DM*s, and (ii) *resources*. Organization's resources that represent non-human physical assets are called *platforms* or *assets*. A *DM* is an entity with information-processing, decision-making, and operational capabilities that can control the necessary resources to execute mission tasks, provided that such an execution will not violate the concomitant capability thresholds. A *platform* is a physical asset of an organization that provides resource capabilities and is used to process tasks. For each asset/platform, we define its maximal *velocity* and its *resource capability vector*, where each entry specifies the number of units of resource for the corresponding type available on the asset. A match between resource requirements of the task and resource capabilities of assets executing this task identifies the success of task processing (see section on task processing specifics). The *asset hierarchy* specifies the resident/parent platform for each asset and thus restricts the asset utilization. The assets typically have diverse operational and execution characteristics. For example, a salient feature of single-hit weapons located on the same platform (e.g., a carrier) is the "duty cycle", which imposes constraints on utilization of weapons of this type. During a duty cycle time, no asset of the corresponding type can be committed from its parent platform.

An *organization* is a *team* of human DMs, who coordinate their information, resources, and activities to achieve their common goal in a complex, dynamic, and uncertain mission environment. The key attributes in modeling a DM are the individual DM *thresholds* with respect to particular DM activities (e.g., information processing and operational load thresholds).

These thresholds quantify human limitations and necessitate the need for distribution and decentralization within a human organization. As a consequence of decentralization in large-scale systems, each DM only has access to a portion of organization's resources and possibly to the information available to the team. The total decision-making and operational load is partitioned among DMs by decomposing a mission into tasks and assigning these tasks to individual DMs who are responsible for their planning and execution. An overlap in task processing capability, wherein two or more DMs possess the capability to individually execute a task, gives the team a degree of freedom to adapt to uneven demand by redistributing the load.

Organizational Structure

In our paradigm, we model the structure of an organization as consisting of three substructures: (1) resource allocation, (2) communication network, and (3) command structure.

Resource Allocation

In general, DMs are provided with limited resources to accomplish their objectives. The distribution of these resources among DMs, and the assignment of these resources to seek information and to process tasks are key elements in an organization's design. A *resource allocation structure* is defined as an assignment of organizational assets and resources to DMs. This assignment specifies the operational control of DMs over their assigned resources. We assume that each asset is assigned to a single DM and cannot be shared during the mission.

Communication Network

Team members must dynamically coordinate resources to process their individual tasks while assuring that team performance goals are met. As a result, communication among DMs is required for efficient mission execution. This communication is due to three main reasons:

(a) Synchronization of resources
(b) Coordination due to simultaneous task processing
(c) Information flow between dependent tasks.

The first type of communication refers to efficiency of resource utilization, and might involve requests by DMs for transfer or employment of platform/asset, which is controlled by other DMs. The second type of communication arises whenever two or more DMs are executing the same task and need to coordinate its processing and potential asset reassignment. The third type is due to the information flow between tasks with input–output relationships. The information flow among DMs occurs whenever these tasks are assigned to different DMs (this communication is 0 when the tasks are assigned to the same DM). Therefore, the organizational design can also specify a *communication structure* among DMs to facilitate coordination and distributed information processing required for completing the mission. This structure specifies the allowable channels to send information among DMs and the parameters of those channels (e.g., capacity, reliability, information loss, etc.).

Command Structure

In addition to assigning each DM his share of information, resources, and activities, the organizational design must explicate a decision *hierarchy* among DMs that designates their *control responsibilities* (through command authority) and regulates the inter-DM *coordination.* A *command structure* of the organization specifies the decision hierarchy among DMs and assigns the responsibility of resolving decision ambiguities among coordinating DMs. The command and communication structures are tightly coupled, and their design problem must account for strong interdependence between command responsibilities and coordination in the organization.

Mission Processing and Organizational Interactions

The mission processing is the execution of tasks, obtained from mission decomposition, by organizational resources/assets, which are controlled/operated by human DMs. The task parameters and interdependencies (e.g., task value, priority, execution time, resource requirements, precedence constraints, etc.) guide the DMs in sequencing the tasks for execution. On the other hand, limited resources and DMs' constraints (operation and communication workload thresholds) restrict task execution. Therefore, the critical issues in team *mission processing* are: *what* should be done, *who* should do what, with *which resources,* and *when*? One of the examples of task execution is a model presented in Fig. 1 (Levchuk, Kleinman, Ruan, & Pattipati, 2003). Generally, we decompose the problem of task execution into several subtasks:

(1) Identification (task must be identified with sensor resources available to the organization)
(2) Asset allocation (assets must be selected to execute the task)

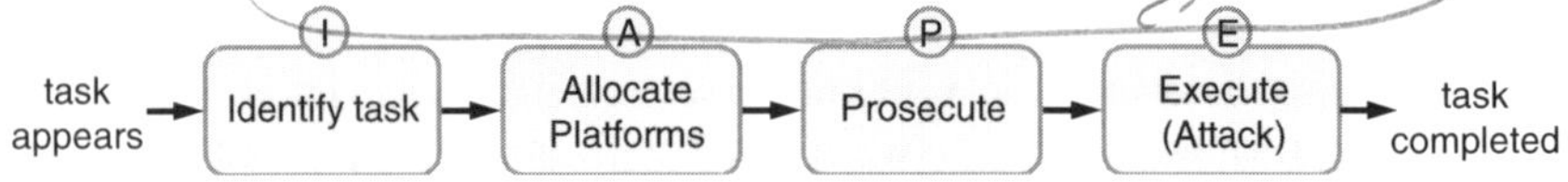

Fig. 1. Task Execution Chain.

(3) Task prosecution (assets must be synchronized and routed to task location)
(4) Attack (actual engagement/processing of a task by assets).

In this model, identification subtask (I), allocation subtask (A), prosecution subtask (P), and execution subtask (E) are performed sequentially (the latter subtasks involve parallel communication among DMs owning the assets in order to synchronize the assets' time-over-target to complete the task in a specified processing time window). During the identification subtask (subtask I), the DM responsible for task completion is specified. Efficient asset-to-task allocation (subtask A) is essential to effective mission execution, since it reduces the delay associated with prosecution of the corresponding task (subtask P). If a single DM, responsible for executing the task, possesses the assets with the requisite resources to complete this task with a high accuracy, the problem of selecting the most efficient asset package to execute a task can be formulated and solved (note that the general problem of resource-task allocation cannot be solved in polynomial time; see Levchuk et al., 2002a, b). However, the problem becomes significantly more complex when a single DM does not possess the required resources. In this case, the allocation subtask should be further decomposed into elementary subtasks that involve asset prioritization, asset request, communication, etc. Informally, the responsible DM would have to coordinate the actions with other DMs to request the commitment of their resources and their direct participation in prosecuting the task. Given the model above, we identify the times required to execute each subtask in the execution chain of a task:

- Time required to identify the task (this time depends on the organization's internal processes, locations of information sensors, etc.)
- Time required to coordinate among DMs to determine the asset-to-task allocation
- Time required to send/route the assets to the task location, including any waiting time needed for asset synchronization
- Time to attack the task – from the first asset attack to the last asset-task completion.

Therefore, the completion time of a task is determined as the sum of its arrival time and the time to execute the subtask chain. The subtask time parameters defined above directly affect the values of task start times in human-in-the-loop experiments.

A successful scheduling of tasks to available organizational resources (assets) under resource requirement and task inter-dependency constraints is a key determinant of organizational performance. The resource-to-DM allocation and structure of organization's command and control place further constraints on the strategy that the organization can use, since they introduce additional communication workload and delays.

The processing of a mission by an organization is formally identified by specifying asset-to-task assignment, and the corresponding DM-task allocation. The asset–task assignment specifies the necessary interaction among assets when processing a task. This interaction necessitates coordination among DMs that have ownership of these assets; the DMs serve as information/decision/action carriers. In the next sections, we outline our modeling of team processes and several measures that quantify individual and team interactions during mission execution.

Internal and External Coordination of Individual DMs

To model coordination-related overhead in an organization, we define two types of coordination: *internal* and *external*. Internal coordination accounts for the need to coordinate among assets assigned to the same DM and operate those assets to accomplish mission tasks. External coordination is the inter-DM dependence that results from cooperative processing of a task by multiple DMs.

The workload associated with operating an asset must be determined from the specifics of asset's operation and its involvement in task processing. We define an asset P_j's *operational workload* as the aggregated load of tasks executed by this asset, which is equal to the sum of the processing workloads associated with using this asset to execute each assigned task. We assume that individual asset–task processing workload parameters are known. Hence, the *internal coordination workload* of a DM is defined as the sum of operational workloads of assets assigned to this DM.

A *direct DM–DM coordination* between two DMs is defined as the aggregated time associated with simultaneous processing of the same set of tasks by these DMs. Thus, we define the *external coordination workload* of a DM as the sum of its direct coordination with other DMs.

Team Load and Workload Balancing

The *workload* of a DM is defined as a weighted sum of the internal and external coordination workload of this DM. The weights for internal and external coordination specify their impact on the aggregated DM workload. While the total aggregated workloads of organizations with the same mission completion time may be similar, their performance is distinguished by the distribution of this workload among team members.

We define the *team workload balance* of an organization as the root-mean-square (RMS) of workloads of team members (Levchuk et al., 2003). The RMS workload measure accounts for both the mean and the variance of workloads, and, consequently, provides a measure of balance of the aggregated workloads of DMs. The minimization of RMS workload measure corresponds to a minimization of both the mean and the variance of workloads across the team (Phadke, 1989). Given that two organizations O_1 and O_2 have the same mission completion time or task gain on a mission M, we say that organization O_1 is more congruent with this mission than O_2, if the RMS workload of O_1 is smaller than that of O_2. That is, the better an organization is matched to its mission, the better will be its workload balance among the DMs.

Processing Specifics: Models of Task Accuracy, Latency and Execution Gain

When all resources required by a specific task are met (i.e., the vector of resource requirements for this task is component-wise less than or equal to the vector of aggregated resource capabilities of assets assigned to this task), then the accuracy of task completion is equal to 100%. However, in realistic applications where the resources are scarce, an organization may wish to reduce the task execution accuracy in order to achieve better timeliness. In order to accommodate timeliness–accuracy trade-off, a model of accuracy has been defined within the DDD-III simulator for scoring the DMs (Kleinman et al., 1996). The accuracy of executing a task is thus defined as the average of squared ratios of the resource used to the resource required over all resource types. The ratio of the resource used to the resource required identifies the percentage of satisfied resource for the corresponding resource type. The squaring of its average penalizes significant resource allocation mismatches.

The *latency* of a task is defined as the time from the appearance of a task to the time when its execution starts. The speed of command that can be achieved by the organization is inversely proportional to its task processing latencies. That is, the better an organization is matched to its mission, the smaller will be its task latencies and higher will be its speed of command.

In the presence of time-critical tasks, an organization may trade-off task accuracy versus timeliness. For an organization that is incongruent with its mission, such engagement practices may result in the same levels of task timeliness as for a congruent organization. However, this timeliness is achieved at the cost of lower accuracy. Therefore, a measure that reflects the task accuracy and timeliness tradeoff can be combined into a single measure, called the *task execution gain*. The *execution gain* of a task is defined as the accuracy multiplied by its value. In order to visualize the dynamic pattern of total gain achieved by an organization over time, we define the *accrued task gain* $G(t)$ (Kleinman, Levchuk, Hutchins, & Kemple, 2003) as an aggregate of task gains achieved by time t. We increment the gain function when each task completes its execution with a gain of this task, hence the *accrued task execution gain* is equal to the sum of execution gains of tasks completed by time t. Thus, $G(t)$ is a piece-wise constant (i.e., stair-case) function as shown in Fig. 2. An organization that achieves better task latency and higher task accuracy is seen as having the accrued gain function rising at a faster rate. On the other hand, the final values of gain functions for both organizations might be the same, since the total achievable mission gain is the same for any organization and equal to the sum of all task values (it will be achieved in case the organization completes all tasks with 100% accuracy). Hence, the ultimate measure of performance of an organization on a mission is the normalized area under the accrued gain function curve for this organization (see Fig. 2):

$$A(s) = \frac{1}{s}\int_0^s G(t)\,\mathrm{d}t, \quad s \geq 0.$$

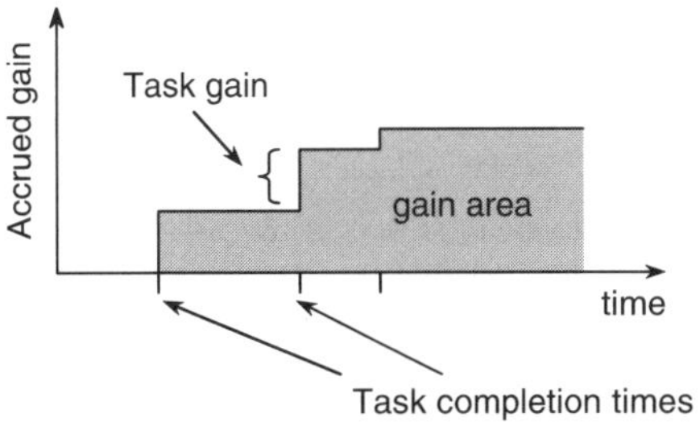

Fig. 2. Accrued Gain Metric.

CONCEPT OF CONGRUENCE

Application of systems engineering techniques to the process of designing human organizations led to several graph-decomposition and combinatorial optimization algorithms to synthesize congruent organizational structures (i.e., structures that are in some sense "matched" with their mission task environment) (Levchuk et al., 1997, 1998, 2002a, b; Pete et al., 1998), and to several graph-theoretic measures of task complexity (Levchuk et al., 1996). Potential benefits of a structural match predicted by the normative model, as well as the ability of a proposed design process to find this match, have been tested empirically in a computer-mediated team-in-the-loop experiment with human DMs in a DDD-III (see Kleinman, Young, & Higgins, 1996 for a description) simulator of Joint Command and Control scenarios (Kleinman et al., 2003). DDD-III and other similar simulators allow one to compare the performance of different organizational designs for a specific mission, and to test the utility of the design procedure. Findings from recent experiments on DDD-III simulator gave the empirical validation of our modeling and design methodology. It clearly showed the advantages of structural optimization since the model-driven non-traditional architectures outperformed their traditional counterparts. The experimental results showed that not only were the system engineering methods successful in constructing the desired architectures, but architecture type differently affected team processes as was hypothesized by the design (Entin, 1999; Hocevar, Kemple, Kleinman, & Porter, 1999; Kleinman, Levchuk, Hutchins, & Kemple, 2003; Levchuk et al., 2003). In the next sections, we present the definition of congruence, and describe a congruent design process methodology and its validation.

Definition of Congruence

An organization is said to be *congruent* with its mission, if its *structure* and *processes* are "matched" to the environmental parameters (Burton & Obel, 1998; Mackenzie, 1986). Informally, the congruence between the organization and a mission can be perceived as the structural fit depicted in Fig. 3. The degree of "match" ("fit") between an organization and a mission can be quantified based on its *performance* or *structure*. A *congruent* organization minimizes the level of workload imbalance, communication requirements, and DM–DM dependence. These three characteristics can be identified via a fit of specific structural parameters of organizations and

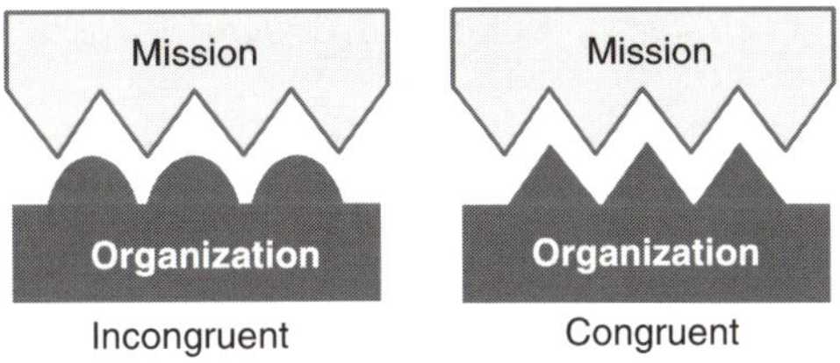

Fig. 3. Informal Visualization of (Mis)Match Between a Mission and an Organization.

missions including:

- Organization: DM-asset allocation and organizational structure (authority and communication).
- Mission: task density, locations, information flow, task precedence, and resource requirements.

The concept of performance-based congruence is relative. The degree to which an organization is congruent to a mission is obtained by comparing its performance to that of an "optimal" organization for the same mission. However, finding this optimal organization is computationally prohibitive for real-time mission monitoring, re-planning and decision support. On the other hand, human-in-the-loop simulations, needed for performance evaluation, present a challenge in uncertain and dynamic environments, where the effort to achieve *dynamic congruence* forces organizations to adapt while they continue to operate (Mackenzie et al., 1996). In situations involving dynamic and uncertain environments, we turn to the concept of structure-based congruence measures.

How precise or loose should the congruence be? A loose match between organizational and mission structures may be better if it is to be robust to changes in the mission. This is because an organizational structure that is precisely matched to a mission may exhibit brittle behavior in an uncertain environment. In addition, a substantial decrease in the degree of congruence can signal the need for dynamic reconfiguration.

We can use an accrued gain metric to define a process-based congruence. For mission M, we say that organization O_1 with normalized gain area $A(O_1, M; T_f)$ (where T_f is the mission end time – assumed the same for all organizations on the tested mission) is more congruent to this mission than organization O_2 with normalized gain area $A(O_2, M; T_f)$, if and only if $A(O_1, M; T_f) > A(O_2, M; T_f)$.

Design of Congruent Organizations

The optimal organizational design problem is one of finding both the optimal organizational structure and strategy (i.e., processes) that allow the organization to achieve desired performance during the conduct of a specific mission. Our previously developed three-phase organizational design methodology (see Fig. 4) and its wide latitude in mixing and matching different optimization algorithms at different stages of the design process led to an efficient matching between the mission structure and that of an organization. A detailed description of algorithms used at each phase of the organizational design process may be found in (Levchuk et al., 2002a, b). The methodology allows one to overcome the computational complexity by synthesizing an organizational structure via an iterative solution of a sequence of three smaller and well-defined optimization sub-problems (Levchuk et al., 2002a, b):

Phase I (*Scheduling Phase*). The first phase of our design process determines the task–asset allocation and task sequencing that optimize mission objectives (e.g., mission completion time, accuracy, workload, resource utilization, asset coordination, etc.), taking into account task precedence constraints and synchronization delays, task resource requirements, resource capabilities, as well as geographical and other task transition constraints. The generated task–asset allocation schedule specifies the workload of each resource. In addition, for every mission task, the first phase of the algorithm delineates a set of non-redundant resource packages capable of jointly processing a task. This information is later used for iterative refinement of the design, and, if necessary, for online strategy adjustments.

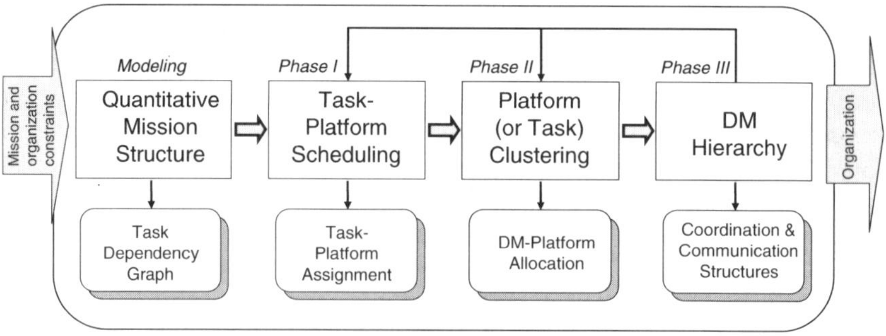

Fig. 4. Three-Phase Organizational Design Process.

Phase II (*Clustering Phase*). In this phase we combine assets into non-intersecting groups to match the operational expertise and workload threshold constraints of available DMs. Next, each group is assigned to an individual DM to define the DM-resource allocation. Thus, the second phase delineates the DM-asset–task allocation schedule and, consequently, the individual operational workload of each DM.

Phase III (*Structural Optimization Phase*). Finally, Phase III completes the design by specifying a communication structure and a decision hierarchy to optimize the responsibility distribution and inter-DM control coordination. Phase III also balances the control workload among DMs with varying expertise.

Congruence Hypothesis

The structure-based congruence is a multi-dimensional concept involving resources, task structure and organizational processes (e.g., workload balance). We define *structure-based* congruence measures by evaluating the closeness of task parameters with the organizational structure and processes. Based on substantial evidence in the management literature (Burton & Obel, 1998; Hollenbeck et al., 2002; Mackenzie, 1986), and our normative organizational design process (Levchuk et al., 2002a, b) developed as part of the A2C2 program, we hypothesize that the better an organization is matched to its mission, the better will that organization perform.

In order to formalize the effects of a structural match between an organization and a mission, and to predict organizational performance, we utilize our 3-phase design methodology (Levchuk et al., 2002a, b). The performance of organization is obtained using the scheduling step (Phase I) of the design methodology; this step defines the processes of an organization executing the mission. We consider the notion of a structure-based congruence measure derived from the following characteristics of the mission:

- Task-resource requirements
- Task precedence/dependence
- Task load per resource type.

These parameters determine the (mis)match between a mission and an organization because they affect the following four primary characteristics of organizational performance:

- Accrued task gain
- Workload balance

- Communication requirements
- DM–DM dependence.

The accrued task gain measure serves as the ultimate "congru-o-meter" for assessing the fit of an organization to a mission.

Empirical Testing of Congruence Concept: Experiment-8

In order to test and validate our hypothesis that the better an organization is matched to its mission, the better that organization will perform, we designed and conducted a team-in-the-loop A2C2 experiment using two different organizational structures and two different missions. The first organizational structure was to be congruent (matched) with the first mission, but highly mismatched (i.e., exhibit low congruence) to the second mission. The reverse was true for the second organizational structure.

For our experiments, we selected two organizations with opposite structural characteristics. In one organization, termed *Divisional*, the DMs had control over diverse resources distributed in one geographical area. In another organization, termed *Functional*, DMs had control over unique resources and had responsibility over the wide geographical area. The experiment – number 8 on the list of A2C2 empirical milestones – was conducted at NPS in August and November 2002. The objective of this experiment was to compare theoretically predicted and experimentally observed measures of congruence between the missions and the organizations. Instead of modeling an organization to execute a specified mission (Levchuk et al., 2002a, b), we used a "reverse engineering" approach of designing mission scenarios that specifically (mis)matched selected organizational structures. The concepts developed in Levchuk et al. (2002a, b) for modeling the DM-resource allocation (Phase II) were used to create matches and mismatches between task-resource requirements and DM-resource capabilities by manipulating the need for multi-DM task processing (reducing the need for multi-DM processing in congruent cases, and increasing it in the incongruent ones). Multi-DM task processing requires communication and asset synchronization among the DMs participating in task execution, thus increasing task execution latency. Based on our scheduling algorithms (Phase I of our design process), we can further increase the DM–DM dependence in incongruent cases by specifying a precedence structure among tasks that must be executed by different DMs. Thus, task latencies at a single DM greatly affect the overall performance of the team. The results for simple congruent and incongruent situations (Levchuk et al., 2003) provided the theoretical insights for the design of A2C2 Experiment 8 (Kleinman et al., 2003).

A major congruence metric tested in Experiment-8 was the degree of inter-node coordination. As this coordination is a function of the organizational structure *and* the mission/task requirements, the scenario design process focused considerable effort on the selection of task resource requirements. Tasks in the congruent situations were designed to require low inter-node coordination, whereas in the incongruent cases tasks were designed to have higher coordination demands (Levchuk et al., 2003; Kleinman et al., 2003). The tasks used for this instantiation included the major mission tasks, time-critical high priority tasks, and several others.

Another metric that enters into congruence is workload imbalance. By adjusting the spatial and temporal arrivals of tasks that dealt with defending against the enemy, we were able to differentially load individual nodes within tested organizations (i.e., Functional and Divisional). We were able to unevenly load the team members in the incongruent cases, while *for the same scenario* having a balanced/distributed workload in the congruent cases. Other, less salient manipulations in the scenarios were also effected (e.g., boundary splitting, information flows, situational awareness) that were geared to make the incongruent cases relatively more difficult than the congruent case. In short, we used the knowledge gained from earlier laboratory-based experiences (Entin, 1999; Hocevar et al., 1999), along with guidance from model predictions, to design the scenarios and "tune" the organizations.

We compared the analytical predictions with empirical data from the human-in-the-loop experiment using similar measures, including the total *accrued task gain* (based on the task scoring method, and identifying the trade-off between task latency and task accuracy), *gain area*, *number of DM–DM assists* (needed for multi-DM task processing, and termed *external coordination* in the 3-phase design process), and total workload distribution measure. Measures from the DDD simulations were extracted using the new DDD Post-Processor (Wong & Kleinman, 2002). We found that the model-predicted structural mismatch between an organization and mission was validated by the experiment. Further, a mission indeed resulted in degraded performance in the non-congruent cases when compared to the congruent ones – specifically in terms of timeliness of task execution, coordination workload, and the total gain attained by the organization. We found that the congruent organization achieves a higher gain area (higher mission tempo) while executing the mission with lower external coordination (higher speed of command – lower number of DM–DM assists) and as a result, higher independence of DMs and lower cognitive load for mission execution (Diedrich et al., 2003; Entin et al., 2003; Levchuk et al., 2003; Kleinman et al., 2003).

Having firmly established the value of congruence as a construct in "optimal" organizational design, our next step in A2C2 research will be to examine: (a) the processes that teams employed to try to overcome poor performance in the incongruent cases, (b) whether players were aware of any factors that caused their performance decrement, and (c) what *human* teams are likely to do about it (e.g., adapt their structure (roles/responsibilities/assets) or just cope?).

Sensitivity of Congruent Organizations

A congruent organization, designed to perform a specific instance of the nominal mission, is sensitive to the uncertainties of the environment not present in this instance and might exhibit fragile performance on unplanned random variations of the original mission (Levchuk et al., 2004). These findings are supported by extensive research in structural contingency theory (SCT) (Burns & Stalker, 1961; Lawrence & Lorsch, 1967; Miller, 1988; Pennings, 1992), and also correlate well with cross-sectional research on both large-scale organizations (Drazin & Van de Ven, 1985) and smaller work teams (Hollenbeck et al., 2002). Various strategies may be utilized to build an organization that is commensurate with the dynamic nature of its environment. At one extreme, one may construct an organization capable of processing a range of expected missions. At the other extreme, one may build a "finely tuned" organization for a specific mission and allow online structural reconfiguration and/or strategy adaptation to cope with unforeseen changes in the mission and/or an organization. The former (multi-mission) organizations, herein termed *robust*, are able to sustain high levels of performance in dynamic environments without having to change their structures. The latter organizations, herein termed *adaptive*, are able to generate new strategies and/or reconfigure their structure to potentially achieve even higher performance.

DESIGN ALTERNATIVE: ROBUST ORGANIZATIONS

The robust design approach originated in quality planning and engineering product design activities (Taguchi, 1986, 1987). Taguchi states that it is often more costly to control causes of process variation than to make the system *insensitive* to the dynamics. An organization is termed *robust* if it can maintain acceptable performance in a changing environment without having to change organizational structure. The robustness is usually achieved by introducing redundancies in DM- and task-resource allocation, which makes organizations more stable with respect to environmental perturbations and/or decision/processing errors. In order to achieve robustness, an organization is designed to process a range of missions. Evidently, this insensitivity results in slightly degraded performance on each specific mission, but minimizes the organization's fragility.

Mission Uncertainty

In the 3-phase organizational design process of Levchuk et al. (2002a, b), we construct an organization based on known task and organizational parameters. However, the parameters could be uncertain. Consequently, the mission environment could "swerve" into unaccountable directions and a fixed organization would fail. This establishes the need for designing organizations that take into account possible uncertainties. The following environment uncertainties, introducing variability in the mission and/or resources, can be considered in the organizational design problem: (a) measurement errors, (b) task precedence errors, (c) task decomposition errors, and (d) unexpected tasks.

Example of Robust Design Methodology

In Levchuk et al. (2004) the 3-phase congruent design methodology has been extended to design a robust organization that accounts for mission uncertainty. The model includes creating a surrogate mission, which consists of *concatenations* of mission realizations of the original mission scenario obtained under specified environment uncertainty parameters. A mission $M_c = M_i \to M_j$ is called a *concatenation* of missions M_i and M_j, if M_c consists of all tasks defined in M_i and M_j, with the restriction that tasks from M_i must be executed before tasks in M_j can commence. Similar to comparison of performance using Monte-Carlo simulations, the robust design methodology constructs an organization to perform (to be congruent to) a surrogate mission consisting of multiple sequential concatenations. This results in the design of an organization with averaged performance over the set of sub-missions that constitute the surrogate scenario. As these sub-missions are random variations of the original mission under environmental uncertainties, they represent the elements of its neighborhood. Constructing an organization using our 3-phase design process to perform the surrogate concatenation mission would therefore produce a robust solution (when number of concatenations is sufficiently large).

Robust Design Complexity

The design of the organization maximally robust to changes in mission environment requires the knowledge of the whole range of uncertainty. In other words, the design must account for all possible variations of the mission or simply all sub-missions from the neighborhood of the original mission under specified uncertainty parameters. Obviously, this is an infeasible task. Instead, the design methodology of Levchuk et al. (2004) allows accounting for a fixed number of sub-missions randomly selected from a neighborhood of the original mission. The larger the number of concatenations, the closer is the designed organization to the maximally robust one. On the other hand, this results in increased complexity of the solution, where the large number of concatenations makes the solution prohibitively complex. Thus, the number of concatenations drives the design process allowing a trade-off between complexity and optimality.

Robust Design Sensitivity

When uncertainty about an environment increases, the relatively small number of mission concatenations required for robust design can no longer "cover" the required range of missions. Moreover, even if the design of an organization maximally robust to these wider changes were possible, the constructed organization would have too much redundancy and be too insensitive to the actual mission realization, thus exhibiting poor performance. In an uncertain environment, it may be more cost-efficient for an organization simply to alter its structure and processes to environmental changes than to waste resources to preserve the redundancy required to cope with many possible mission outcomes.

CAS

ORGANIZATIONAL ADAPTATION: COMBINING BENEFITS OF CONGRUENT AND ROBUST DESIGN

An organization is termed *adaptive* if it allows online structural reconfiguration and/or strategy adaptation to cope with unforeseen changes in the mission and/or in the organization. Thus, adaptive organizations are capable of modifying processing strategies and structure to maintain high performance. Flexibility in design is the key to success of adaptive organizations. Following Tsourveloudis & Phillis (1998), we consider the following types of organizational flexibility:

(1) *Processing flexibility* (task assignment, task-resource allocation, and task processing sequence). This type of flexibility measures the ability of an organization to deal with changes in task processing.
(2) *Planning flexibility* allows for quick reaction to unexpected events such as processing node/resource failures and minimizes the effect of task interruptions on a mission schedule. This type of flexibility is related to *operational commonality*, i.e., the number of common task-resource and DM-resource pairings that the organization can utilize. It is also related to *substitutability*, namely the ability to replan and reschedule tasks by employing equivalent resource packages under failure conditions. Both planning and processing flexibility are interdependent and influence the strategy adaptation employed by an organization.
(3) *Resource allocation flexibility* measures the ability of an organization to reassign its resources in response to changes in a task environment.
(4) *Hierarchy flexibility* pertains to the ability to shift DM–DM coordination/authority structure. Both resource allocation and hierarchy flexibility are interdependent and determine the structural adaptation procedures used by an organization.

Compared to robust design, the approach to construct adaptive organizations is equally attractive. This is motivated by a tendency of robust design methodology to overly engineer each aspect of a system to reduce the chances of failure. Since the projected variations may not occur in practice, typically robust organizations increase the system overhead and decrease the level of system efficiency. In order to improve the ability of an organization to accommodate variations during the course of its mission, without sacrificing its efficiency, organizations should be designed with adaptability in mind.

The dynamic behavior and strategy adaptation in human multi-agent organizations has been recently addressed. Various methods for adaptation and its analysis have been considered, including: dynamic process selection (Handley, Zaidi, & Levis, 1999), tuning and shaking via simulated annealing (Lee & Carley, 1997), local diagnostics with knowledge of new activities and their relevance to performance (Heller, 2000) and interaction models adjusted with local assessment (Foisel, Chevrier, & Haton, 1998). McGrath and Krackhardt developed three different network theories of change, exploring the underlying assumptions and implications of each model and identifying the parameters of organizational structure and processes that facilitate the efficiency and speed of adaptation process (McGrath & Krackhardt, 2003).

Many researches have explored the adaptation of organizational command and communication structures. For example, Epstein (2003) considered the optimal history of structural adaptation for a particular environmental dynamic and found that, depending on environmental parameters, it involved periods of extreme hierarchy separated by relatively "flat" internal trading regimes. In our work we considered the structural adaptation of an organization, which includes the changes in DM-resource-task allocations, and authority/coordination structure (see Levchuk et al., 2004).

Despite many advantages that an adaptive organization offers, it has its own shortcomings. In the context of agile manufacturing systems, Booth (1996) argued that "lean" production concepts have put companies at risk of not being able to recover from unforeseen situations due to reductions in skilled staff, and in the design and development capability in particular. To become agile, companies have to aim for flexibility, speed of response, and adaptability to probable changes. The underlying criticism highlights the fact that there is a compromise in combining the two equally promising design procedures, viz., robustness and flexibility. The notion of organizational adaptability points to the need for an organization to be both robust to accommodate small variations in the system and flexible enough to maintain a high level of performance by adapting strategies and structures to accommodate the effects of *large* changes during the course of a mission. Other work on flexible system design may be found in Kulatilaka (1988), Piramuthu, Raman, and Shaw (1994), Peddie, Banks, and Haslam (1991).

Adaptation Target: Strategy Versus Structure

The first issue in designing adaptive organizations is to distinguish the adaptation of organizational strategy from structural adaptation in the organization. Strategy adaptation usually refers to the mission processing specifics of a single or a group of decision-makers (e.g., changing priority of task execution and information processing, altering the communication patterns, shifting the focus of the mission, changing asset utilization, etc.). The strategy adaptation may be induced by training and preplanned for contingency scenarios.

The structural adaptation refers to changing the allocation of resources to DMs, adjusting the command structure and responsibilities, and reconfiguration of communication network in the organization. Structural adaptation is more difficult to accomplish since it requires the participation of multiple DMs and has an impact on the performance of the organization as a whole. Since prior experience of working under earlier systems influences the newly developed processes and interactions, mediating some changes and preventing others, the reconfiguration history (the dynamics of the organizational structure in which it operated in the previous environment) greatly affects the performance. On the other hand, structural reconfiguration may bring more improvement than strategy adaptation. For example, a strategy adaptation to the new environment might be to change the communication pattern in the organization so that DMs will receive the information and request assets not available to them due to lack of resources. In turn, this creates coordination overhead and reduces the speed of command, although the situational awareness is maintained. On the other hand, structural reconfiguration could be employed to change the allocation of assets so that DMs become self-sufficient and no redundant communication occurs. In the latter condition, situational awareness is maintained and there is no communication workload overhead. The negative effect of redundant communication overhead has been explored in experiment 8 (Diedrich et al., 2003; Entin et al., 2003; Levchuk et al., 2003; Kleinman et al., 2003), and was shown to be a driving factor toward incongruence of an organization to a mission and a decrease in performance.

Adaptation Source: Local Versus Global

In order to determine if adaptation is required, the appropriate mission/organization *monitoring data* should be analyzed. Limited situational awareness of individual DMs affects their ability to capture the state of the organization and environment, and identify the optimal adaptation policy. Therefore, the second issue encountered in the design of adaptive organizations is the specification of the source of adaptation – the organizational DMs empowered to make decisions to employ a specific adaptation policy.

In hierarchical organizations, the authority to declare and enforce on-line reconfiguration belongs to the superior DM (known as the root DM). Hence, it is natural, although not necessary, that a decision to adapt be taken at this highest level of the command hierarchy. The need for global/centralized adaptation might arise due to the following reasons:

- The information needed to make a decision to adapt might not be available at the local DMs.
- The global problem might not be decomposable, and the solution to a set of sub-problems does not match the optimal adaptation policy.

However, the aggregated adaptation problem might be too complex to solve in a centralized manner, and therefore a distributed problem solution must be adopted. In addition, the importance of information about the need for local adaptation (adaptation of the local strategies and substructures of the organization) might be lost when the aggregated problem is considered. Therefore, the trade-off between decentralization, information prioritization, and solution optimality must be carefully considered.

Usually, local adaptation policies are employed to guide the adaptation of strategies of individual DMs, while the global adaptation rules (with some decentralization) are used to devise the structural adaptation in the organization. The individual DMs can also be empowered to make local structural changes (e.g., asset transfers, etc.).

Adaptation Timing: Dynamic Versus Static

In order to maintain its mission schedule in a dynamic environment, an adaptive organization must be able, in a timely fashion, to capture/analyze the necessary information, examine its adaptation alternatives, and implement the right adaptation option. For an organization to be able to adapt and still maintain its mission schedule, the adaptation phase must be compatible with the processing of mission tasks. In some cases, the adaptation time must be significantly smaller than the time to process the corresponding mission tasks to allow for successful completion of the mission. Clearly, the timing of adaptation policy must be explored. While strategy adaptation can easily be made dynamic, the structural adaptation can become dynamic only with strict constraints on the reconfiguration direction. The time required to reconfigure the current organization to a new structure and the cost of probable temporal decrement in performance (due to the need to adjust to a new structure) must be considered. As a result, the structural adaptation policy must explore the trade-off between reconfiguration and performance costs. If a static (off-line) adaptation and requisite training were possible, the optimal adaptation policy would then be to change to the locally optimal structure similar to project-based organizations, which are organized to perform a given task and then dissolved.

Adaptation Method: Proactive Versus Reactive

There are two approaches that the adaptive design can take. In a dynamic and highly uncertain environment, in which there is little or no prior knowledge about the mission, an adaptation process can account for the mission history (current and previous state of the environment) to infer the optimized structure. This is termed a *reactive* adaptation, where a reconfiguration is initiated based on the environment state with salient adaptation triggers. Thus, the adaptive organization reacts to the environmental changes, assuming that those are precursors of the future state of the mission, and changes the organizational structure only if it becomes incongruent with the current mission state. However, a large time lag in detecting the change of mission state might reduce the improvement obtained using such a policy. A more attractive approach is to try and predict the state of the future environment and utilize *proactive* design policy. Such a policy is sought when the benefits of transforming into a new structure, in which to execute the current and future sub-missions, outweigh the gain from staying in the same organization. Note that when the environment can be predicted with high certainty, the actual change occurs before the de facto incongruence mismatch with the current structure occurs.

Notions of Adaptation Cost and Direction of Change

As noted before, the adaptation design must account for both reconfiguration and performance costs. However, little of the empirical research studies teams or organizations that *actually change* their structures from Time 1 to Time 2. Despite the conceptual attractiveness of infinite reconfigurability advocated by SCT (e.g. flexible team-based structures, Townsend, DeMarie, & Hendrickson, 1998, project-based virtual teams, Levitt et al., 1994, 1999, and "cellular structures", Allred, Snow, & Miles, 1996), there are many conditions that make change difficult (Dimaggio & Powell, 1983). Moon et al. (2004) discusses the transformation from *Functional* to

Divisional organization (and vice versa). The concept of "asymmetric adaptability" is introduced as a potential boundary to the application of contingency theories. A direct test of whether teams could actually adapt in the manner implied by the theory indicated that teams responded more favorably to *Functional-Divisional* shifts than they did to *Divisional-Functional* shifts. Team levels of coordination mediated this difference while team levels of cognitive ability moderated this difference. Therefore, authors argued that certain types of adaptation are more natural than others and that the prior experience of working under an earlier system influences how persons react to the adapted system. Hence, there is a need to complement the static logic behind many contingency theories with a dynamic logic that explicitly challenges an assumption of symmetrical adaptation.

Example of Adaptation Strategy Design

The A2C2 experiment-8 researched two extreme cases of mission scenarios, with maximized "distance" between them in terms of structural parameters. The organizations congruent to each one of these missions not only differed significantly in the structure, but also performed poorly on the opposite scenario. This led to a hypothesis that the mission can be decomposed into morphing stages (or sub-missions), each having uniform properties. Adaptive organizational design must account for these sub-missions and distances among them. The adaptation path then must specify the structure of the organization for each morphing sub-mission. The organization that employs this adaptation process is seen as a morphing structure. Hence, to define the adaptation process based on morphing sub-missions, we need first to identify the cost of reconfiguration (adaptation) from one organizational structure to another, and the cost of executing a sub-mission by the organization in a specific structure (that can be thought of *congruence mismatch*). In the following, we describe our adaptation methodology, which is based on a global solution with a dynamic proactive structural adaptation policy.

Reconfiguration Cost

In the following, we consider only organizations with the same resource capabilities and the same number of team members. Evidently, this can be extended to the general case. We define the cost of reconfiguration between two organizations as the difference between their structures. The structure of an organization is defined via two matrices:

- DM-platform allocation matrix $A = [a_{k,m}]$, $k = 1, \ldots, D$; $m = 1, \ldots, R$, where D is number of DMs, $a_{k,m} = 1$ if DM_k is assigned platform P_m, and $a_{k,m} = 0$ otherwise;
- DM–DM hierarchy tree matrix , $H = [h_{i,j}]$, $i,j = 1, \ldots, D$, where $h_{i,j} = 1$ if DM_j is a subordinate of DM_i, and $h_{i,j} = 0$ otherwise.

When DMs are considered to be distinct, these matrices uniquely define an organization and its structure. However, when DMs are indistinguishable, matrices A and H define an organization with respect to permutation of DM ordering.

We define two phases of structural reconfiguration, and their corresponding costs:

- DM-platform reallocation – defined by matrix A; the cost to remove or assign a platform to a DM is W_A
- Hierarchy reassignment – defined by matrix H; the cost of removing or adding a link in the hierarchy is W_H.

Following the above logic, the total *cost of reconfiguration* from one organizational structure to another is equal to the sum of DM-platform reallocation cost and organizational network (hierarchy) reassignment cost. A definition of reconfiguration cost may involve the dependence on: (a) a specific DM, (b) platform, (c) hierarchy, and (d) environment-related parameters. The number of platform reassignments from DM_k of organization O_1 with $A^1 = [a^1_{k,m}]$, $H^1 = [h^1_{i,j}]$ to DM_r of organization O_2 with $A^2 = [a^2_{k,m}]$, $H^2 = [h^2_{i,j}]$ is equal to $\Sigma_{m=1}^{R} |a^1_{k,m} - a^2_{r,m}|$. The number of reassignments needed to bring DM_k of O_1 to have the same superior as DM_r of O_2 is equal to $\Sigma_{j=1}^{D} |h^1_{j,k} - h^2_{j,r}|$. The maximal number of platform reassignments between any two organizations is equal to $2R$ (each platform is reassigned), and the maximal number of hierarchy reassignments is equal $2(D-1)$ (each DM's parent is reassigned, including or excluding the root node).

We consider a simplified definition of reconfiguration cost (equal to the number of platform and hierarchy reassignments multiplied by the corresponding costs) that could be generalized to include various organizational characteristics without loss of validity of the approach. We assume that DMs are distinct, which is true for human teams. Then, the cost of reconfiguration from organization O_1 to organization O_2 having the same resource capabilities and DMs, represented by their corresponding matrices $A^1 = [a^1_{k,m}]$, $H^1 = [h^1_{i,j}]$ and $A^2 = [a^2_{k,m}]$, $H^2 = [h^2_{i,j}]$, is defined as a normalized number of platform and hierarchy reassignments multiplied by the corresponding costs:

$$C^R(O_1, O_2) = \frac{W_A}{2R}\sum_{k=1}^{D}\sum_{m=1}^{R}\left|a^1_{k,m} - a^2_{k,m}\right| + \frac{W_H}{2(D-1)}\sum_{i=1}^{D}\sum_{j=1}^{D}\left|h^1_{i,j} - h^2_{i,j}\right|$$

The cost defined above is just an example of the reconfiguration cost model. Our adaptation process methodology is a generic policy that does not depend on specific cost definitions. In the above, $C^R(O_1, O_2)$ is a symmetric cost and does not depend on organizations' history. It has been argued that the direction of change is in fact asymmetric, with mission execution and history of operation in specific structures affecting the cost of change and having an impact on future performance (Moon et al., 2004). All these factors can be incorporated into the reconfiguration cost definition without loss of the validity of the adaptation method.

Performance Cost

When trying to devise a structural reconfiguration, the main objective is to make the organization reach the best feasible performance at any time. Obviously, this is not possible due to the cost of reconfiguration from one structure to another. This cost could be reduced by training the team members to adapt, but it cannot be removed. Still, the prime driving factor is the actual dynamic performance of the organization. Although this is a very vague definition, it could normatively address utilizing the mission decomposition into morphing stages. Then, the dynamic performance is viewed as performance on a specific sub-mission representing the morphing stage. The mission decomposition could be time-based, utilizing the time instances that the reconfiguration from one structure to another is possible. It could also incorporate the decomposition of original mission into stages with uniform parameters across their time, and thus determine the instances where the adaptation is (or might be) necessary.

For each mission M and organization O (not necessarily optimal), we can calculate the performance parameter$C^P(O,\ M) = \Omega(O,\ M) - \Omega^*/\Omega^*$, where $\Omega(O, M)$ is a workload distribution (RMS measure) that can be achieved by organization O on mission M and Ω^* the optimal workload distribution that can be achieved on mission M. We use the measure of workload distribution based on model of DMs as limited-capacity processors, where bottlenecks occur when the workload threshold approaches the capacity. Therefore, $C^P(O, M)$ can be viewed as the performance-based *measure of structural congruence mismatch* between the organization and the mission and is equal to the relative decrease in performance of organization O on mission M

compared to the optmal organization. We say that an organization O is *relatively congruent* o mission M if congruence mismatch parameter $C^P(O, M)$ is below specified *congruence mismatch threshold*. For each sub-mission in the orphing stages of decomposition, we consider only its relatively congruenorganizations.

Following the ave logic, the *performance cost* of an organization on the mission is equal the structural congruence mismatch parameter. This is just one example the simplified relative performance decrease calculation model and can bdapted to account for organizational history, knowledge, experience in thme structure, training, etc. (Fig. 5).

Adaptation Pol

Lets assume the original mission N is decomposed into morphing sub-missions (sta$M_1, \ldots, M_K$, and can therefore be considered as a con-catenation ofe sub-missions (see Fig. 5). Assume that an organization is to be desigro process this mission N, a concatenation of missions $M_1, \ldots, M_K$at is, $N = M_1 \rightarrow \ldots \rightarrow M_K$. Each of the missions M_i may represent entary environment transformations (e.g., events that occur and chang task environment), and their concatenated sequence is viewed as *phing* process of mission N through missions $M_1, \ldots, M_K$. The orgaon is selected from the set of available structures $S(O) =$ O_j, $j =$, L , for which the reconfiguration costs $C^R(O_i, O_j)$ are iden-tified. Fh mission M_i and structure O_j, we can calculate the congru-ence mi parameter $C^P(O_j, M_i)$.

The *tion policy* of an organization on mission N is defined as a sequenructures π_i, $i = 1, \ldots, K$, where the organization assumes the structi for a sub-mission M_i, for $i = 1, \ldots, K$.

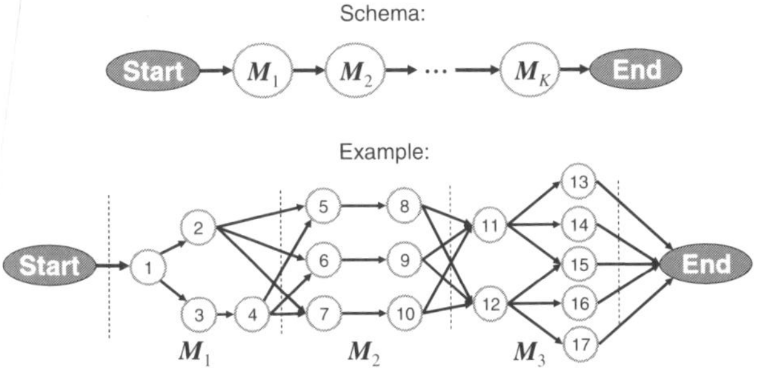

A Schematic Representation of Mission Decomposition into Morphing Submissions.

We define the *reconfiguration cost weight* W^R an the *performance cost weight* W^P, which are designed to trade-off performnce versus structural reconfiguration costs. Then, the *cost of adaptation poly* $\pi_i, \quad i = 1, \ldots, K$ is defined as the weighted sum of reconfiguration and peormance costs: $\Theta_\pi = W^R \cdot \Sigma_{i=1}^{D-1} C^R(O_{\pi_i}, O_{\pi_{i+1}}) + W^P \cdot \Sigma_{i=1}^{K} C^P(O_{\pi_i}, M_i)$ (Fi 6).

Adaptation Process: Finding Optimal Min-Cost Adapton Policy
To find optimal min-cost policy $\pi^* = \arg\min \Theta_\pi$, wonstruct a Viterbi trellis (Fig. 6) wherein each stage i correspnds to a mn M_i, with paths leading only to (from) nodes representing organizationelatively congruent" with the corresponding missions. The cost of ath between two structures O_k and O_m (both relatively congruent witissions M_i and M_{i+1}) is equal to $W^R \cdot C^R(O_k, O_m)$ – the cost of structreconfiguration from O_k to O_m multiplied by the weight of reconfigura cost W^R. The cost of visiting a node on the path (executing mission M tructure O_k) is equal to $W^P \cdot C^P(O_k, M_i)$ – a corresponding congruencsmatch multiplied by the performance cost weight. To obtain the least adaptation strategy (bold line in Fig. 6), we find the least-cost terminth via Viterbi algorithm, a recursive optimal solution to the problem ofng the shortest path in a trellis. For more details, see Forney (1973).

A node in Viterbi trellis (Fig. 6) is represented as a e with two parameters – the cost of visiting the node (number above ne) and the

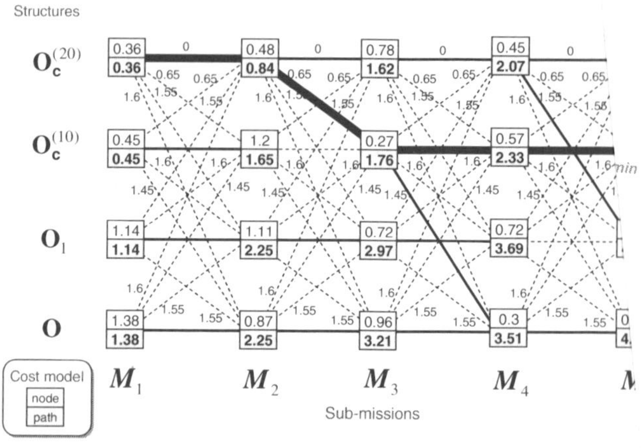

Fig. 6. Adaptation Process. Example of Policy Selection via Viterbi (for Cost Weights).

cost of adaptation path leading to this node (number below the line). The Viterbi algorithm finds the least-cost path to each node (including the cost of visiting the node) at the current stage, considering its predecessors at the previous stage. At each stage of the trellis, the least-cost path is found to each of its nodes (including the node's cost) from the nodes at the previous stage, the corresponding edge is marked, and the length of the path is updated. At the last stage, the terminal path with the shortest length is selected (indicated with the bold line in Fig. 6).

Reconfiguration and performance cost weights W^R and W^P are selected to achieve a trade-off between performance and structural reconfiguration costs. This trade-off is determined by the performance to reconfiguration cost weight ratio $\rho_{PR} = W^P/W^R$. The designer can choose to put more emphasis on minimizing reconfiguration cost by increasing the reconfiguration weight W^R (hence, decreasing ρ_{PR} ratio), or more emphasis on optimizing performance (thereby minimizing the congruence mismatch) by increasing the performance weight W^P (hence, increasing ρ_{PR}).

When the reconfiguration cost weight is significantly larger than the performance cost weight ($\rho_{PR} << 1$), the adaptation option is rejected, and the optimization process will result in a single organization across all morphing stages, which produces the best-aggregated performance cost. When the performance weight is significantly larger than the reconfiguration weight ($\rho_{PR} >> 1$), the reconfiguration cost can be disregarded. This results in an adaptation policy that employs the best organizational structure for each morphing mission M_i.

Adaptation Triggers and Perception of Congruent Design

Organizational adaptation process is significantly simplified if specific causes for adaptation, or *adaptation triggers*, are anticipated a priori. These are the unexpected changes in the mission environment, resource failures, DM failures, etc., that require an organization to adapt. After a suitable adaptation option is selected, the organization needs to coordinate among its members to realize the selected change. However, identifying the specific events as adaptation triggers might be difficult, since triggers must be the indicators/predictors of the long-lasting environment changes. Some of the events are non-reversible (e.g., DM failure, resource loss, change of mission objectives/goals, etc.) and therefore clearly fall into the set of potential signals for adaptation. Other events, such as changes in the mission task parameters, might indicate only a temporal alternation of the mission structure, and therefore the best policy is to stay in the same organizational configuration and make strategy adaptations to cope with temporary mission bifurcations. Events that cause only short-term environmental changes should not be considered as adaptation triggers. However, the accumulation of such events may bring the long-lasting transformation to the environment state. Therefore, the adaptation process must account for the whole environment state and its history in order to perceive the direction of the environment transformation.

One of the perceptions of congruence theory might be that the change must occur only when the organization can no longer sustain the high level of performance. First, this seemingly implies that, when the performance of the organization decreases, it might be a trigger for adaptation. While certainly an appealing concept, it is easily challenged by noting that the notion of optimality is subjective (Keeney & Raiffa, 1993). Moreover, different aspects of organizational performance are deemed important when assessing the efficacy of an organization. In general, however, there is little consensus on what constitutes organizational performance and there is no universally best set of performance measures (Cameron, 1986). Even if the set of performance measures has been chosen for a specific organization, their values strongly depend on the faced the mission environment, and do not actually indicate whether there exists a better organization. Hence, the better approach is to find the optimal organization for the current environment, and determine the congruence of current organization to its mission by comparing the current organization's performance to the optimal one.

Second, it seems that congruence theory implies that the timing of adaptation must be connected with incongruent situations. However, if the adaptation triggers are known a-priori and their occurrence would predict the future mission state transformation (into a state incongruent with current organization), a better adaptation strategy would be to make "proactive" and gradual changes before the actual incongruent situation transpires. This policy will reduce the cost of reconfiguration and decrease a potential lag in performance improvement due to adjustment to the new structure.

CONCLUSIONS

In this chapter, we overviewed analytic methods, applications, and measures, which form the basis for current A2C2 research on organizational design and adaptation for large-scale human-machine systems. We described several strategies for cost-effective design of mission-based organizations to efficiently process missions with various degrees of uncertainty. Specifically, we illustrated the methodology to design *congruent*, *robust*, and *adaptive* organizations, and discussed the performance and design trade-offs involved. We defined a set of *performance measures* to generate the objective function (s) for our design process and to analyze the sensitivity of organizational performance to changes in the mission and/or organizational parameters.

The notion of structural congruence between a mission and an organization has been generalized to define a measure of congruence mismatch based on workload measures; it can serve as a criterion to signal the need for structural adaptation. This may be extended to include the structural and process (i.e., scheduling and resource allocation) match between two organizations as well. Another possible extension is the inclusion of DM-related adaptation triggers, the mismatch between DM's dynamic *capacity* for task processing and the operational requirements placed on the DM. Predicting these conditions before their onset would allow the prevention of their deleterious effects, which is a key in effective team management and adaptation.

In several human-in-the-loop experiments conducted under the A2C2 program, we found that the model-predicted structural mismatch between an organization and a mission indeed resulted in degraded performance in the non-congruent cases when compared to the congruent ones – specifically in terms of timeliness of task execution, coordination workload, and the total gain attained by the organization. We found that the congruent organization achieves a higher mission execution tempo while performing the mission with lower external coordination (higher speed of command – lower number of DM–DM assists) and, as a result, higher independence of DMs and lower cognitive load for mission execution. The latter results indicate that our research will be valuable to the design of novel Army and Navy organizations, as they strive to define organizational configurations to achieve a higher degree of autonomy in distributed operations.

REFERENCES

Allred, B. B., Snow, C. C., & Miles, R. E. (1996). Characteristics of managerial careers in the 21st century. *Academy of Management Executive*, *10*, 17–27.

Booth, R. (1996). Agile manufacturing. *Engineering Management Journal*, *6*(2), 105–115.

Burns, T., & Stalker, G. M. (1961). *The management of innovation*. London: Tavistock.

Burton, R. M., & Obel, B. (1998). *Strategic organizational diagnosis and design: Developing theory for application* (2nd ed.). Boston, MA: Kluwer Academic Publishers.

Cameron, K. S. (1986). Effectiveness as paradox: Consensus and conflict in conceptions of organizational effectiveness. *Management Science*, *32*(5), 539–553.

Carley, K. M. (1998). Adaptive organizations and emergent forms. *Proceedings of the 3rd international conference on multi agent systems*, Paris, France.

Carley, K. M., & Svoboda, D. M. (1996). Modeling organizational adaptation as a simulated annealing process. *Sociological Methods and Research*, *25*(1), 138–168.

Diedrich, F., Entin, E., Hutchins, S., Hocevar, S., Rubineau, B., & MacMillan, J. (2003). When do organizations need to change – part I: Coping with organizational incongruence. *Proceedings of the 9th international command and control research and technology symposium*, Washington, DC.

Dimaggio, P. J., & Powell, W. W. (1983). The iron cage revisited: Institutional isomorphism and collective rationality in organizational fields. *American Sociological Review*, *48*, 147–160.

Drazin, R., & Van de Ven, A. H. (1985). Alternative forms of fit in contingency theory. *Administrative Science Quarterly*, *30*, 514–539.

Entin, E. E. (1999). Optimized command and control architectures for improved process and performance. *Proceedings of the 1999 command & control research & technology symposium*, Newport, RI.

Entin, E., Diedrich, F., Kleinman, D., Kemple, B, Hocevar, S., Rubineau, B., & Serfaty, D. (2003). When do organizations need to change – part II: Incongruence in action. *Proceedings of the 9th international command and control research and technology symposium*, Washington, DC.

Epstein, J. M. (2003). *Growing adaptive organizations: An agent-based computational approach.* Working paper, The Santa Fe Institute, http://www.santafe.edu/sfi/publications/Working-Papers/03-05-029.pdf.

Federal Aviation Administration (FAA). (1993). Pilot fatigue, sleep and circadian rhythms: NASA fatigue countermeasures program. *Aviation Safety Journal*, *3*(1), 20–25.

Foisel, R., Chevrier, V., & Haton, J. (1998). Modeling adaptive organizations. *Proceedings of the 4th international conference on multi agent systems.*

Forney, D., Jr. (1973). The Viterbi algorithm. *Proceedings of the IEEE*, *61*(3), 268–278.

Handley, H. A., Zaidi, Z. R., & Levis, A. H. (1999). The use of simulation models in model driven experimentation. *Proceedings of the 1999 command & control research & technology symposium*, Newport, RI.

Hankins, T. C., & Wilson, G. F. (1998). A comparison of heart rate, eye activity, EEG and subjective measures of pilot mental workload during flight. *Aviation, Space and Environmental Medicine*, *69*(4), 360–367.

Heller, T. (2000). If only we'd known sooner: Developing knowledge of organizational changes earlier in the product development process. *IEEE Transactions on Engineering Management*, *47*(3), 335–344.

Hocevar, S., Kemple, W., Kleinman, D., & Porter, G. (1999). Assessments of simulated performance of alternative architectures for command and control: The role of coordination. *Proceedings of the 1999 command & control research & technology symposium*, Newport, RI.

Hollenbeck, J., Moon, H., Ellis, A., West, B., Ilgen, D., Sheppard, L., Porter, C., & Wagner, J. (2002). Structural contingency theory and individual differences: Examination of external and internal person-team fit. *Journal of Applied Psychology*, *87*, 599–606.

Keeney, R., & Raiffa, H. (1993). *Decisions with multiple objectives*. New York: Cambridge University Press.

Kleinman, D., Levchuk, G., Hutchins, S., & Kemple, W. (2003). Scenario design for the empirical testing of organizational congruence. *Proceedings of the 2003 international command and control research and technology symposium*, Washington, DC.

Kleinman, D., Pattipati, K., Luh, P., & Serfaty, D. (1992). Mathematical models of team performance: A distributed decision-making approach. In: R. Swezey & E. Salas (Eds), *Teams: Their training and performance* (pp. 177–218). Norwood, NJ: Ablex.

Kleinman, D., & Serfaty, D. (1989). Team performance assessment in distributed decision-making. *Proceedings of the symposium on interactive networked simulation for training*, Orlando, FL.

Kleinman, D., Young, P., & Higgins, G. (1996). The DDD-III: A tool for empirical research in adaptive organizations. *Proceedings of the 1996 command and control research and technology symposium*, Monterey, CA.

Kulatilaka, N. (1988). Valuing the flexibility of flexible manufacturing systems. *IEEE Transactions on Engineering Management*, *35*(4), 250–257.

Lawrence, P. R., & Lorsch, J. W. (1967). *Organization and environment*. Boston, MA: Harvard University Press.

Lee, J. S., & Carley, K. M. (1997). Adaptive strategy for improving C2 performance. *Proceedings of the 1997 command and control research and technology symposium*, Washington, DC.

Levchuk, G. M., Kleinman, D. L., Ruan, S., & Pattipati, K. R. (2003). Congruence of human organizations and missions: Theory versus data. *Proceedings of the 2003 international command and control research and technology symposium*, June, Washington, DC.

Levchuk, G. M., Levchuk, Y. N., Luo, J., Pattipati, K. R., & Kleinman, D. L. (2002a). Normative design of organizations – part I: Mission planning. *IEEE Transactions on Systems, Man, and Cybernetics – Part A: Systems and Humans*, *32*(3), 346–359.

Levchuk, G. M., Levchuk, Y. N., Luo, J., Pattipati, K. R., & Kleinman, D. L. (2002b). Normative design of organizations – part II: Organizational structure. *IEEE Transactions on Systems, Man, and Cybernetics – Part A: Systems and Humans*, *32*(3), 360–375.

Levchuk, G. M., Levchuk, Y. N., Meirina, C., Pattipati, K. R., & Kleinman, D. L. (2004). Normative design of project-based organizations – part III: Congruent, robust, and adaptive organizations. *IEEE Transactions on Systems, Man, and Cybernetics – Part A: Systems and Humans*, *34*(3), 337–350.

Levchuk, Y. N., Pattipati, K. R., & Curry, M. L. (1997). Normative design of organizations to solve a complex mission: Theory and algorithms. *Proceedings of the 1997 command and control research and technology symposium*, Washington, DC.

Levchuk, Y. N., Pattipati, K. R., Curry, M. L., & Shakeri, M. (1996). Design of congruent organizational structures: Theory and algorithms. *Proceedings of 1996 command and control research and technology symposium*, Monterey, CA.

Levchuk, Y. N., Pattipati, K. R., & Kleinman, D. L. (1998). Designing adaptive organizations to process a complex mission: Algorithms and applications. *Proceedings of the 1998 command & control research & technology symposium*, Monterey, CA.

Levitt, R. E., Cohen, G. P., Kunz, J. C., Nass, C. I., Cristiansen, T., & Jin, Y. (1994). The 'virtual design' team: Simulating how organization structure and information processing tools affect team performance. In: K. M. Carley & M. J. Prietula (Eds), *Computational organization theory*. Hillsdale, NJ: Lawrence Erlbaum Associates.

Levitt, R. E., Thomsen, J., Christiansen, T. R., Kunz, J. C., Yan, J., & Nass, C. (1999). Simulating project work processes and organizations: Toward a micro-contingency theory of organizational design. *Management Science*, *45*, 1479–1495.

Lin, Z., & Carley, K. M. (1993). Proactive and reactive: An analysis of the effect of agent style on organizational decision-making performance. *International Journal of Intelligent Systems in Accounting, Finance and Management*, *2*(4), 271–288.

Mackenzie, K. D. (1986). *Organizational design: The organizational audit and analysis technology*. Norwood, NJ: Ablex.

Mackenzie, C. F., Jefferies, N. J., Hunter, W. A., Bernhard, W. N., Xiao, Y., & Horst, R. (1996). Comparison of self reporting of deficiencies in airway management with video analysis of actual performance. *Human Factors*, *38*(4), 623–635.

Mayk, I., & Rubin, I. (1988). Paradigms for understanding C3, anyone? In: S. E. Johnson & A. H. Levis (Eds), *Science of command and control: Coping with uncertainty* (pp. 48–61). Washington: AFCEA International Press.

McGrath, C., & Krackhardt, D. (2003). Network conditions for organizational change. *The Journal of Applied Behavioral Science*, *39*(3), 324–336.

Miller, D. (1988). Relating Porter's business strategies to environment and structure: Analysis and performance implications. *Academy of Management Journal*, *31*, 280–308.

Moon, H., Hollenbeck, J. R., Humphrey, S. E., Ilgen, D. R., West, B., Ellis, A. P. J., & Porter, C. O. L. H. (2004). Asymmetric adaptability: Dynamic team structures as one-way streets. *Academy of Management Journal*, *47*, 681–695.

Papastavrou, J. D., & Athans, M. (1992). On optimal distributed detection architectures in a hypothesis testing environment. *IEEE Transactions on Automatic Control*, *37*, 1154–1169.

Peddie, R. A., Banks, J. H., & Haslam, T. J. (1991). Electricity privatization-IT's role in facilitating rapid organizational change. *Engineering Management Journal*, *1*(4), 178–186.

Pennings, J. M. (1992). Structural contingency theory: A reappraisal. In: L. L. Cummings & B. M. Staws (Eds), *Research in organizational behavior* (Vol. 14, pp. 267–309). Greenwich, CT: JAI Press.

Pete, A., Kleinman, D. L., & Pattipati, K. R. (1994). Structural congruence of tasks and organizations. *Proceedings of the 1994 symposium on command and control research and decision aids*, Monterey, CA (pp. 168–175).

Pete, A., Pattipati, K. R., Levchuk, Y. N., & Kleinman, D. L. (1998). An overview of decision networks and organizations. *IEEE Transactions on System, Man, and Cybernetics – Part C: Applications*, *28*, 172–192.

Phadke, M. S. (1989). *Quality engineering using robust design*. New York: Prentice-Hall.

Piramuthu, S., Raman, N., & Shaw, M. J. (1994). Learning-based scheduling in a flexible manufacturing flow line. *IEEE Transactions on Engineering Management*, *41*(2), 172–182.

Roberts, F. (1979). *Measurement theory, with applications to decision-making, utility and the social sciences*. Reading, MA: Addison-Wesley.

Sage, A. P. (1981). Behavioral and organizational considerations in the design of information systems and processes for planning and decision support. *IEEE Transactions on Systems, Man, and Cybernetics*, *11*(9), 640–678.

Salas, E., Dickinson, T. L., Converse, S. A., & Tannenbaum, S. I. (1992). Toward an understanding of team performance and training. In: R. Swezey & E. Salas (Eds), *Teams: Their training and performance* (pp. 3–29). Norwood, NJ: Ablex.

Scott, W. R. (1981). *Organizations: Rational, natural, and open systems*. New York: Prentice-Hall.

Taguchi, G. (1986). *Introduction to quality engineering*. White Plains, NY: UNIPUB/Krauss International.

Song, A., Mathur, A., & Pattipati, K. R. (1995). Design of process parameters using robust design techniques and multiple criteria optimization. *IEEE Transactions on Systems, Man, and Cybernetics*, *25*(11), 1437–1446.

Taguchi, G. (1987). *System of experimental design* (Vols. 1 and 2). White Plains, New York: UNIPUB/Krauss International.

Townsend, A. M., DeMarie, S. M., & Hendrickson, A. R. (1998). Virtual teams: Technology and the workplace of the future. *Academy of Management Executive*, *12*, 17–29.

Tsourveloudis, N. C., & Phillis, Y. A. (1998). Manufacturing flexibility measurement: A fuzzy logic framework. *IEEE Transactions on Robotics and Automation*, *14*(4), 513–524.

Vincke, P. (1992). *Multicriteria decision-aid*. New York: Wiley.

Wasserman, S., & Faust, K. (1994). *Social network analysis: Methods and applications*. Cambridge, UK: Cambridge University Press.

Wellman, B. (1991). Network analysis: Some basic principles. *Sociological theory*, *1*, 155–200.

Wellman, B., & Berkowitz, S. (1988). *Social structures: A network approach*. Norwood, NJ: Cambridge University Press.

Wong, A., & Kleinman, D. (2002). *DDD post processor V1.2 user guide*. Technical Report. Naval Postgraduate School.

Xiao, Y., & Mackenzie, C. F. (1997). Uncertainty in trauma resuscitation. *Proceedings of the human factors and ergonomics society 41st annual meeting*, Santa Monica, CA.